The Social Gospel Today

The Social Gospel Today

Edited by Christopher H. Evans

Westminster John Knox Press
LOUISVILLE
LONDON · LEIDEN

Book design by Sharon Adams
Cover design by Night & Day Design

First edition
Published by Westminster John Knox Press
Louisville, Kentucky

This book is printed on acid-free paper that meets the American National Standards Institute Z39.48 standard. ∞

PRINTED IN THE UNITED STATES OF AMERICA

01 02 03 04 05 06 07 08 09 10 — 10 9 8 7 6 5 4 3 2 1

Library of Congress Cataloging-in-Publication Data

The social gospel today / Christopher H. Evans, editor.—1st ed.
    p. cm.
  Includes bibliographical references and index.
  ISBN 0-664-22252-8 (pbk. : alk. paper)
  1. Social gospel. 2. Sociology, Christian—United States. I. Evans, Christopher Hodge, 1959–

BT738 .S614 2001
261.8—dc21   00-054082

*To the faculty, staff, and students
of Colgate Rochester Divinity School/Crozer Theological Seminary:
Past, Present, and Future*

Contents

Acknowledgments

My introduction to the social gospel, as a historical topic and as a vital theological legacy, came through seminary courses I had years ago at Boston University School of Theology from Earl Kent Brown and Dean Emeritus Walter G. Muelder. These two scholars modeled for me the social-gospel emphasis that united a compelling vision of personal faith and social transformation. They also taught me that the full power of divine grace comes to faith communities who not only honor the wisdom of past traditions, but who have the ability to diligently engage these traditions to find new meaning in the present.

The genesis for this book emerged at the 1999 Social Gospel Conference held at Colgate Rochester Divinity School/Crozer Theological Seminary. I am grateful to Gary Dorrien, Susan Lindley, Janet Fishburn, and Rosemary Keller, whose presentations at that event provided a nucleus in which this volume grew. My gratitude is extended to my faculty colleagues at Colgate Rochester, including Melanie May, William R. Herzog, and President G. Thomas Halbrooks, who graciously agreed to provide the book's preface. Special thanks also needs to be given to Ann Marie Berner, whose word processing wizardry provided invaluable assistance in compiling this book, and to Naomi Annandale, Colgate Rochester Master of Divinity student, who assembled the book's index. To all the book's contributors, I give thanks for your commitment and enthusiasm to this project and for putting up with my insistent prodding about meeting deadlines.

Many additional persons offered critical assistance in various ways as this project took root and was brought to completion. I would especially like to thank Robin Olson, Wendy Deichmann Edwards, Ellie Stebner, Dale Davis, and Bob Hill, who have engaged me on matters pertaining to the social gospel's significance as a historical-theological tradition. My gratitude is extended to Deborah Van Broekhoven, Stuart Campbell, and Karen Sundland of the American Baptist Historical Society for their gracious hospitality in allowing me access to the Walter Rauschenbusch Papers, housed at Colgate Rochester Divinity School/Crozer Theological Seminary. I'm grateful to G. Nick Street, my former editor at Westminster John Knox Press, for his constant encouragement and valuable suggestions in the process of bringing this project to completion. I am also grateful to my current editor, Donald McKim, project editor Linda Watkins, and to all at Westminster John Knox who saw this book through to its publication. Finally, to Peter and Andrew Olson Evans I give loving thanks for teaching me that God's grace is real and for the glimpses they give me of a joyous future.

It is an honor to teach at an institution that directly contributed to the legacy of the social gospel associated with the teaching career of Walter Rauschenbusch. My work is enriched by my association not only with wonderful faculty and staff colleagues, but by our students, whose own pilgrimages to reconcile personal faith and social justice in the tradition of the social gospel continuously inspire me to become a better teacher and Christian. It is to all those representing that spirit of deep faith and critical reflection who have and will continue to pass through the doors of Colgate Rochester Divinity School/Crozer Theological Seminary that this volume is dedicated. Their witness embodies the essence of what needs to endure in the social gospel today.

Christopher H. Evans

Contributors

Christopher H. Evans is Associate Professor of Church History and Director of United Methodist Studies at Colgate Rochester Divinity School/Crozer Theological Seminary, Rochester, New York.

Susan Hill Lindley is Professor of Religion at St. Olaf College, Northfield, Minnesota.

Darryl M. Trimiew is Dean of Black Church Studies and Martin Luther King Jr. Professor of Christian Social Ethics at Colgate Rochester Divinity School/Crozer Theological Seminary.

Melanie A. May is Vice President of Academic Affairs and Dean of the Faculty and Professor of Theology at Colgate Rochester Divinity School/Crozer Theological Seminary.

Rosemary Skinner Keller is Academic Dean and Professor of Church History at Union Theological Seminary in New York City.

Dianne Reistroffer is Assistant Professor of Ministry and Dean of the Seminary at Louisville Presbyterian Theological Seminary, Louisville, Kentucky.

Gary Dorrien is the Ann V. and Donald R. Parfet Distinguished Professor at Kalamazoo College, Kalamazoo, Michigan.

Janet Furness is Associate Professor of Social Work at Roberts Wesleyan College, Rochester, New York.

Timothy Tseng is Associate Professor of American Religious History at the American Baptist Seminary of the West, Berkeley, California.

Janet Forsythe Fishburn is Professor Emerita at Drew University in Madison, New Jersey, where she taught American Church History in The Graduate School and Practical Theology in The Theological School.

Max L. Stackhouse is the Stephen Colwell Professor of Christian Ethics at Princeton Theological Seminary, Princeton, New Jersey.

Pamela D. Couture is Associate Professor of Pastoral Theology at Colgate Rochester Divinity School/Crozer Theological Seminary.

Preface

The social gospel has been making an impact on churches and individuals for almost a century. My own experience serves as a single example. Some time ago during my seminary studies, I chose Walter Rauschenbusch's *A Theology for the Social Gospel* as one of the required primary texts I would review in my historical theology course. Having come from a very conservative, pietistic background, I thought it was important that I learn firsthand about some of the writings of "liberal" theologians.

Although this experience of reading *A Theology for the Social Gospel* took place almost fifty years after its publication, it was a transforming event. The Bible had always been authoritative for me, and no part of it was more authoritative than the life and teachings of Jesus. I had understood it to teach of individual sin and salvation. Christ came to provide the way of salvation from sin for all individuals who would repent of sin and believe in him.

Rauschenbusch did not deny any of my prior understanding, but he did assert that it was a truncated understanding. Having seen the great needs as he served as pastor of the German Baptist Church on the edge of Hell's Kitchen in New York City, he set forth his clarion call for the movement in 1907 with the publication of *Christianity and the Social Crisis*. There and in his subsequent work, he argued that a gospel of individual salvation was only a half gospel, for the gospel had social dimensions as well. He pointed out that Jesus continued the call of the prophets for justice and mercy by proclaiming the coming kingdom of God in which unconditional love would eventually triumph over all obstacles in society. Rauschenbusch called on the church to respond to Jesus' call for bringing in the kingdom of God and to struggle for its realization. Such an understanding of the gospel was a revelation to me.

I also learned that Rauschenbusch held together both piety and social action. He refused to give up one for the other. He viewed them both as necessary for the life of the church. Rauschenbusch's favorite of all his works was his book of prayers, *For God and the People: Prayers of the Social Awakening*.

Although some of the language and issues appeared dated, the prayers still soared with beauty and timeless truths.

As I struggled with the development of my own theology during my seminary pilgrimage, certainly I did not fully embrace all aspects of the social gospel any more than I embraced all aspects of its underlying liberal theology. Much of it appeared dated. Many of the presuppositions from its cultural milieu were problematic. Nevertheless, that encounter with Rauschenbusch changed my perspective forever.

This book is a call to allow the social gospel to speak to our current context much as I found Rauschenbusch speaking to my context several years ago. It is a call to encounter the social gospel again. It does not suggest that we accept all its ideas or presuppositions, nor does it advocate that we go back to the social gospel—quite the contrary. Rather, it proposes that we consider again the messages of some of its proponents to find their relevance for our lives in the church today. Perhaps, if we will listen to its message again through these pages, the social gospel can provide us with fresh insights and enriched perspectives and become for us again a new revelation.

G. Thomas Halbrooks
President, Colgate Rochester Divinity School/Crozer Theological Seminary

Introduction

Historical Integrity and Theological Recovery: A Reintroduction to the Social Gospel

Christopher H. Evans

In 1939, F. Ernest Johnson delivered the annual Rauschenbusch lectures at Colgate Rochester Divinity School. Established in 1929 in honor of Walter Rauschenbusch, America's leading exponent of the social gospel and a long-time professor of church history at the seminary, the lectures featured many prominent theologians and ethicists of post–World War I American Protestantism.[1] At the height of American neo-orthodoxy, when the liberal theological suppositions of the social gospel were under harsh scrutiny, Johnson's lectures were published under what might have struck many of his contemporaries as a somewhat peculiar title: *The Social Gospel Re-Examined*.[2]

Johnson lamented what he believed was the haste of church leaders to dismiss the social gospel, arguing that the tradition needed to be reformulated, in light of what was taking place in the church and society at that time. Writing in an era when many neo-orthodox and postliberal theologians held, at best, an ambivalent attitude toward the social gospel, Johnson argued that the church jettisoned that theological tradition at its peril. He affirmed, "the very continuity of tradition means that there is an ongoing concern, an abiding value to be conserved, but no less important is the reconstructive process which results from the fact that emergent needs continually challenge old concepts and formulas. The theological task of our time is to find an adequate expression for meanings that . . . are timeless in their nature, in terms that will be relevant to the facts of our temporal existence."[3]

This book is an effort to follow Ernest Johnson's call for a reappraisal of the theological tradition that historian Charles Howard Hopkins called "America's most unique contribution to the great ongoing stream of Christianity. . . ."[4] From the outset, it needs to be stated that this book, like Johnson's, is not a plea for Christian faith communities to uncritically embrace the social gospel. As Johnson observes, "a *recovery* of theology can never be equivalent to a *return* to theology."[5] However, the book is an effort to show how an important theological tradition that rose to prominence in the early twentieth

century can be reinterpreted, in ways that challenge Christian faith communities to redefine their mission and identity at the opening of the twenty-first
century.

As many of the book's chapters make evident, defining what we mean by
"social gospel" is subject to a range of interpretations. Shailer Mathews's often
quoted definition, that the social gospel represented "the application of the
teaching of Jesus and the total message of the Christian salvation to society,
the economic life, and social institutions . . . as well as to individuals," has been
critiqued in light of recent scholarship.[6] However, the definition reflects how
church leaders like Mathews, Rauschenbusch, Washington Gladden, Richard
Ely, Vida Scudder and many others called upon the church of their era to wrestle with the following question: How does Christian faith make a difference
for a church and a society that is in a state of theological and societal flux? The
social gospel emerged out of a late nineteenth-century context of social and
theological transition—one with parallels to our own era of technological
transition and growing ambiguity regarding the church's role in American culture. As Johnson argued, however, what made the social gospel vital to church
history was that it accentuated the social imperative of Christianity. Christian
faith must center upon "the conviction that a sustained dynamic for ethical
action is furnished only by a religious faith and that such a faith is effectively
nourished only by the corporate life of the community."[7] This basic theological premise for the social gospel—that Christianity must be rooted in faith-
based communities committed to social transformation—is worthy of reassessment and fleshing out considering the complexities that confront churches at
the beginning of the twenty-first century.

Even though historians and theologians have recently shown renewed
interest in recovering aspects of the social-gospel legacy, today many Christians, as was the case in Ernest Johnson's era, view that legacy with a degree of
ambivalence. Although the social gospel is linked to a wide variety of social
reform movements in the twentieth century, the tradition's usefulness for
modern faith communities remains ambiguous.

Part of the negative reaction against the social gospel rests upon the critique that the tradition lacked any formative theological base. Many scholars
identified the social gospel's significance primarily through its impact upon the
institutional character of twentieth-century Protestantism. The prominent
American church historian Sidney Mead argued that the social gospel spawned
no new churches or denominations, but "was in reality a movement in the
denominations looking for theological roots."[8] Mead and other scholars
largely saw the social gospel as a sign of late nineteenth-century Protestant
institutional virility, or perceived virility. The tradition symbolized an era
when many Protestant churches assumed a taken-for-granted hegemony upon

American morals and public values. More recently, Susan Curtis, in an expansion of Mead's argument, saw the social gospel as part of how white middle-class Protestant churches uncritically accommodated themselves to an ideology synonymous with an emerging consumer culture, born in the Progressive Era of the early twentieth century. "Protestants in the social gospel tradition increasingly relied on the standards of business, entertainment, and the state to evaluate their religious efforts. They assumed that churches spoke with authority only insofar as they measured up to secular standards of expertise, efficiency, and entertainment."[9] One could argue that Curtis's assessment applies more to the rise of various genres of twentieth-century American evangelicalism, whose constituencies far outstripped liberal-mainline traditions in terms of embracing and mastering the marketing language and technology of modern culture.[10] Her point, however, highlights the frequently argued critique by historians, ethicists, and theologians that the social gospel lacked any formative or original theological synthesis, apart from its foundations in theological liberalism. As William McGuire King observed, "The consensus of opinion seems to be that the social gospel was basically a theological variant of nineteenth-century liberalism . . . and that it was heavily dependent on the intellectual suppositions of that tradition: its theological idealism, its ethical intuitionism, its stress on the immanence of God in nature, and its uncritical confidence in evolutionary progress."[11] As King points out, however, this perspective does an injustice to many social gospel representatives who believed they were engaged in an important and vital process of theological construction and synthesis.

At the same time, it is my contention (a view shared by many writers in this book) that one cannot understand the social gospel as a theological movement apart from its liberal theological heritage.[12] In our era, the word *liberalism* is often used pejoratively and is interpreted in ways far removed from how the term was understood in its late nineteenth-century context. For those who view themselves as theological "conservatives," the term *liberal* often signifies that one's theological identity lacks a clear commitment to specific beliefs. Liberalism connotes negative caricatures of how theology promotes an innocuous faith in pluralism, denying the core values of Christian belief related to sin and the importance of personal conversion and salvation. For those who identify their theological beliefs stemming from currents of liberation theology, the term *liberalism* can also carry negative connotations. To identify oneself as a liberal from this perspective is to accept a status-quo gradualism that eliminates possibilities for radical social change in America. Finally, both theological poles often associate liberalism with the curse of *modernity* (another imprecisely defined term), whereby those who carry the liberal label are caricatured as holding a myopic faith in the social institutions, values, and scientific innovations of contemporary culture. Given the weight of misappropriated historical and theological baggage assigned to the social gospel over the course of the twentieth century, is it any wonder that many view the tradition as a legacy that offers little of substance to contemporary theology?

These caricatures of liberalism, however, fail to capture the spirit in which the term was understood by the men and women who historians identify as part of the social gospel movement. It is certainly true that many social gospel liberals like Gladden and Rauschenbusch were deeply influenced by emerging liberal ideals related to biblical criticism, understanding Jesus' ministry in its historical context, and the effort to reconcile Christian beliefs with nineteenth-century developments in the natural sciences. To be a social gospel liberal, however, was not just a designation that described how individuals reinterpreted traditional Christian doctrines such as the Trinity, the virgin birth, or personal salvation (although contrary to some later arguments, many social gospelers were deeply concerned about matters of doctrine). To be a social gospel liberal was an assertion that one cared passionately for the world and that the task of Christianity was primarily geared toward a creative engagement with the social currents of the present (or, to use the German word, to engage the *zeitgeist*, "the spirit of the times"). What made the social gospel a distinctive liberal movement was the way it attempted to instill in the society of its era the message that a Christian's personal faith could not be separated from the contemporary problems and issues that plagued the public conscience. Social gospel leaders believed that they lived in an era of unprecedented social change, an era when American society was experiencing seismic economic, political, and cultural shifts. In juxtaposition to the rise of late nineteenth-century premillennialism, whose leaders and followers largely abandoned hope in social reform and social progress, opting instead to preach an otherworldly faith in Christ's second coming, the social gospel leaders saw their historical era as a time of unprecedented opportunity. The social crises of the late nineteenth century caused these leaders to view salvation not just as an individual quest to be saved *out* of the earth, but to see the question of salvation *interconnected to* one's struggle to build a better society in the present—and future. As King accurately notes, "what set the social gospel apart was the way that its understanding of the social dimension of human experience was used to rethink the categories of Christian theology."[13] For many, this enterprise of theological reformulation was nothing short of a second Reformation. As Rauschenbusch argued in 1904, the purpose of Christianity was not to jettison the past in the face of that which was considered "modern." The purpose of Christianity was to make an ancient heritage relevant to the pressing social concerns of the day.

"The tongue of fire will descend on twentieth century men and give them great faith, joy and boldness, and then we shall hear the new evangel, and it will be the Old Gospel."[14]

The social gospel injected into Western theology an insistence that theological questions pertaining to sin and salvation were inseparable from one's struggle to work for social justice. Even amidst the hostile reaction against the social gospel by neo-orthodoxy in the 1930s, no less a theologian than H. Richard Niebuhr recognized that there was something theologically powerful about the social gospel that was distinctively liberal, yet was also in continuity with historical Christianity. What Niebuhr found promising about the social gospel (even amidst his concerns about the tradition's liberal-anthropomorphic theology) was that it offered a new and distinctive way for Christianity to revision the relationship between more traditional notions of soteriology and the contemporary imperative for social action.

> The Social Gospel has seen sin and righteousness as characteristics of group life; it has noted that vicarious suffering is laid upon group for group rather than upon individual for individual; it has seen the problem of salvation as a social problem and it has worked for the conversion or "change" of societies rather than of individuals who, no matter how much they may be changed, yet remain bound by common social evils and participants in common social sin.[15]

Today, what we commonly remember about the social gospel is its often myopic vision of a church that was dedicated to making America, and by extension, the world, conform to the hegemonic cultural values associated with American Protestantism of that time. What we often lose sight of, however, is the way that representatives of the social gospel heritage were devoted to propagating theologies that stressed the importance of what has been termed *social salvation*. This latter vision challenged churches to promote an awareness of how God was present through the *zeitgeist* of modern culture, and called upon Christians to work for major institutional changes that would lead to an egalitarian, democratic society.

In many respects, this major ideal of the social gospel has been adapted into the intellectual and political cultures of twentieth-century America.[16] The social gospel's insistence that government should and must play a role in regulating the economic practices of the nation, with an eye toward alleviating the plight of the poor, was partially actualized during the New Deal administrations of Franklin D. Roosevelt in the 1930s and 1940s.[17] Even as debates rage in contemporary American politics concerning the proper role of government to regulate the private sector in national (and international) affairs, few would argue (or even envision) returning to an era in which government played no role in determining economic practices within American society. Most powerfully, the social gospel's legacy became a major intellectual cornerstone for a variety of twentieth-century political reform movements, notably the Civil Rights movement led by Martin Luther King Jr.[18]

At the same time, however, there is little discussion today in theological and secular circles that has attempted to relate the social gospel legacy to contemporary social problems. A few secular scholars, notably Todd Gitlin and Richard Rorty (the grandson of Rauschenbusch), have argued for the renewal of a liberal-democratic vision related to contemporary American politics, but their ideal of a just society has been cut clean from its theological moorings.[19] Gitlin and Rorty champion a contemporary engagement with an earlier progressive legacy, in which Americans would abandon self-interest to embrace a shared egalitarian-democratic vision for America's future. Yet these scholars overlook the faith-based visions of social reform that were central to the main exponents of the social gospel. Although social gospelers were driven by the liberal-progressive desire to renounce self-interest in favor of serving the needs of the greater public good, the tradition, at its best, did not draw a sharp line between faith and political engagement. Of paramount importance to the social gospel was that the pressing social issues of the day—the elimination of child labor, the alleviation of economic and educational disparities between the rich and poor, the establishment of a safe working environment, and the creation of a living wage for every working American—were not simply problems that warranted political solutions. They were deeply moral and spiritual issues that could only be addressed and solved from a faith-based perspective. As expressed by William McGuire King, what united many adherents of the social gospel was their belief that "knowledge of God was only available when theological reflection became one with social action and with participation in the social struggles of humanity."[20] This theological core of the social gospel was expressed eloquently in the last Sunday-morning sermon preached by Martin Luther King Jr., when he commented that the eradication of poverty in America was not simply a matter of America's ability to galvanize material and political resources.

> This is America's opportunity to help bridge the gulf between the haves and the have-nots. The question is whether America will do it. There is nothing new about poverty. What is new is that we now have the techniques and the resources to get rid of poverty. The real question is whether we have the will.[21]

For Martin Luther King Jr., as for the major exponents of the social gospel, optimum political engagement against societal injustice arose not only from a strong personal faith; it emerged when that faith actively critiqued and engaged the dominant principalities and powers of contemporary society. The danger of such an approach is that it can easily lead to a "Christ of culture" faith, whereby Christianity, as neo-orthodox theologians like Reinhold Niebuhr warned, can easily become a means of endorsing the values of a dominant culture. The essays in this book highlight that the social gospel, at times, was held captive by the cultural suppositions of white Euro-American Protestantism, synonymous with Robert Handy's notion of a "Christian America."[22] At the same time, however, this "liberal" aspect of the social gospel theological legacy, as many of the book's authors point out, has the potential to call upon churches and church leaders to engage in an ongoing critique of the dominant theological and cultural suppositions of our era.

If there is one assertion that unites the perspectives offered in this book, it is this: The social gospel, while perhaps not a unified theological movement, compels future generations of Christians to wrestle with the essential tension between an individual's personal faith and the social gospel ideal of social salvation. It is irresponsible to argue that the social gospel "invented" the distinctive Protestant orientation that the church's ultimate goal was to influence the moral contours of secular society (in this regard, a strong case can be made to credit John Calvin for defining this modern view of the church, as opposed to any representative from the social gospel tradition). Nevertheless, it would be difficult to deny that the social gospel infused Western theology with the conviction that basic questions of Christian doctrine, in particular questions related to sin and soteriology, were inseparable from questions of social transformation. It is ironic that Rauschenbusch's book *Christianizing the Social Order*, a book seen by many as his most theologically "naive" work, contains some of his most eloquent words about the nature of salvation. "To concentrate our efforts on personal salvation, as orthodoxy has done, or on soul culture, as liberalism has done, comes close to refined selfishness. . . . Our religious individuality must get its interpretation from the supreme fact of social solidarity."[23] Rauschenbusch's words serve as a powerful reminder that any talk of Christian mission for the next century that does not take seriously the integration between personal faith and social transformation is an incomplete vision for the church.

The general question that this book poses is this: How might a recovery of the social gospel legacy empower contemporary churches to recover and restate the theme of social salvation within early twenty-first-century Christianity? As the editor of this book, I might put the question differently, postulating the following question to the reader: Do the conditions of the contemporary church warrant the introduction of a "new social gospel," a new theological Reformation based upon many of the theological, ethical, and historical themes introduced by the "first" social gospel movement in America?

The effort undertaken in this book, to reinterpret how the social gospel legacy might enable churches to redefine questions of personal faith and social transformation in the context of twenty-first-century Christianity, moves against many of the polarizing currents within contemporary North American churches. Current conversations agree that earlier paradigms, shaped by taken-for-granted assumptions of the church's dominant role in American culture, need to be jettisoned. However, these contemporary debates often fall within two polarities, each offering valid insight on the travail of contemporary Christianity and each vision, in its own way, incomplete.

One view redefines the church in light of patristic tradition, especially calling for churches to accept what are called "confessing" standards of early church doctrine. The effort of mainline churches to clarify their doctrinal heritages has produced renewed, and fruitful, conversations concerning the proper role of doctrine for contemporary churches. The movement has created a significant interest in liturgical renewal and has heightened the need to redress the historical imbalance within most Protestant traditions between Word and Sacrament.

Another polarity that has emerged in the past generation argues that contemporary churches need to redefine their agendas in ways that reconstruct religious symbols and rituals in light of modern cultural trends. Many exponents of the "church growth" movement fall under this perspective, arguing that traditional understandings of Christian worship are unable to address the rapidly shifting value structures of those living in what is termed *postmodernism*. Citing the increasing alienation of the American middle class from traditional religious institutions, it is argued that churches need to develop forms of mission that can reinterpret church tradition, using symbols and language that contemporary Americans can understand.[24]

Both of these perspectives accurately highlight the ongoing quest of many Americans for spiritual meaning, amidst the chaos of postmodern life. They both see the church's future success through an ability to foster distinctive models of community that can reinterpret essential Christian truths. Yet the critical question that needs to be raised is this: Do the current stresses on recovering patristic doctrine or the emphasis on church growth support Johnson's plea that a theologically vital Christianity depends upon the disciplined faith of an ethically driven community?

I believe the record of both contemporary currents is mixed. Whereas the doctrinal perspective attempts to hold the church accountable to its historical past, tradition runs the risk of becoming dogma that is held up beyond contemporary scrutiny. Current efforts within many mainline churches to use doctrine as a means of placing prohibitions on the leadership roles of gays and lesbians highlight the tendency of some to view doctrine as a simple matter of proper interpretation—a way of uncovering a "pure" Christian tradition from the recesses of an ancient past.[25] Such an enterprise is a dubious undertaking, not only because it often assumes that early church history is a monolith, but because it often turns early church history into a narrative expunged from what are seen as the corrupt excesses of modern culture. In effect, early church history becomes an icon for a golden-age era of Christianity, negating subsequent historical periods as irrelevant, or secondary, to contemporary circumstances.

While it is essential to see how past historical themes give clarity to the present, the historian always faces the danger of viewing certain periods in church history uncritically. Consequently, one can ignore the fact that the early church, as with all periods of Christian historical formation, dealt with numerous questions of cultural and theological ambiguity that never produced clear-cut doctrinal winners and losers. As J. Philip Wogaman has observed, the quest of Christians to recapture a "nostalgic vision" of a real or perceived past only gives us a fragmented portrait of our history and is of little use to us in the present.[26] One of the problems facing those who call for contemporary Christians to embrace an exclusive identity based upon the model of the early church is that the call is often more romanticized than theologically authentic. In every era in church history, the proponents of such a call (including the proponents of the social gospel) believed that they were recovering the teachings of early Christianity. The effort of reinterpreting church doctrine, however, has always meant an ability to make tradition vital to the needs of faith communities living at specific moments in time. As Johnson accurately notes, "Traditionalism must always be in some measure combated if history is to be accorded any really significance—that is to say, if anything new really happens."[27] Johnson's assertion expresses the fundamental truth espoused by Jaroslav Pelikan, who warned, "Tradition is the living faith of the dead, traditionalism is the dead faith of the living."[28] Pelikan's assertion reminds us that when we cling with unflinching fidelity to traditions, no matter how deeply rooted they may be in the church's historical past, we run the risk of losing touch with the ways Christian communities spawned, nurtured, challenged, and modified currents of tradition throughout the course of church history. To venerate a particular doctrine or a component of tradition in a fashion that removes it from its historical context is like ripping a plant out of its soil. Instead of sustaining life, doctrinal rigidity can turn living traditions into a dead faith that only serves the limited needs of segmented groups in the church.

Many proponents of the church growth perspective face a different problem—a tendency to disregard tradition. Several church-growth writers reflect a keen sense of the current alienation that many Americans (especially younger generations) feel from the values and symbols associated with mainline denominations. There is, however, within this movement a tendency to be ahistorical—to see little in the past that is relevant to the present. Discipleship for this group becomes solely focused on personal needs, without any regard for how an individual's beliefs relate to larger faith communities. Church-growth proponents are often insightful in identifying the deep spiritual yearnings of contemporary Americans. However, I'm not convinced that these movements have found a way to relate this yearning for greater spirituality to larger historical and theological formulations of Christian belief and practice. In some ways, the contemporary language of church growth sounds similar to the language spoken by some of the liberal modernists who emerged from the ashes of post-World War I liberalism: Both groups put a tremendous emphasis on contemporary culture at the expense of a deeper reservoir of historical and theological memory.

What both of these perspectives lack is a clear articulation of a compelling vision for social salvation—a vision that takes seriously Rauschenbusch's concern that Christianity avoid the dualism between a vital personal faith and the imperative for social transformation. Like many of his contemporaries, Johnson recognized how historical events of the 1920s and 1930s shattered the idealistic reform visions of the kingdom of God articulated by many social gospelers. Nevertheless, he feared those who embraced Christianity as "a political fire escape," where the purpose of faith was to bolster individual happiness, denying the ethical and moral responsibilities of living in the present.[29]

The issue at stake for our time is how do we recover, critique, and reappropriate the social gospel legacy in ways that avoid a myopic treatment of the past, yet also take seriously the vital questions of faith and meaning that face a diverse array of early twenty-first-century Christian faith communities. The authors of this book take seriously the idea that contemporary theology can, and must, engage in a critical reappropriation of past traditions. As one of this book's contributors noted elsewhere, "Rootlessness is neither an intellectual virtue nor a theological one, especially if we are concerned about moving the present in a direction that corrects our past."[30] We believe that the social gospel is one such tradition that has significance for twenty-first-century faith communities; this significance deserves closer scrutiny, because it calls upon Christians to wrestle with how the ramifications of a distinctive tradition can enable us who care about the church's future to engage the complex social realities of our era.

The question of how contemporary Christian communities might grapple with the meaning of social salvation, in the tradition of the social gospel, is central to part 1 of the book. Chapters 1 and 2, by Susan Lindley and Darryl Trimiew, respectively, wrestle from different perspectives with the question of defining and reassessing the social gospel's historical and theological legacy. Both writers reach different assessments concerning how the movement's legacy should be understood in the context of today's church. For Lindley, a primary task for understanding the historical significance of the social gospel is expanding earlier definitions of the movement to include the experiences of white and African American women of the late nineteenth and early twentieth centuries. She argues that earlier definitions of the social gospel, limiting the movement primarily to white-male clergy, fail to take into account how a diversity of women engaged reform issues in ways that expand traditional social-gospel definitions of social salvation. Darryl Trimiew's essay on race and the social gospel revisits a longstanding debate, related to the movement's lack of engagement with American racism. The social gospel's impact has been documented upon the life and thought of America's greatest social prophet, Martin Luther King Jr. Trimiew, however, argues that the lack of engagement on racial issues by white social gospel leaders accentuates how the movement's Euro-American cultural suppositions excluded African Americans as major participants in the movement. Highlighting Martin Luther King. Jr.'s vision of "the beloved community," Trimiew argues that contemporary churches need a compelling vision for a "new social gospel." Such a vision would acknowledge some of the social gospel's contributions to a legacy of social justice, yet move beyond the racism that plagued the original movement.

The remaining essays in part 1 deal with various themes that flesh out significant aspects of the social gospel's historical and theological legacy. Melanie May examines how a key theological theme of the social gospel, the doctrine of the kingdom of God, helped define the theological contours of the twentieth-century ecumenical movement. While highlighting the critical role played by the social gospel in shaping modern ecumenical thought (especially through what is today the Church and Society wing of the World Council of Churches), May argues that future ecumenical conversations must move beyond many of the Western theological and cultural premises that social gospel leaders commonly associated with the kingdom of God doctrine.

The social gospel played a major role in the institutional evolution of American mainline churches in the twentieth century. At the same time, its goal of "Christianizing" American society is seen as one of its great follies. Is there any way to revision this latter theme in our time? My essay examines how Rauschenbusch's understanding of "Christianizing" American society was embodied in his own family. By examining his relationship with his oldest daughter, Winifred, I argue that Rauschenbusch's understanding of the kingdom of God, while culturally tied to the conservative values of Victorian America, suggests that Rauschenbusch held a more elastic view of gender issues than that suggested by previous scholars. Rosemary Keller's essay highlights how women's leadership in the nineteenth and twentieth centuries challenged traditional historical and theological definitions of the social gospel.

Her chapter discusses how these historical models of church leadership, including the deaconess and settlement house movements, accentuate critical themes for women in the church today. In a similar vein, Dianne Reistroffer demonstrates how women in the social gospel heritage redefined stewardship practices at the end of the nineteenth century. Comparing women's ways of giving to more traditional stewardship models of social gospel men, she shows how women exercised leadership and power in the church of their era, and how these models reflect upon our understandings of stewardship in the present.

Part 2 of the book looks at how the social gospel legacy relates to specific social problems facing the church and society of our era. Gary Dorrien's chapter revisits the important question of how the social gospel contributes to modern economic practices. Focusing his analysis chiefly on Washington Gladden, considered by many to be the father of the social gospel movement in America, Dorrien examines how twenty-first-century American society can reappropriate the legacy of the social gospel in dealing with contemporary issues of economic justice.

Several strands of historical and theological scholarship have made appropriate distinctions between the terms *liberalism* and *social gospel*. The identification of the social gospel, however, as an outgrowth of late nineteenth-century liberalism remains dominant. Janet Furness's and Timothy Tseng's essay, however, points out that liberal church leaders were not the only Christians involved in significant social ministries. Their analysis of conservative American evangelicalism reveals significant strands of social ministry that echo and, at points, diverge from an earlier generation of "liberal" social gospel Christianity. Janet Fishburn examines the social gospel heritage in light of recent controversies surrounding the full participation of gays and lesbians in mainline churches. Church leaders in the social gospel heritage often led American Protestantism toward constructing holistic visions of justice and social transformation. Fishburn contends, however, that male social gospel leaders were responsible for a gender dualism in which social gospel men continuously defined women's roles in ways that marginalized their leadership in church and society. Her essay examines how this dualistic perspective has reemerged in contemporary mainline Protestant debates concerning discussions of gender equality and sexual orientation.

The final two essays in the book examine some of the ramifications of the social gospel legacy beyond a North American context. Max Stackhouse's essay explores how the social gospel's legacy can enable churches to deal constructively with emergent issues and tensions associated with twenty-first-century globalization. He argues that we are witnessing the emergence of a new incantation of the social gospel, one that challenges North American churches to deal effectively and prophetically with questions of theological pluralism, interfaith dialogue, and the construction of a globally based social ethic. Pamela Couture's concluding essay explores the relationship of the social gospel heritage to emergent models of pastoral theology that point beyond predominant North American therapeutic models of pastoral care. She discusses how the social gospel heritage might suggest new directions for pastoral care ministries in the twenty-first century, models that both respond to emergent problems in North America and in an increasingly global context.

To write a book of this nature is difficult, because one always risks misappropriating history in ways that do an injustice to the past. However, as Rauschenbusch affirmed in his last book, *A Theology for the Social Gospel*, "If theology stops growing or is unable to adjust itself to its modern environment and to meet its present tasks, it will die."[31] On a purely historical level, the social gospel is dead. The theological and reform aspirations hoped for by Rauschenbusch and other social gospelers were shattered by subsequent historical events of the last century. However, if one understands theology, as Rauschenbusch did, then being part of an ongoing process of historical reformulation and readjustment, but ignoring the legacy of the social gospel, may result in one's peril.

PART I

Historical and Theological Legacy

Deciding Who Counts: Toward a Revised Definition of the Social Gospel

Susan Hill Lindley

Though a layperson, N. H. Burroughs held a prominent position as a national leader in a Protestant church body from 1900 to 1961. In addition, in 1909 Burroughs opened and served as the head of a Washington, D.C., school designed to help urban workers, convinced that the teachings of Jesus and the concept of salvation must be applied to both individuals and to social structures; thus Burroughs was consistently outspoken about economic and political injustice in the United States. While Burroughs appears to have had few connections with traditionally acknowledged leaders of the social gospel movement, such concerns and perceptions would seem to make one an obvious part of the social gospel—but Nannie Helen Burroughs was an African American woman. The church body with which she worked was the National Baptist Convention, and she served as the corresponding secretary of the Baptist Women's Convention. The urban laborers upon whose plight she focused were black women domestic workers, and the school she founded was the National Training School for Women and Girls, where young African American women could, indeed, receive industrial training for the kinds of jobs they were most likely to find but where they also received a "classical education" that included required work in black history.

One might argue that the exclusion of someone like Nannie Helen Burroughs is primarily due to a racist and sexist myopia on the part of both the social gospel's leaders and its historians, yet it is also related to the matter of definition of the movement and to presumptions, even unconscious ones, that have underlain those definitions. Thus despite numerous existing definitions of the social gospel exhibiting a wide range of approaches, definitions occasionally in tension if not mutually exclusive, it may be fruitful to once again revisit the issue.

One justification for periodic redefinition is what Christopher Evans has called "historical integrity." Descriptions of the social gospel by its best-known participants and by a first generation of historians have carried implicit assumptions about "who counts." The focus was on a white middle-class male Protestant leadership that articulated social gospel ideals and analyses and that promoted programs, particularly through the churches, to correct perceived problems. The "objects" of the leadership's concern were primarily lower-class white men who labored in the industries of the growing urban centers of the Northeast and the Midwest. While the traditional leadership expressed some concern for other groups, like African Americans and women factory workers, such attention was peripheral or at best secondary to its central project. Yet these white men were not the only persons who perceived a disjunction between Christian beliefs and structural injustice in their day, nor were white male factory workers the only ones who suffered from the contemporary economic and political systems. Historical integrity thus demands that we pay attention to what has been overlooked: other leaders and workers in the social gospel; other areas where structural injustice impacted the lives of the poor or dispossessed; arenas other than the churches for addressing the problems of poverty and injustice.

Some classic definitions and descriptions have also presumed a particular theological basis for the social gospel or have highlighted various theological assertions as key for the social gospel. They, too, have sometimes been effectively if not always intentionally exclusionary. The issue of "who counts" thus impacts the matter of theological recovery as well as historical integrity. While other authors in this book address more directly such issues of theological recovery, some of the neglected voices can contribute valuable perspectives and correctives that may serve well those contemporary theologians who hope to recover enduring theological insights from a movement whose heyday occurred a century ago. My own focus, however, is on the matter of historical integrity, on casting a wider net. The catch may then prompt not only a redefinition in a formal sense but, equally important, modify summative descriptions of the social gospel as it flourished in the late nineteenth and early twentieth centuries in the United States.

For a simple and direct definition, it would seem difficult to quarrel with the one offered by a participant, Shailer Mathews, and cited by C. Howard Hopkins in his landmark study on the movement: ". . . the application of the teaching of Jesus and the total message of Christian salvation to society, the economic life, and social institutions . . . as well as to individuals."[1] While it is hard to improve upon Mathews's simple definition, subsequent attempts to redefine the movement were needed to unpack that definition, delineating more clearly its implications. Such a process is both inevitable and necessary as scholars uncover new evidence and view old evidence with new perspectives.[2] The first generation of scholars presented a movement that lasted from roughly the end of the Civil War through the end of World War I and was defined by its roots in theological liberalism, particularly the emphasis on "the fatherhood of God," "the brotherhood of man," and the kingdom of God as the center of Jesus' teaching, and by its response to human problems and dislocations precipitated by urban industrialization.[3] Successive students questioned that definition on various grounds: Was the social gospel simply or primarily a reaction to external events? Was nineteenth-century Protestant liberalism too narrow a theological basis? Weren't evangelical roots and the nineteenth century tradition of revivals and reform equally important?[4] Was the social gospel a uniquely American phenomenon, or was it part of a broader movement in the English-speaking (or Protestant) world?[5] Is the real key not the problems addressed—those of urban labor—but the focus on social salvation? Did social salvation take precedence, temporally and substantively, over individual salvation, or did the movement's proponents see both as equally critical?[6] Did social gospel theologians reject any concept of the kingdom of God as a future and otherworldly hope in favor of its temporal establishment, or did they attempt to interpret that biblical image as both present imperative and future vision?

Other revisionists have focused on the matter of inclusion and exclusion. The parameters, if not the center, of the movement have been significantly challenged in recent decades by scholars who have focused on the activities of Christians who were not white middle-class males located in those sections of the United States where urbanization and industrialization were having their greatest impact in the last decades of the nineteenth century and the first ones of the twentieth century. While it is true that the vast majority of those traditionally identified as the movement's leaders were, indeed, white men—and most, though not all, of them Protestant ministers—there were others, particularly white women, African American men and women, and working-class people, who shared social gospel ideals and goals. Nor was the movement absent in the predominantly rural South.[7] The question then becomes one of "who counts?" White men were, indeed, more likely to have the level of education and the connections with centers of power and credibility in American culture that made them more visible and influential, and it is hardly surprising that the first generation of scholars, themselves educated white males, focused on such familiar leadership and on the strength of the movement in the Northeast and Midwest of the United States. But a second generation of scholarship has uncovered significant activity in areas less noticed by that first generation. Episcopalian and socialist Vida Scudder, one of the few women noted in the first generation of studies, must be joined by well-known women like Frances Willard, who, as president of the Woman's Christian Temperance Union, moved beyond temperance to broad concern about structural urban problems and her own membership in the Knights of Labor, as well as by

numerous other women who wrote novels or worked as deaconesses, in settlement houses, or through their churches' women's groups to address social
issues that impeded the progress of the kingdom of God. Edgar Gardner Murphy was a white Southerner and former Episcopal priest who worked to
improve race relations and child labor conditions. Although he "has not until
now . . . been ranked among the social gospelers," concluded Ronald White
and C. Howard Hopkins in their 1976 revisionist volume on the social gospel,
"he deserves to be."[8] Henry Hugh Proctor, a black Congregational pastor in
Atlanta, made his own church a center for social services and worked to defend
the civil rights of African Americans. Reverdy C. Ransom, preacher and later
bishop in the African Methodist Episcopal Church, consistently linked Christian faith and social mission, founding the Institutional Church and Social Settlement in 1900 for Chicago's blacks. He worked with the Niagara Movement
and later the National Association for the Advancement of Colored People,
and wrote, especially in the *A.M.E. Review*, on the political and economic
injustices suffered by African Americans. Black women also acted on social
implications of their Christian faith, women like Nannie Helen Burroughs[9]
and Mary McLeod Bethune, who initially hoped to serve as a foreign missionary to Africa. Denied that opportunity because of her race, Bethune went
on to a long career as educator, reformer, and political activist. A helpful definition of the movement needs to be broad enough to encompass those man-
ifestations that cultural and historical myopia excluded.

Yet the issue of "who counts" goes beyond asking whether southerners,
white women, African Americans, or other "outsiders" should be considered
as part of the social gospel movement if they shared some or all of its presuppositions and goals. Even to express the question in that way implies that the
center of the movement, as represented and delineated by its traditionally
acknowledged leadership, is both stable and definitive, so that if others wish
to count, they need to fit a classic definition of the movement. But are they
merely to be integrated, where possible, into a set, existing understanding?
This is problematic, for at times they do not fit very well; this also leaves in
place an implicit assertion that the real heart and core of the movement is what
it always was, the product of a relatively privileged group of white middle-class
males. A definition of any movement which, *by definition*, implicitly excludes
previously neglected voices is both inadequate and misleading. (This is not to
suggest that some movements, like the KKK, may not *explicitly* exclude certain
voices, but such exclusion then becomes a central part of the definition and
nature of that movement. Social gospel leaders professed as theologically central a belief in "the brotherhood of man"—terms presumed at the time to be
generic. However inadequate the breadth of vision of those leaders may have
been, they never *by definition* excluded some groups of humans from the con-

cept, and it would surely be ironic for later historians to insist on a definition that denied neglected voices the possibility of participation as actors and not merely objects of sympathy.)

Inauthentic and implicitly exclusionary definitions of a movement can take different forms. For example, one may define the movement in terms of Christian response to particular historical concerns, principally urban labor in the last decades of the nineteenth century and the early ones of the twentieth century, thus ignoring or marginalizing Christian response to social problems in the South or rural areas. One could insist that "the" social gospel was predominantly concerned with economic structures that needed to be "Christianized" since American political structures were already "democratic" and hence "Christian," and it was only abuse of the basic system that needed attention—but to women and African Americans, systemic *political* change was crucial. One could identify "the" movement with a particular theological tradition like nineteenth-century Protestant liberalism and consequently overlook not only the evangelical roots of the movement but also the Baptist piety of a Walter Rauschenbusch or the Anglo-Catholicism of a Vida Scudder. To be sure, correctives to these limited definitions of the movement have been part of social gospel scholarship for decades.

Alternatively and more subtly, one can continue to assume a core leadership as definitive and then deduce "the" movement's ideas about a particular issue from those leaders. For example, a historian of social Christianity like Paul Phillips concludes that issues of women's rights at the turn of the twentieth century, particularly woman suffrage, were of peripheral interest at most to social gospel leaders.[10] True, a Washington Gladden or a Walter Rauschenbusch may have had minimal concern for women's rights, but woman suffrage and women's working conditions were much more central to women like Frances Willard or Vida Scudder and their colleagues in the Woman's Christian Temperance Union or the Women's Trade Union League. Similarly, racism was not one of the highest priorities for most white male leaders—though recent works have suggested that these leaders were less oblivious to its import than older critiques suggested—but race relations were surely "front and center" for people like Proctor, Ransom, Burroughs, and Bethune.

In expanding the concerns that count in the movement, the point is not to argue that the best-known core of white male leaders of the classic social gospel were more sensitive and activist in areas of racism or sexism than they were, though the picture is more complex than earlier critics' dismissals. The critiques were and are justified, and historical integrity demands balanced assessments of the traditional leaders' "blind spots."[11] Yet the more crucial point is to insist that as the roster of "who counts" is expanded, so too may the roster of issues addressed by "the" movement because some social gospelers held as central what others saw as peripheral in terms of structural change. A more accurate generalization then becomes, for example, that most of the white male middle-class leadership of the social gospel, not "the" social gospel, placed a relatively low priority on racism and was conventional in its views of women.

In one sense, historiography of the social gospel movement, like other particular historical foci, is a microcosm of scholarship on American history as a whole. One may envision the changes precipitated by greater sensitivity to the "white male bias" of history in two stages. First is the necessary work of recovering the neglected stories, the lives, problems, and contributions of those who by reason of class, race, gender, or geographical location have been underrepresented and underappreciated. In terms of the social gospel, an excellent start has been made on this stage, though further work, of course, remains to be done, particularly among the rank and file—the men and women who through church groups and other local organizations heard or read social gospel ideas and tried to act upon them in their immediate setting. A second stage is, however, much more difficult: to produce an account that genuinely integrates the "new" (in terms of historical awareness) stories into the traditional account so that it becomes a new story for all, not simply the old story with a few more asides and footnotes. In the case of the social gospel, this is particularly challenging because of the varieties of theological viewpoints, goals, and methods even within traditional understandings of the movement, not to mention the results of revisionist scholarship.[12] Yet this is a critical goal, both for historical integrity and because the "new" voices may contribute different perspectives and insights valuable for current theology and action.

At the same time, it is important not to propose a definition so broad as to be functionally useless to historians and theologians. To baptize virtually every impulse for social reform as "social gospel" is a kind of religious imperialism that also fails to credit particular Christians with a distinctive contribution as they responded to what they understood as the imperatives of the gospel. A further concern about excessive breadth is the matter of historical location. Is the movement's distinctiveness best preserved by limiting it to the last decades of the nineteenth century and the early ones of the twentieth century? Is the term *social gospel* best kept for the manifestation in the United States of a broader movement of social Christianity during that time period? Should one argue that "the" social gospel did not die shortly after the first World War but rather continued, at times in new forms and with new concerns and leadership? Proponents of both a narrower and a broader conception of the movement can mount persuasive arguments, and it may be that *the social gospel*, like *evangelicals*, will remain a multileveled term in American religious history, a term whose usage must be clarified in particular contexts.

Even if a multileveled and contextual approach is adopted, continued concern with some kind of basic definition is justified because, for better or worse, the term has become part of the ongoing conversation of twentieth-century Christian theology. As Max Stackhouse wrote in a preface to the 1999 book *Perspectives on the Social Gospel*, "It is simply not true that the social gospel is dead. It is alive and well in the preoccupations of many thinkers and preachers; it generated a number of public policy initiatives that live on; it has entered and altered, by intermixture with other movements and developments, the social and religious genetic code of twentieth century thought across the spectrum."[13] Moreover, if the theses of this collection are correct, that contemporary theology can, and must, engage in critical reappropriation of past traditions and that Christians need a compelling vision for social salvation, and if one believes that the insights and contributions of the social gospel, whatever its limitations, represent a significant and enduring perspective on the Christian gospel, there is a continuing need to be clear about how one is using the term.

My own attempt at a definition arose from personal conviction and pragmatic need. Introduced to the social gospel during the 1960s and 1970s as part of the history of religion in America, I accepted the conventional wisdom in critique of its limitations: that it had been theologically, politically, and economically naive; that its leadership had virtually ignored issues of race; that it was bound by middle-class assumptions and prejudices; that it ended after World War I through a combination of external circumstances (disillusionment in the aftermath of the "Great War" and the isolationist and materialist preoccupation of the next decades) and the decisive theological critique of "Christian realism." Yet I was also drawn by its concern to link Christian theology and the practice of justice in the world in its time as the Civil Rights movement and liberation theology did a half century later. It seemed then to me, as it still does, to be a faithful response to the gospel, necessary not only in the heyday of the "classic" social gospel movement but also as a continued reminder to Christians thereafter. Second, I have been a teacher of undergraduates for more than a quarter century, one whose daily work necessitates the formulation of relatively clear and concise descriptions of movements and ideas for an audience that is often neither theologically sophisticated nor historically informed. In the third place, much of my own scholarly work has been part of the explosion of interest in the neglected voices and activities of women in American religion, which has in turn led me to increased sensitivity to the absence of other voices. Beginning to hear those new voices as part of the social gospel raised exciting possibilities for reassessment of the nature and breadth of an important movement in American religious history, but it also necessarily raised questions of definition.

Thus the modest proposal: an attempt at a working definition of the movement that allows for both historical integrity and theological recovery, one that finds a kind of via media, neither baptizing every impulse for social justice as social gospel nor excluding alternative or less traditionally obvious voices and loci. It is my "working classroom definition," and I proposed it at the opening panel of the social gospel conference at Colgate-Rochester in March 1999:

> The social gospel was distinguished, on the one hand, from general charity and humanitarian work by the religious motivation behind its ideas and activities and its insistence on connecting social ideals with the Kingdom of God, at least partially realizable in this world. On the other hand, the social gospel moved beyond traditional Christian charity in its recognition of corporate identity, corporate and structural sin, and social salvation, along with concern for individual sin, faith, and responsibility.

Such a definition allows the inclusion of less traditional voices and concerns but includes key and distinctive points of the social gospel: its recognition of structural problems and its goal of social salvation. In addition, connection with Christian faith and specifically a vision of the kingdom of God—though not necessarily the institutional church—is foundational. Faith in the kingdom of God as a present reality as well as a future goal means that social gospelers have some level of optimism that progress in this world toward greater justice and harmony is possible. Belief in the kingdom's full realization as a future beyond history may be a corrective to excessive naivete; belief in the kingdom as present reality and this-worldly potential disallows cynicism or fatalistic resignation in the face of injustice. Finally, the definition attempts to repudiate the caricature of some critics that social gospelers didn't care about individual salvation or destiny and attempts to avoid an overly broad claim that any vaguely religious social activity was part of the movement.

As a working definition, it leaves open certain continuing questions. First, what should be the relative weight of thought and action in determining "who counts" as part of the movement? Might the mix be different in less prominent advocates than in the traditionally acknowledged leadership? How much is thought dependent on access not only to some form of higher education (or the leisure to become self-educated) but also to public fora of one kind or another? Yet if the premise is accepted—that one may be truly part of the movement without being either a creative theologian or an effective publicist—how are such persons to be discovered and their relative contributions assessed by historians? Finding the answers may not be easy, but to ignore the resources undercuts our historical integrity in understanding the movement itself and may well bear on our conclusions about its impact.

Another question concerns the degree of self-consciousness about the actions one needs to have had in order to count as part of the social gospel, a question in turn related to but distinct from the complex issue of motivations. Did a person have to identify himself or herself as part of the social gospel movement? How articulate must one have been about his or her activities as a challenge to social structures or about the idea of social salvation? Can these be read from deeds instead of words? When a Methodist deaconess, citing the imperative of Christian faith, calls for laws limiting child labor (or at least the enforcement of existing laws), public support of kindergartens for the poor, and a machinery of juvenile courts and probation rather than incarceration for young offenders, even if she never uses the term *social salvation,* is she not an advocate of the social gospel?[14] I would argue for the possibility of a spectrum here, acknowledging that for some it was a matter of partial or growing awareness. That some of the best-known leaders of the movement, like Gladden and Rauschenbusch, were awakened by personal contact with the devastating poverty of urban workers to a conviction that traditional charity was an insufficient solution to the needs of the poor has long been noted. I would argue that a similar process held for many women. My own study of deaconesses, while neither systematic nor definitive, has been suggestive. Here were women whose religious commitment was clearly evidenced in their joining of an order but whose personal and practical experiences sometimes moved them, like their male ministerial counterparts, to the questioning of structures. Seeing how transitory was the change that could be made for the poor by traditional charity, deaconesses were often forced to question the causes of poverty and, in turn, to seek out structural solutions that addressed those causes. The point is not that all deaconesses were part of the social gospel, any more than all Protestant ministers were, but that here is a locus neglected by traditional social gospel historians which might prove fruitful in expanding and reshaping our understanding of who and what counted.

The search for historical integrity by expanding notions of "who counts" in the social gospel has made substantial progress in the revisionist work of the last few decades, but further tasks remain. First is one of publicity: conveying to nonspecialists the results of revisionist work, so that pastors, teachers, and academic historians and theologians whose primary field of research is not the social gospel no longer repeat out-dated and exclusionary descriptions of the movement. Second is the need for continuing work on the neglected voices, areas of concern, and activities designed to challenge unjust structures of American society during the heyday of the social gospel. Third and related is the need to explore questions such as the ones I have raised (and surely others will raise additional questions). How does one balance thought and action in proponents of the social gospel? What degree of theological sophistication and self-conscious identification with the social gospel, as it was, admittedly, led and articulated publicly primarily by white middle-class men in its own time, is necessary for someone to "count"? Finally, we need new broad accounts of the social gospel that truly integrate the wider range of voices, concerns, and activities with what has been historically viewed as the core of "the" social gospel. The resultant fuller understanding is important not only for the matter of historical integrity but also for the hope that the theological insights of the social gospel may continue to speak fruitfully and prophetically to the church today.

2

The Social Gospel Movement
and the Question of Race

Darryl M. Trimiew

For W. E. B. Du Bois the primary question of the twentieth century was how to remedy the color line.[1] Du Bois also maintained that the most pressing social-political-ethical question for future generations would be how to resolve the problem of international racism. Social gospel leaders were aware of this problem. While most of them were in favor of more humane treatment for blacks and others, their understanding of the mission of the Christian social gospel invariably exacerbated racial subjugation. The primary reason concerns the teleology of the social gospel. One common denominator among social gospelers was their belief that the gospel of Jesus Christ should work to alleviate social, political, and economic problems. This duty was not, in their opinion, fulfilled by the Christian culture that had evolved on American shores. These problems were believed to be amenable, however, to incremental improvement, a form of gradualism, primarily by means of a more faithful and intelligent process of intervention in the affairs of the world. In this theory, as people were informed of the true social responsibilities enjoined by the gospel, as they acted in a revolution of the saints to solve those problems, such difficulties would yield to the active intervention of the church. There were two problems with this approach. First, the commitment to incremental change presupposed that gradualism was the best method for implementing and achieving social justice. Second, the intervention that was proposed misunderstood the basic problem. For the problem of the color line is, among other things, a subtle but broad-based commitment to a form of white supremacy.[2] This commitment results mainly from a failure to undertake critical self-examination in white society and therefore is amenable to redress only when the majority culture is willing to effect change within itself.

Such a change was not possible historically, however, because, in particular, the commitment to white supremacy, the loyalty and fervor for whites-only led interventions held by social gospelers, was not considered problematic by them. On the contrary, their proposed ideal society was one in which white

27

domination was considered normative and ideal. Thus one of the goals of the social gospel was also the goal of achieving the assimilation of nonwhites into an orderly submissive minority in which they would not differ in any appreciable way from the majority. God's will on earth was presumably to be carried out in a world dominated by whites.[3]

This assumption of the desirability of assimilation as a *telos* was predicated more specifically on the belief that only Anglo-American males were moral agents fit to make changes in society. In this understanding of moral activism, the black community could never transcend its assigned position of inferiority as a mission community. As such, blacks could only be objects of mission and ministry, not partners in any mission designed to combat racism or any other important problems.

Accordingly, the social gospelers failed to combat racism because the mission goals of the Christian social gospel, though designed in theory to help and uplift the black community, did so in ways that furthered white supremacy and did so with the intent to achieve racist goals (namely an uncritical assimilation of nonwhites into submissive, supportive roles in a white-dominated majority). In short, the Christian social gospel could not address the problem of the color line because it never perceived its participation in the preservation of the color line as a problem.[4] Quite to the contrary, it saw as one of its tasks the duty to participate in the preservation of a permanent white-dominated society.[5]

The importance of this reevaluation of the Christian social gospel movement lies in its ability to help us better understand the current streams of Christian activism. Some of the successors to the social gospel movement are still unable to imagine or participate in a multiethnic, multiclassed American society, precisely because such a movement no longer reserves exclusively for European Americans positions of leadership in the formation of a socially and morally progressive society. Further, many white Christians still have difficulties in envisioning a Christian society that is not predicated upon white domination. Yet in a world in which exclusive white domination is no longer achievable, and clearly not morally justifiable, movements for the same are doomed to fail eventually. Thus the continued commitment to white domination dooms many current would-be progressive Christian movements in their attempts to better race relations in the same way as it did the social gospelers.[6] A recognition of the erroneous understandings of their history has at least the potential of helping current struggles refrain from making the same mistakes.

This historical commitment to white domination in the process of exercising moral agency can be demonstrated in two ways. The first demonstration examines the interaction, or lack thereof, between social gospelers and black would-be allies such as Reverdy Ransom, Ida B. Wells-Barnett, and Nannie Helen Burroughs. Since no serious rejection of social gospel praxis and theory was entertained by Ransom, Wells-Barnett, or Burroughs (other than the implicit wholesale adoption of white supremacy), it may seem surprising to some that they were routinely ignored by social gospelers.[7] This historical fact suggests the inability of social gospelers to follow or work with black leadership. This historic failing is the primary proof of the commitment of social gospelers to whites-only moral leadership.

The second demonstration examines the influence that the social gospel had on a major civil rights activist while simultaneously highlighting his rejection of white domination and uncritical wholesale assimilation. The distinct difference between someone who was deeply influenced by the social gospel and someone who was an exponent of the social gospel is important. Often claimed as a successor to the social gospel movement, Dr. Martin Luther King Jr. rejected white domination. Instead he fought for the realization of a multiethnic, multicultural society, the *beloved community*, a community inherently in contradiction to the idealized white-dominated communities sought after and fought for by social gospelers.

Accordingly, this argument will proceed with two historical-ethical examinations. The first examines how the leadership of black contemporaries to the social gospelers was not accepted, along with a demonstration of a systemic refusal to work with or follow any significant black leadership that was available and amenable to alliances with the Christian social gospel. The second examination will assess how Martin Luther King Jr. employed some of the theology of the social gospel, yet rejected the white supremacy implicit in it. We will conclude this argument with an examination of King's beloved community and how it constitutes a superior moral community more likely to be realized in the twenty-first century.

The Classic Social Gospel Tradition

Social gospel theorists have been aware of the alienation between black Christian contemporaries of the social gospel movement and the commonly acknowledged white social gospel leaders. Some have attempted to address this gap by pointing out the similarities between the praxis and theology of blacks and/or women with that of the social gospelers. In doing so, they seek to correct the shortcomings of the classic social gospel and extol the virtues, practices, and theology of rejected and neglected black and/or women Christians. These efforts are worthwhile and useful provided that they do not obscure basic historical facts. Much of this work is laudable in the same sense as the historical revisionism often seen in selecting members of the Baseball Hall of Fame at Cooperstown, New York. Competent baseball historians routinely cull the records of the old Negro leagues and talk to surviving players, coaches, reporters, and fans of that era. From the information gleaned, they determine that Josh Gibson, Buck Owens, or some other black notable should be inducted into Cooperstown. Some of these revisions are posthumous, some are not; most if not all are justifiable since the criteria are high and prejudice against blacks still lingers. What cannot be changed is the actual historical record. Buck Owens did not play in the major leagues. His exclusion was unjust but there it stands, an immutable historical fact, one that means that the world of baseball was a poorer, more unjust and less competitive place. To say that these players should have been allowed to play is correct. To say that they would have changed baseball and even America is also correct, but it is wrong to talk of major league baseball of that era as if these players and others of lesser acclaim had indeed played there. They did not. Who would have won what pennants and indeed what white players would now be in Cooperstown is, accordingly, unknowable and speculative. Such an outcome can be more easily seen by examining early twentieth-century prizefighting champions who refused to fight black fighters of their era.[8] That their world was significantly different from what it could have been is easier to see in the head-to-head competition that boxing entails.

A similarly misleading result can be obtained by characterizing black contemporaries of the social gospel as "neglected social gospelers," for it obscures the fact that such blacks were "playing" as moral agents while social gospelers were also simultaneously "playing," to continue the baseball metaphor, but the games were not played in the same league. Unlike baseball, where the balls and bats, field and mitts, rules and regulations were relatively the same for all participants, the moral interactions and struggles of blacks and whites were of significant difference. Consider how one historian, Susan Lindley, addresses this issue:

> The neglected voices of persons like Vida Scudder, Reverdy Ransom, and Nannie Helen Burroughs add depth and eloquence to the message of the social gospel. Some of what they said echoed themes of better known white male leaders, but they also sounded their own distinctive notes. Even as we continue to see urban labor as the central concern of the social gospel, their voices remind us that the woman factory worker, the black man whose option for work at the time was often to be a despised "scab," and the black female domestic were part of the urban labor force. They remind us that the theological grounding of a social gospel could range from Anglo-Catholicism to the black religious tradition as well as the more typical white evangelical liberalism. And these three, at least, also suggest commitment and activity that began in the movement's heyday but lasted well beyond the watershed of World War I into the third and fourth decades of the twentieth century.[9]

Lindley is correct that Ransom, Burroughs and others, such as Wells-Barnett did establish and promulgate Christian social activism movements. There is an unmistakable affinity between the ideas held by these moralists and the thinking of white social gospel leaders. It may even be demonstrated historically that black Christian reformers such as Wells-Barnett, Francis J. Grimke, or Bishop Henry McNeal Turner promulgated a black "social gospel" in the alternative universe that they occupied, struggled in, and died in. Yet that social gospel was no more a part of what we now call the Christian social gospel than the Negro leagues were a part of the major leagues. This reality can be seen in the instances where the alternate universes collided and black Christian activists interacted with white gospelers. In such cases of convergence, the theological ideas of white social gospelers were affirmed by black social gospelers without a reciprocal affirmation of the theology of black activists. This lack of reciprocity by white social gospelers is particularly apparent concerning the issue of race.

One historical example of this convergence without agreement can be seen in the dispute between Wells-Barnett and Frances Willard. By all accounts, Willard is an acknowledged proponent of the historic social gospel tradition. While there is an affinity of ideas shared by Willard and Wells-Barnett for the primary goal of Wells-Barnett's mission, namely the eradication of the practice of lynching, she received little or no support from Willard. Indeed, she and Willard clashed publicly and privately on this issue. Willard's institution, the Woman's Christian Temperance Union, did not actively oppose lynching. Willard showed her own racism by opposing the proposed Federal Election Bill, which would have given the federal government control over national elections. This bill would also have paved the way for the full enfranchisement of blacks and would have allowed for the eventual creation of a multiethnic, multiclassed society in which white domination was no longer normative. Willard's opposition to Wells-Barnett on this point is revealing. With reference to Wells-Barnett's opposition to lynching—that the practice encouraged oppression and social control based on racist sexual mythology, namely that black men were beasts, and in modern parlance, sexual predators—Willard rejected all of Wells-Barnett's documentation and held to the racist standard of her generation that black men were inherently savage. She publicly categorized southern blacks as "a great dark faced mob."[10] With reference to the sexual proclivities of blacks in general, she noted that "[they multiply] like the locust of Egypt. The grog-shop is its center of power. . . . The safety of women, of children, of the home is menaced in a thousand localities so that men dare not go beyond the sight of their own roof-tree."[11] In short, such bestial people could possibly, over a very long period of time, be trained like good dogs to stay to themselves and to behave but could not responsibly be given the right to vote. They certainly could not be considered candidates for being neighbors. In short, at every turn where Willard might have resisted white domination, she not only failed to resist but joined in the preservation of the institution.

What this means is not just that white social gospel leaders were racist, which of course, they were (like most Americans of that era) but also that they completely lacked the inherent resources to criticize themselves on this point. Moreover, they lacked the ability to hear the voices of would-be allies in the social gospel movement who were critical of them, such as Wells-Barnett. She and other black contemporaries were ignored except where those voices merely parroted the social, political, and theological ideas of the Christian social gospel movement. In other words, Ransom, Wells-Barnett, and Burroughs were not merely neglected voices of the social gospel movement, but rather Christian social activists whose "other" social gospel was rejected by their social gospel contemporaries. Clearly, they were not recognized as genuine moral agents whose opinions mattered, whose insights needed to be regarded with care, whose criticisms might be inspired by God as correctives to the moral praxis and aspirations of social gospelers. And, further—quite rightly—white social gospelers saw their black counterparts as champions of a different and invidious gospel—a gospel in which equality might reign and white hegemony might be destroyed. In other words, this historical period was not a time when a variety of social gospelers—some black, some white—were actively serving God together. Rather, it was a time when parallel Christian social activist movements fought for differing visions of the "kingdom of God in America."

The two movements cannot be equated but must be recognized as two or more distinct movements. In a sense, the quest for the continuation of a white-dominated society was carried on simultaneously by social gospelers and another contemporary "Christian" organization, the Ku Klux Klan. Both declared their belief in a Christian God and in white domination. Yet it seems much easier for us now, in the twenty-first century, to see these movements as oppositional in the early twentieth century. Indeed, the two movements were in no way identical. However, black Christian social activists and white social gospelers were profoundly different in their respective understanding of moral agency and the conditions necessary for a morally just society. It is only when the commitment to white supremacy as an acceptable feature of early twentieth-century America is acknowledged as normative for white social gospelers that the social gospel movement can be fully understood for what it was. Only then can we understand how it succeeded and how it failed.

Painful as this acknowledgment may be, it is necessary to accept it in order to understand, among other things, why white liberal theologies continued to fail so miserably at addressing the question of the color line later in the twentieth century. The short explanation for this failure is that the portion of white liberal theologies that may rightfully be designated as successors to the social gospel movement carried the commitment to white supremacy into their mission and ministry. The inability to see blacks as moral agents—rather than merely as moral entities for whom moral agents (such as white males) might have a responsibility—blinded and cursed the social gospel movement, and similarly blinded and cursed its successors. Meanwhile, the successors to the black Christian activism of the early twentieth century—the successors to the work of Ransom, Burroughs, and Wells-Barnett—were busy internalizing some of the theological sentiments and themes of the social gospel. At the same time, they rejected the inherent racism of the social gospel and continued the quest for an egalitarian, multiethnic society in which blacks and others are not assimilated into a white majority so completely as to extinguish their identity.

Instead the desired Christian mission is to work with all people to create a new society. How this new generation struggled and how a new "social gospel" evolved can be seen in the person of Dr. Martin Luther King Jr.

Martin Luther King Jr.: A Christian Social Gospeler?

> In spite of the noble affirmations of Christianity, the church has often lagged in its concern for social justice and too often has been content to mouth pious irrelevances and sanctimonious trivialities. It has often been so absorbed in a future good "over yonder" that it forgets the present evils "down here." Yet the church is challenged to make the gospel of Jesus Christ relevant within the social situation. We must come to see that the Christian gospel is a two-way road. On the one side, it seeks to change the souls of men and thereby unite them with God; on the other, it seeks to change the environmental conditions of men so that the soul will have a chance after it is changed. Any religion that professes to be concerned with the souls of men and yet is not concerned with the economic and social conditions that cripple them is the kind the Marxist describes as "an opiate of the people."[12]

It was for this kind of criticism of the church as well as for his activism that Martin Luther King Jr. has been characterized as having been deeply influenced by the social gospel tradition.[13] He designated himself as such.[14] It is, of course, clear that he shared many of the theological positions of the classic social gospel tradition of the late nineteenth century and early twentieth century. It is also equally clear that, chronologically speaking, he was born in a different generation than the social gospel tradition and was most active in an even later generation. How then can he be correctly characterized as a social gospeler? Such a designation could still be defensible if he, though later born, carried out as much as possible the theology and *praxis* of the social gospel. By all accounts, he did not. Like all prominent black Christian social activists of nearly every generation, he did not espouse white domination and supremacy, as we have argued was normative for the social gospel movement. Indeed he should be rightly regarded as one of the foremost opponents to such a movement. King's mission to encourage and develop the beloved community—a community in which all people would be morally equal and morally responsible—is the antithesis of the white-dominated society promoted by the early social gospel.[15]

Since King's opposition to white supremacy is indisputable, and the commitment to white supremacy by the classic social gospel similarly clear, why then is King associated with the social gospel movement? The answer lies in the characterization of Christian social gospel practices and objectives by its putative successors. At least some current exponents of Christian activism are clearly capable of recognizing the black community and the merit of black leaders to act as moral agents with whom alliances can be established. But they are able to do so *because* they have been converted to the social gospel of Dr. Martin Luther King Jr., not to the social gospel of Washington Gladden, Walter Rauschenbusch, Josiah Strong, or Shailer Mathews. Modern Christian social activism movements are also capable of conceiving of a multiethnic society in which blacks would not simply be assimilated to the point of invisibility *because* of a similar conversion. In short, this "new" social gospel is substantially different, ethically speaking, from its predecessor and is, therefore, capable of attracting and keeping blacks who are also in opposition to unfettered industrialism, capitalism, and theological escapism. These latter themes were, of course, core ideas in the classic social gospel. This ability to recognize blacks as a moral community with which to act in concert, rather than simply to act on behalf of as a paternalistic guardian, coupled with the recognition that a better America would have to be a multiethnic, multiclassed society that recognized itself as such, removes this African American Christian activist movement from consideration as a mere continuation of the social gospel movement. The characterization of this new movement as a simple continuation of the Christian social gospel is an interpretative mistake that does not allow scholars to properly understand and appreciate the classic social gospel movement nor to account for the developments in Christian activism in post-World War II America.

Of what advantage is this categorical separation? Its primary advantage is explanatory. Part of the confusion in the modern Christian American activism movement continues to center on the question of the nature and mission of the church. Historical structures in communities, churches, classes, ethnicities, political parties, and cultural movements continue to keep certain people together and certain people apart. Currently there does not exist a broad Christian activist movement that transcends these particularities and that attempts to address the racial, economic, political, and cultural divisions that beset America. Nonetheless there are a variety of organizations—the National Council of Churches, Habitat for Humanity, and others—that attempt to bridge this gap. Hence Americans remain divided into a variety of camps in which a number of different churches and Christian groups work, generally not in cooperation with each other, in a piecemeal fashion to achieve some of the objectives sought by the classic social gospel. The question of the color line remains an important unresolved problem. Indeed much of the division of modern Christian groups can be attributed primarily to this one factor alone. Blacks will no longer serve as obedient pawns in white-dominated institutions. Whites remain unwilling to have nonwhite leaders in charge of their major organizations. Accordingly, in some respects there is no successor to the classic social gospel movement.

Again, as previously mentioned, the closest figure who might be able to serve as the foundation for a newly developed social gospel is Martin Luther King Jr. King had all of the attributes of a social gospeler, a stringent criticism of capitalism, an empathy for the working poor, a love of God, and a commitment to leading people into a life and death struggle for equality of opportunity and development as full-fledged citizens. King is considered to have created a new incantation of the social gospel. Preston Williams writes of King on this point:

> In the work of Martin L. King, Jr., the social gospel received new life. Conditions had so progressed that it could now act to bring radical change to blacks in the heart of the South. The direct-action technique which Negroes had used throughout their history was to become under King and others an adjunct to legal and court reform.[16]

Yet even Williams acknowledges with regard to King, "Since this strategy had its roots more in the practice of Gandhi than in American Social Christianity, it too was to lead King further in the direction of nonviolence as a way of life."[17] Williams engages, accordingly, in a form of revisionism (which we are trying to avoid doing also) when he tries to link King to the social gospel. He notes, "In the person of Martin L. King Jr., the social gospel brought its own world view. It was to lift as well as to make equal, and, like integration, it looked toward the destruction of much if not all black folk culture."[18] He goes on to note:

> King, unlike other social gospelers, made race central and stressed more coercion and direct action within the context of nonviolence;

but, like other social gospelers, he too possessed an optimistic conception of man and human progress, an idealistic conception of love, and a notion that a purified Western culture most resembled the Kingdom of God.[19]

What is problematic about Williams's interpretative approach is not his reading of King; he is insightful in his assessment of the man and his mission. Williams's mistake is in finding theological ideas and themes in King that were central to the classic social gospel, and subsequently placing the mantel of the new social gospel leader upon him simply because he shared such ideas and advanced certain social gospel initiatives. This would make King a social gospel successor to figures such as Gladden and Rauschenbusch. But though King is deeply influenced by that movement and by the work of Reinhold Niebuhr, what he offered was an entirely new approach to Christian social activism. Arguably King can be seen as a successor to Ransom, Turner, Wells-Barnett, Grimke, and others because he was a continuation of their Christian struggles for freedom and equality for blacks and for the creation of a multi-ethnic, multiclassed society. Even with these similarities, King is very different from these black Christian activists because of changes in his much later historical era, particularly in the area of the third-world struggles against Western Christian world imperialism.

King lived in an era in which it became increasingly clear that, domestically and overseas, people of color could advance themselves and the gospel with or without the help of whites and even, in some cases, in opposition to them. He advances Christian social activism precisely because he picks up some of the ideas of the social gospel, and does so without also holding on to the racist elements. But Ransom achieved the same approach as a contemporary of social gospelers without being recognized as a leader or included in their number. King goes further than Ransom in that he adapts race-blind ideas—along with the liberal theology of personalism, Gandhi's nonviolence, and the theology, praxes, and ethics of the black church—to lead a new movement toward a new telos: the beloved community. This is not a continuation of the classic social gospel, but a revival of the social activism of Ransom and other black leaders—contemporaries of white social gospel leaders whose activism was rejected by white America.

King's Christian activism, though not a continuation of the social gospel tradition, can serve as a foundation for the creation of a new social activism. This new movement could be called the new social gospel. It would be a social gospel shared with that of Cesar Chavez, Dorothy Day, Nannie Burroughs, Fannie Lou Hamer, Jesse Jackson, and many others. It would not be the possession of any ethnic group but would be the expression of a new and liberated activist Christian community. No longer bound by the chains of racism or classism, no longer constrained by truncated visions from the past, this new social gospel could learn from and note the achievements of Gladden, Rauschenbusch, and others, without being bound by the baggage of that era.

It is with the hope of establishing such a new movement that studies on the classic social gospel movement are useful, as well as studies on all American Christian activism, and it is to advance that cause that this essay has been written. Other useful essays that look at the social gospel era will, no doubt, turn up other neglected voices of Christian activists; there are many out there. These other voices—along with King's and those of other current Christian activists—form the theological basis for a new, vigorous social gospel.

The Kingdom of God, the Church, and the World: The Social Gospel and the Making of Theology in the Twentieth-Century Ecumenical Movement

Melanie A. May

The place of the kingdom of God in a theology of the social gospel was clear to Walter Rauschenbusch: "If theology is to offer an adequate doctrinal basis for the social gospel, it must not only make room for the doctrine of the kingdom of God, but give it a central place and revise all other doctrines so that they will articulate organically with it. . . . This doctrine is itself the social gospel. Without it, the idea of redeeming the social order will be but an annex to the orthodox conception of the scheme of salvation."[1]

Given the centrality of the kingdom of God to the social gospel, Rauschenbusch was also clear that God is active in all the world, not only in the church. "The social gospel tries to see the progress of the Kingdom of God in the flow of history; not only in the doings of the Church."[2] The social gospel, therefore, was engaged in issues of industrial labor, the conditions of the working class and poverty, and urban problems. This is to say, it was the kingdom of God here on earth that was so central to the social gospel. Social sin was to be eradicated and social salvation established, corporately and institutionally and governmentally. In short, the social order itself was to be Christianized.[3]

In this essay, I will explore the role of the social gospel in the making of theology in the twentieth-century ecumenical movement by attending to ecumenical discussions of the kingdom of God, in relation to the church and the world. I will first of all focus on the century's first major ecumenical conference[4]—the Universal Christian Conference on Life and Work, held in Stockholm, Sweden, in August 1925. At this formative conference, social gospel themes were pervasive and strongly pronounced; sustained talk of the kingdom of God was unprecedented. But the consequent controversy was equally strong and sustained. By focusing on the Stockholm conference, therefore, both the formative theological streams and the perduring debates of the twentieth-century ecumenical theological conversation become apparent.

In a second section, I will elaborate on these perduring debates and trace shifts in the making of theology in the ecumenical movement. These shifts, which began in the late 1920s, became more defined by two conferences in the late 1930s. At the heart of these shifts was continued debate about the nature and mission of the church, in relation to the kingdom of God and the world, and about the nature and task of theology.

On one hand, the faith and order movement concentrated on assisting the churches to achieve the goal of visible unity by overcoming divisive doctrinal and liturgical differences, by reappropriating a common apostolic tradition, and, thereby, becoming a credible sign of God's plan for humanity and all creation. On another hand, the life and work movement was dedicated to setting forth a Christian way of life in the world, clear that a divided church could not withstand the world's evils, temptations, and trials. Only by working together ecumenically could the churches, by the power of God's Spirit, upbuild the kingdom of God in a world of great social and spiritual upheaval.

One consequence of these post-Stockholm shifts was a definition of faith and order themes as theological, and a definition of life and work themes as "nontheological." The social gospel, accordingly, became marginal to the making of what has counted as theology in the ecumenical movement.

In a third section, I will consider the extent to which, and the ways in which, the social gospel may or may not contribute to theology emerging in the twenty-first-century ecumenical movement. Here I think the key consideration is whether the social gospel is too intrinsically shaped by its originating Western cultural circumstances to be as formative in the twenty-first century as it had been in the twentieth century. In the twentieth century, Western cultural dominance had been noted and criticized. I will exemplify this critique as I introduce the significant involvement of the Eastern Orthodox churches during the twentieth-century ecumenical movement, as well as perspectives from African, Asian, Latin American, Pacific, and Caribbean regions of the world. I will conclude with comments about the trends I see as the ecumenical movement goes into the twenty-first century. I foresee no end to the debates of the twentieth century. Indeed, I think these debates about the nature and mission of the church, in relation to the kingdom of God and the world, and about the nature and task of theology will be more complex and even conflictual. Amid all, these words of Walter Rauschenbusch aid me as I attempt to put the Christian calling in proper perspective. Perhaps they too may be perduring: "The saving power of the Church does not rest on its institutional character, on its ordination, its ministry, or its doctrine. It rests on the presence of the Kingdom of God within her. . . . Unless the Church is vitalized by the ever nascent forces of the Kingdom within her, she deadens instead of begetting."[5]

Lasting Debates

The influence of the social gospel on the making of theology in the twentieth-century ecumenical movement is nowhere more pervasively present than at the opening ecumenical conference of the twentieth century in Stockholm in August 1925. The preparatory process leading to the conference had been a long one. Indeed, as one chronicler, speaking for many chroniclers, said: "The story must begin with the War."[6] At first, it seemed as if the Great War precluded any prospects for ecumenical initiatives. Yet, even as churches were preoccupied with national interests, such initiatives were sustained throughout the war. And then, when the war ended, churches asked themselves why, in August 1914, they had been so ill-prepared to speak to the nations. In the end, the Great War offered a newly urgent occasion to ask about the responsibility of the churches to societies, nations, and the world.

Definite proposals for an international ecumenical gathering came from a number of countries midway through the war. Then, in 1917, Nathan Söderblom, archbishop of Uppsala, in Sweden, took active steps toward convening a conference. At a meeting in Uppsala, a memorandum was drafted to set forth crucial points "regarding Christian unity, social life and so on . . . for consideration and for guidance in the continued work of the Church.[7] The following attests to the affinity between this ecumenical commitment and that of the social gospel:

> The Church ought to be the living conscience of nations and of men. . . . The Church ought to employ all its resources in working for the removal of the causes of war. . . . The Church ought to work for international understanding. . . . The Church has to vindicate the sanctity of Justice and Law in Christ's Name.[8]

It is, therefore, not surprising that, in taking these steps, Söderblom worked closely with Dr. Frederick Lynch, general secretary of the Federal Council of the Churches of Christ in America. In the United States, themes of social ethics and social action had been central to the ecumenical agenda. At the first meeting of the Federal Council, in Philadelphia in 1908, the churches adopted a statement on "the social ideals of the churches" (later known as "The Social Creed of the Churches"), which simultaneously articulated and symbolized Protestant churches' social conscience and commitment to social responsibility. By 1912, Rauschenbusch declared that this ecumenical commitment, together with other lay movements of the time, had made social Christianity orthodox.

After the war, Söderblom brought his proposal for a conference "to consider urgent practical tasks before the Church at this time, and the possibilities of co-operation in testimony and action,"[9] before the International Committee of the World Alliance for Promoting International Friendship through the Churches,[10] meeting in 1919 at The Hague. The proposal was adopted and the continued support of the Federal Council of the Churches of Christ in America was secured. In the early 1920s, Söderblom, in league with leaders of the Federal Council of Churches, took the lead in planning.

Preparations for the conference were bolstered by initiatives being taken in England. Drawing on a strong tradition of Christian socialism,[11] in 1919 the free churches and the Church of England began preparations for their own national interchurch Conference on Politics, Economics and Citizenship (COPEC). The conference was held in 1924, with William Temple as chair.[12]

That same year, an official letter of invitation to the conference was sent to the churches around the world. The purpose of the conference was clearly stated:

> Our prayer and hope is that through this Conference a new impetus will be given to the various movements and strivings for reunion, but the world's need is so urgent and the demand for common action on the part of all Christians is so insistent at this juncture, that we cannot afford to await the fulfilment of that great hope of a reunited Christendom before putting our hearts and our hands into a united effort that God's will may be done on earth as it is in heaven. To this end we will consider such concrete questions as that of industry and property, in relation to the Kingdom of God; what the Church should teach and do to help create right relations between the different and at times warring classes and groups in the community; how to promote friendship between the nations and thus lay the only sure foundation upon which permanent international peace can be built.[13]

But the conference was marked more by controversy than by concord. As the delegates gathered, two potentially conflictual notes were struck. There was a resounding call to the churches to upbuild the kingdom of God on earth. There was also a call to the churches to repent. This dual calling was articulated already in the opening sermon, preached by the bishop of Winchester, F. T. Wood. His text was from the Gospel of Matthew: "Repent ye, for the Kingdom of Heaven is at hand" (4:17).[14] Still, Wood's accent fell on upbuilding the kingdom on earth: "We believe in the Kingdom of Heaven. We are conspirators for its establishment. That is why we are here. That is the meaning of this Conference."[15]

In contrast, M. le Pasteur Wilfred Monod, a professor of theology in Paris, articulated a more ambivalent note when he avowed: "Why are hundreds of delegates, officially appointed by the Churches of the whole world (except by the Church of Rome[16]) assembled in Stockholm? Because Christendom has barely awakened from a terrible nightmare which has left it troubled, weakened, and bitterly humiliated; because the 'Great War' has reduced and diminished it in its own eyes."[17] Monod was clear that the churches are called "to attain the humanizing of humanity, the formation on earth of a family in which the Son of Man will be 'the first born among countless brothers' formed in His image."[18] Then, however, he recalled the 1910 World Missionary Conference held in Edinburgh, and remarked: "The commentators and theologians had rediscovered by gigantic labour the idea of the Kingdom of God, buried, like Pompeii, under the ashes of secular error. . . . The Kingdom of God, the supreme goal to which all the Churches and all the nations should remain subordinate. . . . Where then shall we find the necessary audacity for such a proclamation?"[19]

The bishop of Saxony, Ludwig Ihmels, spoke even more adamantly against social gospel sentiment:

> Nothing could be more disastrous than to suppose that we mortal men have to build up God's kingdom in the world. We must be careful how we express this. We can do nothing, we have nothing, we are nothing. Even if the Lord calls us to be His instruments and sanctifies us by His Spirit, this can only mean that He will give us grace to manifest Him in the congregation by word and sacrament, that He may bring our hearts into subjection to Himself and constrain us to the obedience of faith.[20]

He allowed that the church could rejoice when Christian ideals are "held in public life," but hastened to assert that the church "must make no mistake that all true Christian life . . . can only spring from faith. This is the reason why the tranformation of society by Christianity can only be achieved by the conversion of the individuals who constitute society."[21]

Amid all these voices, the Stockholm conference was, nevertheless, theologically centered on the kingdom of God. In fact, as noted above, this was the first sustained discussion of the kingdom of God in the twentieth-century ecumenical movement. Moreover, it was a discussion thoroughly peppered with social gospel themes. For example, Shailer Mathews, who was present and spoke, said, "the permanent success of a sacrificial social-mindedness is the modern equivalent of the apostolic preaching of the Kingdom of God. We seek the Kingdom of God when we express its spirit of love in human relations."[22] Another speaker, M. le Pasteur Elie Gounelle, quoted Rauschenbusch's call: "Let us christianize the social order," and continued: "To christianize means *humanize* in its fullest meaning"[23]

But the discussion in Stockholm led to sharp controversy that has, in some measure, continued in the ecumenical movement to the present day. In brief, at Stockholm, the controversy was between two views of the kingdom of God and its relationship to the church and the world. Can there be seen, here and now on earth, signs of the kingdom of God? Is it the responsibility of the churches to promote progress in human social affairs and thereby endeavor to establish the kingdom of God on earth? Are we indeed to be "conspirators" with God's action? Or is the kingdom of God an eschatological reality to be revealed only at the end of time? In the meantime, do not Christians live amid the tension of two realms—the world, which is not a realm of progress but decline, and the church, in which there may be a foretaste of the kingdom of God? But is not the establishment of God's kingdom God's work, not our love of neighbor that has devolved into "mere humanitarianism"[24]? One participant put these two contested views of the kingdom of God concisely, commenting: "There has been much controversy as to whether [the kingdom of God] signifies something of this life or of the other life."[25]

It is not surprising that many of the voices critical of those who conspired to build up the kingdom of God on earth were German Lutherans. They were heirs of Martin Luther's teaching that the kingdom of God is discontinuous with life on earth. More than this, of course, they were the defeated in the Great War. In the war's wake, not only was there economic, political, and social disarray in Germany, but there was theological disarray. Theologians who had made significant contributions to Christian social thought—Ernst Troeltsch, Paul Tillich, Christoph Blumhardt—were no longer as compelling to the churches, while the so-called dialectical theologians—Karl Barth, Emil Brunner, Friedrich Gogarten—were beginning to be more influential.[26]

From one perspective, therefore, the Stockholm controversy reflected a very complex and fluid theological situation in which the churches did not know, or even necessarily trust, one another. From another perspective, however, it is clear that the decision not "to deal with matters of Faith and Order,"[27] the assumption that matters of church doctrine and governance could be separated from the churches' cooperation on practical tasks, was easier said than done, especially because the conference began with a series of six speeches on "the purpose of God for humanity and the duty of the church." The addresses in this series, which were an attempt to clarify a firm theological foundation for social ethics and the churches' social responsibility, were not only deeply doctrinally defined, but they were, on major points, contradictory. In short, from the beginning, theological controversy, at times confusion, reigned at a conference dedicated to not being theological in any traditional sense.

At the next ecumenical conference of the twentieth century, the First World Conference on Faith and Order, held in Lausanne in 1927, the theological focus was not on the kingdom of God, but on the church. Interestingly, the text for the opening sermon, preached by Berlin University Professor Adolf Deissman, was the same text for the opening sermon at Stockholm. In Lausanne, however, the text was interpreted to proclaim a different message:

> The Church must . . . preach the fearfulness of sin and the glory of grace. . . . It must not set forth the Kingdom of God as an institution . . . it must present the Kingdom . . . as the unum necessarium, the one thing needful, as judgment to come, and a redemption to come. . . . The Church must give up the attempt to demonstrate the rationality of the Kingdom of God to the healthy intelligence of mankind. It must have courage and joyfulness to proclaim paradox to the world and to expect paradox from the world.[28]

The church, this is to say, is "God's chosen instrument by which Christ, through the Holy Spirit, reconciles men to God through faith . . . until His Kingdom comes in glory."[29] Among the main themes explored at the conference were the church's message to the world—the gospel, the nature of the church, the church's common confession of faith, the ministry of the church, the sacraments, and the unity of Christendom.[30] A new and different theological note had been struck, and has continued to be struck, in the ecumenical movement.[31]

What, then, may be said at this point about the significance of the social gospel in the making of theology in the twentieth-century ecumenical movement? First of all, the social gospel was formative for the emergence of an early and transformative ecumenical insight—social, racial, political, and economic injustice and divisions in the human community are not only the church's responsibility, but this injustice and division threatens the very nature, mission, and unity of the church itself. Accordingly, the church's responsibility for this injustice and division is both an ethical imperative and an integrally theological imperative, since what is finally at stake is the church being the church in and for the world.

At Stockholm and afterward, the ecumenical movement has addressed matters of peace and justice, poverty and sharing of resources, political struggle, and war. But, as was already apparent in Lausanne, the making of theology came to be centered on the church—its doctrine, institution, and sacramental acts—not on the kingdom of God. Although it was acknowledged that the church has a mission in the world, since the late 1930s, matters of peace and justice, poverty and sharing of resources, political struggle, and war have been referred to as "nontheological" factors in most twentieth-century ecumenical conversations.[32]

Along these lines, the persistent, the perduring, debate in the ecumenical movement—about the kingdom of God in relation to the church and the world, as well as about the making of theology—has been carried out. Almost all ecumenical theologians would say that church and world, and accordingly the two ecumenical streams of Life and Work and Faith and Order, are integrally related. But most ecumenical theologians also agree this debate is responsible for "the most troublesome divide within the ecumenical movement."[33]

Continuing Conversations

At the second conference sponsored by the Universal Christian Council on Life & Work, the Oxford Conference on Church, Community and State, there was talk once again about the kingdom of God. Echoing Stockholm, one conference report declared: "The kingdom of God is the reign of God which both has come and is coming. It is an established reality in the coming of Christ and in the presence of his Spirit in the world."[34] But too much had happened since the 1925 conference in Stockholm and this Oxford conference, which met in 1937. There had been worldwide economic crises. There had been civil wars and partitions of lands.

Most crucially, there was the *Kirchenkampf*, the conflict within the church in Hitler's Germany, from which, in 1934, came the Barmen Declaration and the Confessing Church.[35] And so the kingdom of God, avers the Oxford section report, "is, however, still in conflict with a sinful world which crucified its Lord, and its ultimate triumph is still to come."[36] Indeed, Christians who attempted to identify any particular economic, political, or social system with the kingdom of God were said to be erroneously, even heretically, attempting to equate God's realm with a historical and human realm.[37]

The task of Christians, and of the ecumenical movement, therefore, was to enable the church to be the church. In the face of injustice and moral havoc and social disintegration and poverty, the church, "which came into being through God's gift of Jesus Christ as the Saviour of men in all their sinful impotence to find the true way of life," was said to be called by God to be "his witness and the chief instrument of his redeeming work in the world. . . . It is . . . to be 'a colony of heaven' in a fallen world, exemplifying by contrast the true way of human living."[38]

"A Message from the Oxford Conference to the Christian Churches" confirmed: "The first duty of the church, and its greatest service to the world, is that it be in very deed the church—confessing the true faith, committed to the fulfillment of the will of Christ, its only Lord, and united in him in a fellowship of love and service."[39] Accordingly, in contrast to Stockholm's call to establish the kingdom of God on earth, the watchword going forth from Oxford was "Let the church be the church." Christians were no longer identified as conspirators on behalf of the kingdom on earth, but as colonists of heaven in hostile circumstances. The social gospel was set aside as dialectical theology came into ascendancy.

This focus on the church being the church—rather than a focus on the mission of the church in the world or on the kingdom of God on earth—was reiterated at the Second World Conference on Faith and Order held in Edinburgh a few months after the Oxford Conference.[40] Here a correlative theological focus emerged with equal strength—a focus on the Lordship of Jesus Christ as the center of salvation history.[41] This ecumenical affirmation of the Lordship of Christ, of course, also reflected the theological renaissance that dialectical theology represented for many churches.

It is, however, too simple to say this affirmation eclipsed talk of the kingdom of God. Rather, the affirmation of the Lordship of Christ pointed to a new realm of life, which is God's history of salvation. This is not a realm to be built, but to be entered into—as the final end of all things. Jesus Christ as Lord both introduces the kingdom of God into human history and consummates all things at the end of time. In the meantime, Christians and the churches live in a tension with the world—live amid the "already" and the "not yet."

This affirmation of Jesus Christ as the center of salvation history, supported by a rediscovery, amid the crisis of a Second World War, of the Bible as the faithful witness to God's acts in history, was the unwavering theological focus in the ecumenical movement through the 1940s and 1950s. Then, on January 25, 1959, Pope John XXIII convoked "an ecumenical council for the universal church."[42] Pope John XXIII was clear about his purpose for calling the council. It was twofold: He hoped for a new Pentecost, for *aggiornamento*, or an updating of the church in modern times; and for a new initiative toward the unity of the church.

Although the council was an event of the Roman Catholic Church, it was enormously formative of the making of theology in the wider ecumenical movement. Here it is important to note that delegated observers from almost all the world's confessional families were invited to and were present at all sessions of the Second Vatican Council.

Perhaps the most significant theological statement to emerge from Vatican II was this affirmation about the church: "By her relationship with Christ, the Church is a kind of sacrament or sign of intimate union with God, and of the unity of all mankind."[43] This became the watchword going forth from the Fourth Assembly of the World Council of Churches, meeting in Uppsala in 1968: "The church is bold in speaking of itself as the sign of the coming unity of mankind."[44]

The Fourth Assembly, like Vatican II, signaled a new openness to the world in the ecumenical movement, thereby resounding social gospel themes. Worldwide issues of economic disparity and racism, of technological interdependence and political independence were engaged ecumenically. In short, the term *sign* helped the ecumenical movement to bridge "the most troublesome divide" and to speak in a new way about the relationship of the church and the world, particularly about the church's prophetic witness in the world. The church and the world, this is to say, were said not to be separate spheres in conflict. Both were affirmed as realms of God's activity. The task of the church in the world is to be a sign and an interpreter of signs toward the realization of the kingdom of God.

In the early 1970s, this new way of thinking about the kingdom of God, the church, and the world led to a new theological study, sponsored by the World Council of Churches' Commission on Faith and Order, on "The Unity of the Church—Unity of Mankind." As the theology of the social gospel attempted to place the kingdom of God in human history, not only in the church and salvation history, so this study attempted to place the call to the unity of the church within the context of humankind as a whole.[45] Moreover, also reaffirming social gospel theology claims, the framers of the study were clear: "This attempt is deliberately made in the context of a theological argument."[46] The study was, not surprisingly, quite controversial inasmuch as it challenged Faith and Order to rethink the focus, and the locus, of its theological work. The study, this is to say, viewed the church not only as an institution with its doctrines and orders and liturgies, but also as an instrument of God's saving activity in the flow of human history in the world.

Accordingly, the study was clear: Reflection on the church as institution and instrument in the world are both intrinsically theological. This challenge to the decades-old divide of church and world—a divide buttressed by an identification of the kingdom of God with the church and not the world, and by a clear delineation of things theological and things nontheological—long characteristic of Faith and Order studies was too threatening. This study came to a precipitous end in 1974, without a conclusive outcome.

Nevertheless, during the late 1970s, discussion of the church as sacrament, sign, and instrument in relation to the world continued in various ecumenical arenas, including the Joint Working Group of the Roman Catholic Church and the World Council of Churches.[47] The discussion of the church as sacrament, sign, and instrument was perhaps most powerfully related to talk about the kingdom of God at the World Conference on Mission and Evangelism, held in Melbourne in 1980. The conference's message to the churches declares: "The good news of the Kingdom must be presented to the world by the Church, the Body of Christ, the sacrament of the Kingdom in every place and time."[48]

Elsewhere in the Melbourne report, this mandate is elaborated: "The world-wide Church is itself a sign of the Kingdom of God because it is the body of Christ on earth. It is called to be an instrument of the Kingdom by continuing Christ's mission to the world in a struggle for the growth of all human beings into fullness of life."[49] The conference saw the church as sacrament, sign, and instrument in relation to the coming kingdom of God on earth, not in relation to the church's own institutional life. Social gospel themes were articulated, as is clear in this central affirmation found in the conference report—the church does not exist for its own sake, but for the sake of the coming unity of humankind in God's kingdom.[50]

Continuing ecumenical conversation led to a follow-up study on "The Unity of the Church and the Renewal of Human Community" in the early 1980s. This study was even clearer about its intent:

> How can the church be understood in such a way that the nature of the church, and the mission of the church, are seen as integral and inter-related elements of the being (the esse) of the church itself? How can the inter-relation between the church, thus conceived, and humanity 'outside' the church be understood—beyond their obvious relation, following from the fact that the church lives in the world and is sent to the world—in a coherent theological perspective? Does the kingdom of God, within the wider framework of the triune God's plan of salvation from creation to new creation, offer such a perspective?[51]

The consequent understanding of the church and the world and the kingdom of God locate God's action in human history, not only in "salvation history." The church and the whole of humanity together have their goal in the kingdom of God:

> The church is that part of humanity which has been led to accept, affirm and acknowledge ever more fully the liberating truth of the kingdom for all people. It is the community of those who are experiencing the presence of the kingdom and actively awaiting its final fulfilment. The church is therefore called to live as that force within humanity through which God's will for the renewal, justice, community and salvation of all people is witnessed to. . . . In all this the church participates in the paradoxes and dynamic of the kingdom within history.[52]

But the attention given this study was overshadowed by another study, "Baptism, Eucharist and Ministry," which incorporated some reflection on the kingdom of God, for example, in discussing the eucharist and the call to reconciliation.[53] But the church as institution—its ordinances and ministry—remained theologically central.

In the last decade of the twentieth century, one other significant study attempted to heal the historic divide between Life and Work and Faith and

Order, between things theological and things "nontheological." This was the "Ecclesiology and Ethics" study begun in 1993 at a consultation in Ronde, Denmark. At this consultation, the church was said to be a "moral community," meaning, "It is not sufficient to affirm that the moral thrust of JPIC [Justice, Peace and the Integrity of Creation] is only related to the nature and function of the church [which is] itself in a 'moral' reality."[54] A second study consultation, held in Tantur Ecumenical Institute near Jerusalem in the fall of 1994, explored the church's responsibility for "moral formation," emphasizing the role of the church in shaping a "whole way of life."[55] This exploration led to the use of the biblical image of the church as *oikos* or "household" to express the integral relatedness of life, economically, ecologically, and ecumenically.[56] A third and final consultation extended the discussion to an exploration of "malformation," a danger from which the church as institution is not immune.[57]

This study, which echoed social gospel emphasis on the church's role in redeeming the social order yet again, also ended rather precipitously, having perhaps posed more questions than pressed to conclusions. Some churches and theologians were and are concerned that the church must first and foremost be the church, rather than risk engagement with potentially divisive ethical and moral dilemmas in the world. Some think talk about ecclesiology and ethics smacks of a latter-day Pelagianism. Such talk diverts ecclesiological attention from the centrality of eucharistic celebration. Others are concerned lest moral debates undo the "classic" Faith and Order agreements and impede further work toward agreement on matters of baptism, eucharist, ministry, and the confession of faith. In short, "the troublesome divide" at the heart of the twentieth-century ecumenical movement has not been healed.

The Social Gospel and Theology in the Twenty-First-Century Ecumenical Movement

The possible contribution that social gospel thinking may make to theology in the twenty-first-century ecumenical movement is qualified by the extent to which both the social gospel and the ecumenical movement are identified with an order of things now passing away. Specifically, critics argue that the social gospel and the twentieth-century ecumenical movements have not only called for churches to "Christianize the social order," but to Christianize the world in Western fashion. Moreover, critics point out that leaders of these movements, mostly from North Atlantic nations, have simply assumed access to power and privilege that would make this Christianizing mission possible.

More specifically, Western cultural dominance in the ecumenical movement has been challenged from various perspectives. Theologically, advocates of a dialogic, experiential way of "doing" theology in context have seriously challenged more classical, doctrinal approaches. This newly emerging way of "doing" theology, especially as it is being done in Latin America, Africa, and Asia, echoes social gospel thinking by insisting that theology take account of and enable transformation of social and historical situations. But theology being done in Latin America, Africa, and Asia is distinguished from the social gospel both by who is doing it and where it is being done. While the social gospel movement was clergy dominated, the newly emerging theology is theology being done by the whole people of God. Moreover, it is theology being done in solidarity with people in places of poverty and struggle, without any ability to assume power and privilege that could make change possible.[58]

With regard to social witness, particularly with regard to positions taken on issues of justice, peace, disarmament, the international debt, unemployment, and drug abuse, Mark Ellingsen has observed:

> What is striking . . . is that the churches' areas of ethical consensus are uncannily consistent with the values of Western democratic liberalism. . . . Is it possible that certain values and patterns of theological thought associated with the West are of perduring and central value to the Christian faith, which accounts for the consensus of the church statements regarding these 'Western' values? . . . Or is it rather the case that the church statements reflect Western values because the social-statement format is essentially a Western innovation which inevitably forces the Western ethical agenda on those who employ it?"[59]

Western cultural dominance is also being challenged by Eastern and Oriental Orthodox churches, the vast majority of which have long been engaged in the ecumenical movement.[60] Indeed, it is in this regard important to recall that two of the earliest ecumenical initiatives of the twentieth century were taken by Orthodox leaders. In 1902, Joachim III, patriarch of Constantinople, addressed an encyclical to all local Orthodox churches, in which he dealt with the relationships of the Orthodox churches to the Roman Catholic Church, to Protestant churches, and to other ancient oriental churches. He also raised issues that have only rather recently come to the forefront of the ecumenical agenda, for example, the question of a common Christian calendar.[61]

In 1920, the patriarch of Constantinople addressed an encyclical, "Unto the Churches of Christ Everywhere," that affirmed that churches "should no more consider one another as strangers and foreigners, but as relatives, and as being a part of the household of Christ and 'fellow heirs, members of the same body and partakers of the promise of God in Christ'" (Eph. 3:6).[62] Concretely, the encyclical proposed that the churches create "a contact and league (fellowship) between the churches."[63] This proposal, of course, reflected the optimism at the time of the formation of the League of Nations. In fact, the encyclical proposing a league between the churches was issued in the very month that the League of Nations was inaugurated.[64]

But the encyclical also reflected a sense of danger unique to the non-Western, post-World War I situation of many Orthodox churches. Behind the rather abstract words about "dangers that attack the very foundations of the Christian faith and the essence of Christian life and society,"[65] were the very real consequences of the collapse of the Ottoman and Russian empires. While the Ottoman Empire had curtailed the freedom of the patriarchate of Constantinople, it had also allowed the church to carry on the main aspects of its life and worship. In the postwar period, rising secular Turkish nationalism seriously threatened this fragile status quo. The militantly atheist Russian Revolution was an even more radical threat to the well-being of the Orthodox church, and brought still untold persecution in its wake.

These political upheavals, together with tragedies such as the Armenian genocide of 1915 and the multitudes of post-World War I refugees in Greece, helped shape the Orthodox ecumenical vision in the twentieth century. The call for a league between churches like the League of Nations aside, the Orthodox churches' vision was formed in a crucible of suffering.

Another face of this suffering was the proselytizing of the non-Orthodox churches that came to offer aid. This remains a major ecumenical stumbling block between Orthodox and non-Orthodox churches. Indeed, tensions have heightened since the collapse of the former Soviet Union opened the floodgates to Protestant and Roman Catholic churches. The words of the encyclical of 1920 are no less relevant today than they were then: "So many troubles and sufferings are caused by other Christians and great hatred and enmity are aroused, with such insignificant results, by this tendency of some to proselytize and entice the followers of other Christian confessions."[66]

Orthodox criticism of Western cultural, and accordingly Protestant dominance, of the ecumenical movement, and especially of the World Council of Churches, has theological and ethical aspects. The Orthodox churches have shown particular interest in Faith and Order studies of mutual recognition of baptism, eucharist, and ministry, of a common confession of the apostolic faith through the Nicene-Constantinopolitan Creed (381), and of common ways of decision making and of teaching authoritatively. Although Orthodox churches have joined in World Council of Churches' initiatives for justice, peace, and the integrity of creation, these matters like the trials and suffering noted above, are taken to be "nondogmatic" or "nontheological" factors. From an Orthodox perspective, the Christian social thought and action, the whole subject of the church and the world, is most appropriately viewed through an understanding of the church as a reflection of the Holy Trinity, as the reign of God realized in the world. And it is the eucharistic liturgy that draws together all things on earth and in heaven, the vertical and horizontal dimensions of Christian life. In sum, Orthodox view the Western theological and ecclesial mind as primarily practical, while they think worship is central to all else. The theological and ecclesiological differences include differences in language and thought form, including inclusive language. They also emerge in great divides on theological anthropological issues such as homosexuality and the ordination of women.

Orthodox criticism of Western dominance heightened into a crisis in the spring of 1998. In December 1998, a Special Commission on Orthodox Participation in the World Council of Churches was appointed to discuss the organization of the World Council, the ethos of life in the World Council, and theological differences between Orthodox and other churches.

Conclusion

Sketching the significance of the social gospel in the twentieth-century ecumenical movement, and surveying more recent trends, it seems likely that the ecumenical movement in the twenty-first century will be quite different. There will be new structures, new ways of thinking theologically, and the churches will be called to new ways of witness in the world. Whatever contributions are brought from Western churches, including the social gospel and its imperative to establish the kingdom of God on earth, will be part of a much more complex and no doubt more conflictual conversation.

Voices from Eastern and oriental Orthodox churches and voices from churches of Africa, Asia, and Latin America will be stronger, although not always or often similar. Perduring debates about the relationships of the kingdom of God, the church, and the world will persist. Throughout, the Western cultural penchant for an overweaning confidence in human capacities will be challenged.

Nonetheless, the originating insights of a theology for the social gospel are that "the saving power of the Church does not rest on its institutional character, on its ordination, its ministry, or its doctrine. It rests on the presence of the Kingdom of God within her," and that the kingdom of God is active "in the flow of history; not only in the doings of the Church."[67] Thereby to redeem the social order will endure as formative to the making of ecumenical theology. But its formative influence will flourish only as the Western and Protestant theology for the social gospel is baptized into diverse cultural and religious contexts. Thereby theologies for the social gospel will be born that can indeed continue to be catalytic and creative for the making of ecumenical theology in the next century.

4

Gender and the Kingdom of God:
The Family Values of Walter Rauschenbusch[1]

Christopher H. Evans

In January 1908, Walter Rauschenbusch, on sabbatical leave from Rochester Theological Seminary and residing with his family in Marburg, Germany, wrote a New Year's greeting to a friend in America. In his letter, Rauschenbusch discussed the recent Christmas celebrations of his family and mused over the unexpected success of his book *Christianity and the Social Crisis*, published just as he began his sabbatical several months earlier. Preparing to return to America to a fame unimaginable only months before, Rauschenbusch confided in the letter his delight at the book's success, but also the growing responsibility he felt to live out the vision espoused on the book's pages. "Here I am in another country, and without further effort on my part these thoughts, which were part of me, are doing their work beyond any power of mine to follow, control, or estimate. *It is like a child that detaches its life from ours and goes to live its own life. But it has given me a deepened sense of responsibility*" (emphasis mine).[2] The analogy that Rauschenbusch drew between the book that scholars judge as a major social gospel magnum opus and his family is more than a metaphor. It highlights the central value that he placed upon the family as the primary social institution that embodied his theology of the kingdom of God.

Scholarship on the life and thought of Walter Rauschenbusch has explored the integral connection between Rauschenbusch's theology and his views toward gender and family. Janet Fishburn has argued that Rauschenbusch's liberal vision of social reform revealed a strong current of social conservatism, especially with regard to gender equality. Although supportive of women's suffrage, he repeatedly displayed an ambivalence about the advisability of women assuming roles in the public sphere of American society. According to Fishburn, Rauschenbusch's reform vision was truncated by a desire to preserve traditional middle-class family structures. "He wanted an economic revolution without a change in the family unit. Against socialist and feminist demands on behalf of freedom for women, Rauschenbusch never changed his basic conviction that a woman belonged at home."[3] In a similar vein, Betty

DeBerg notes the relative congruency on gender issues between social gospel advocates and proponents of fundamentalism in the early twentieth century: both theological traditions viewed the role of women through the confines of maintaining a Christian home and raising children. "Like the fundamentalists, these 'liberal' churchmen spoke of the home as the most sacred and important social institution and recommended that women remain within its confines."[4] Fishburn and DeBerg share a common conclusion related to recent scholarship on gender and the social gospel. Social gospel men, like Walter Rauschenbusch, perpetuated a late nineteenth-century "separate-sphere" ideology, in which building the kingdom of God in America depended upon men who were willing to champion social justice in the public realm of society and women who were willing to assume the roles of wives and mothers in the domestic sphere.

Scholarly evidence suggests that Rauschenbusch's theology was centered upon maintaining this Victorian view of a woman's place within the nuclear family. But is this the only conclusion one can reach regarding Rauschenbusch's view toward gender? Perhaps not. An important question remains to be addressed: How did Rauschenbusch's relationship to members of his *own* family corroborate or challenge his public views on gender and family, and what do these primary relationships reveal about his theology of the kingdom of God?

For Rauschenbusch, the family was not just a social institution that symbolized the virtues of middle-class social order; the family was a distinctively theological organism that embodied, in miniature, the kingdom of God. "No other social organization is so distinctly the institution of love as the home," Rauschenbusch noted in his 1912 book, *Christianizing the Social Order.* "As the knee joint of a man is a complicated system of ligatures, so a home is an interlocking system of loves. The more the economic activities have passed from the home to the shop, the more completely has the home become an institution of love."[5]

For Rauschenbusch, the family, like the kingdom of God, was a living reality only to the extent that God's love manifested itself in loving relationships between members of a community. "Almost every personal relation of affection connects us with a group of people who have the same interest or who are somehow identified with persons whom we love," he wrote in 1914. "So the love for one man promptly widens out into the love of many and weaves more closely the web of social life."[6] In this regard, "family" was not a static or confined concept for Rauschenbusch; it was a series of dynamic and evolving social relationships between persons within society. As the embodiment of the kingdom of God, the family was a constantly evolving social organism, reflecting the possibilities of social transformation.

Rauschenbusch also viewed the family as the prototype for a healthy democratic society. "The family contains the utmost diversity of sex, age, ability, and education, yet exhibits complete social equality among its members."[7] In this regard, he viewed the suffrage movement as a positive development that would "abolish one of the last remnants of patriarchal autocracy by giving woman a direct relation to the political organism of society, instead of allowing man to exercise her political rights for her."[8]

At the same time, Rauschenbusch lacked a coherent portrait of how social equality for men and women would be embodied in a future "Christianized" society. His struggle, one he experienced within his own family, was defining how his theological understandings of social equality related to late nineteenth-century cultural understandings of social equality, especially pertaining to gender roles. His relationship to his own family reveals an ongoing tension between the conservative cultural suppositions of his era and the dynamic character of his kingdom theology, which stressed personal and social transformation. Many leaders in the Progressive Era, like Rauschenbusch, uncritically embraced late-Victorian "separate-sphere" ideology that confined women to domestic family roles. At the same time, however, many of these leaders were exposed to emerging feminist arguments that challenged these taken-for-granted Victorian suppositions.[9] Extant family correspondence suggests that Rauschenbusch's view of gender was not so much stuck in the Victorian era but caught between two eras: the Victorian era of his youth and the emerging era of his children, all of whom came of age in the early decades of the twentieth century. Inevitably these generational differences caused tension between himself and his five children. Rauschenbusch took great pain that his children never wholeheartedly embraced the cultural and theological values of his generation. At the same time, however, all of his children, sons *and* daughters, embraced vocational identities in the public sphere, and they espoused, in varying degrees, many of their father's theological values pertaining to social transformation.[10]

Rauschenbusch's effort to work out these tensions between his theological and cultural values was especially evident in his relationship to his oldest child and daughter, Winifred. Born in 1894 and named after her father's older brother, Winfrid, who died in infancy, she attended Oberlin College, graduating in 1916 with a degree in sociology. After graduation and, despite her father's concerns over her safety, she became an organizer for the Ohio Woman's Suffrage Association. In 1917, she began graduate work at the University of Chicago, studying with two sociologists who symbolized emerging intellectual currents in modern feminism, George Mead and Robert Park. For several years, she worked as Park's research assistant on a study into the causes of race riots in post–World War I Chicago. In 1921, she was offered a teaching position at the University of Iowa, an offer rescinded, according to Winifred, because of a university bias against her German ancestry. For most of her adult life, Winifred worked as a freelance writer, publishing articles in numerous periodicals on topics ranging from immigration and race relations to contemporary popular culture.[11]

On one hand, Rauschenbusch's relationship with his eldest child reaffirms his conservatism on gender issues. Correspondence between Winifred and her father reveals that Rauschenbusch attempted to hold his daughter accountable to the standards of late-Victorian womanhood—and the resistance of Winifred to those standards. In her later correspondence with her father, Winifred repeatedly declared her independence from his worldview on contemporary gender roles. "I'm not a lady; I'm merely chaotic youth, formless, full blooded, strong and soaring," she wrote to her father after her graduation from Oberlin College. "And so it may hurt you to have a daughter who is a feminist. I'm one by process of growth."[12]

As Winifred struggled to break free of her father's world, her father struggled, partially successfully, to understand his daughter's desire to embrace a world so alien from his own.[13] The relationship between Walter and Winifred Rauschenbusch was in large part a struggle over cultural definitions of gender roles in the early twentieth century. But it also embodied a father's struggle to accept in his personal life what he had taught in his public theology. Like his earlier comment on the power of words to take on meaning independent of their original source, Rauschenbusch struggled to understand that the ultimate purposes of the kingdom of God could never be fully disclosed through the values of any one specific person, culture, or society. As he attempted to accept his oldest daughter's emerging sense of personal and vocational identity, Rauschenbusch was confronted with the fundamental truth he espoused in his famous conclusion in *Christianity and the Social Crisis*: "The kingdom of God is always but coming."[14]

The Kingdom of God and the Rauschenbusch Family

For Walter Rauschenbusch, the key to a loving family centered upon the relationship between a husband and wife. "It [family] is formed when a man and a woman love each other. In their case the natural friendship of two human beings is diversified by the play of sex difference and intensified by sexual love."[15] When Rauschenbusch wrote these words, he was describing an ideal missing from his own parents.

His parents, August and Caroline, shared a relationship characterized by conflict and animosity, as opposed to love and intimacy. Although August was a respected German-Baptist pastor and professor in the German Department of Rochester Theological Seminary, life for Walter Rauschenbusch as a boy and adolescent was far from tranquil. In addition to his father's harsh authoritarianism, young Rauschenbusch lived in a house torn apart by August's violent verbal confrontations with his wife. Additionally, August was prone to be absent from home for extended periods of time. As an adult, Walter Rauschenbusch was determined not to repeat the sins of his own father. In contrast to the dogmatism and lack of affection embodied by his own father, he attempted to model family relationships of collegiality, friendship, and love.

When Rauschenbusch wrote that a loving family started with the bond between husband and wife, he clearly was thinking of his wife, Pauline. Born in Prussia, Pauline Rother came to America as a young girl, not long after her father's death. She settled in Wisconsin where she became a schoolteacher, meeting Walter while he was attending a Baptist convention in Milwaukee in 1889. After a four-year courtship, Pauline and Walter married in 1893.[16]

Pauline Rauschenbusch embodied the role of many women in Protestant parsonage families of that era. She came of age at a time when American Protestantism was defining the minister's spouse through the roles of wife, mother, and hostess who maintained the spiritual sanctity of the family.[17] At least publicly, Pauline ascribed to that family model, where she played the central role in raising the Rauschenbusch children and tending to the domestic responsibilities of maintaining the home. At the same time, the copious correspondence between the couple reflects an intense and passionate bond.

The bond of love between Rauschenbusch and Pauline was also embodied in his relationship with his children. Historian Susan Curtis observed, "[Rauschenbusch] tried to become the ideal father about which he had written in his theology—an indulgent, loving companion rather than a wrathful judge."[18] In many respects, however, Rauschenbusch did not escape the sins of his own father, and his paternal role was at times marked by a stern and aloof demeanor.

The paradoxes in Rauschenbusch's role as a parent can be seen in the voluminous correspondence with his children. Like his father, Rauschenbusch expected intellectual excellence from all of his children and became terse when he felt that they were not living up to their intellectual potential. However, Rauschenbusch was quick to castigate himself for his harshness, expressing several times a contrite attitude toward his outbursts of anger. Most significantly, he displayed a persistent fear that he would become a stranger to his children as they grew older. This sense of alienation, no doubt, was exacerbated by Rauschenbusch's deafness, developed while he was a pastor in New York City in the 1880s. "A hundred little things that would give us a peek into your soul when it is open by chance, escape me because I can not hear," he confided to Winifred.[19] Rauschenbusch's correspondence also reveals something of the guilt he felt over his long absences from home, which became more frequent as his fame grew. On a visit to New York City in 1911, he wrote to his family about the experience of walking the streets of the city where he had once lived and served as a pastor. "I'd rather be home and play with the children," he noted with a degree of melancholy. "Forgive me if I am sometimes impatient or severe. I always suffer for it myself afterward. I can't tell [you] how much I love you all."[20] He lamented to son Hilmar in 1910 that time was running out on their father-son relationship. "I hope we shall understand each other better all the time and be real chums," Rauschenbusch wrote hopefully. "We have only a few years more together, perhaps. Then you will be going away for education and work, and the close companionship of these years may be over. So we must get all the joy of it and make it a dear memory for always."[21]

Yet he could also be extremely humorous in his letters, describing events of his day with a great deal of levity and wit. Amidst the seriousness and, at times, melancholy tone of his letters, Rauschenbusch frequently displayed a whimsical spirit—often at his own expense. He loved to describe the mundane routines of his travels, retelling daily occurrences in ways that were humorously self-deprecating. When he and Pauline made an annual visit to a health spa in Dansville, New York, in 1911, Rauschenbusch wrote to his children a vivid account of his ordeal of enduring a steam bath.

> We went to bed at 9:30 and slept till after eight. . . . Breakfasted on fruit only and were raving hungry by noon. We were told to consult the doctor as part of the fun and he prescribed baths for us. . . . I was put into the hands of a man who has been here 40 years, called Louis. . . . He made me strip and sit in a sheet which I draped around my manly form in close imitation of Cicero's toga. Then he put me naked in a big box, with my head projecting through a small hole and turned h— loose inside. First he stewed me in my own juice, then he turned some gravy on and parboiled me, so that the moisture ran off me like a thousand potato-bugs crawling over my skin. It was scrumptious.[22]

The humor displayed in this passage would also be evident in his children's letters to their father.

Rauschenbusch's correspondence makes it clear that he deeply loved his children and shows how he attempted to relate to them as an older and wiser friend—even as he struggled to make them conform to his values. His relationship to Winifred, however, highlights both his larger impact upon his children and the generational divide that separated him from their world.

The Family Ties of Walter
and Winifred Rauschenbusch

Walter Rauschenbusch wrote whimsically of his oldest child's birth: "She was a little confused in her ideas yet, for she didn't recognize her own father and didn't seem to think he was anything much."[23] The tone of that statement in some way reflects upon the unique relationship that would develop between father and daughter. Although Rauschenbusch wrote numerous letters to all of his children, extant letters to Winifred dominate his personal collection. It was a relationship that produced hundreds of letters between the two, from the time Winifred was a young girl until her father's death in 1918.

The letters between Walter and Winifred reveal the paradox in the elder Rauschenbusch's view toward women. On one hand, the correspondence highlights the Victorian sentimentality of Rauschenbusch—especially his desire that Winifred, like her mother, prepare herself to be a faithful and loving wife and mother. After returning to America from his 1907–1908 sabbatical, he wrote to Winifred, still in Germany with her mother and her siblings, outlining his hope that she would become a role model of American womanhood. Rauschenbusch somewhat callously commented on the responsibilities that would befall Winifred, a young teenager at the time, if something happened to her mother. "Often when a mother dies, the oldest daughter steps into her place and her character quickly matures and becomes nobler and riper through the responsibility. . . . There is nothing else that we love so much in a woman as such gracious helpfulness."[24]

In juxtaposition to this Victorian sentimentality, however, Rauschenbusch's letters reveal his deep love for his daughter and his desire to affirm her gifts. What emerges in his letters are powerful personal confessions of his inability to fully understand his daughter's pains and struggles. In a 1910 letter, written when Winifred was sixteen, he spoke candidly of the generation gap that separated her from her parents. The words in Rauschenbusch's letter reflect upon a timeless theme of a parent's struggle to understand his child's generational perspective.

> Children misread their parents, often cruelly. They have not yet the experiences of work and suffering that would give them understanding by sympathy. I am sure they never gauge how much we love them. . . . On the other hand we fail to understand you children. Partly because we have lost your point of view, your emotions, dreams, and passions . . . it takes a lot of love to comprehend entirely.

In that same letter, Rauschenbusch commented on the communication problems with his children caused by his deafness, but also praised Winifred for her budding interest in writing, encouraging her to share her work with him. He concludes on a theme present in many of the letters: his unconditional love for his children. "You will never have a friend who will love you as steadfastly as we do. And no lover or child will ever love you as unselfishly."[25]

Rauschenbusch worried constantly that his children's maturity would cause him to lose touch with their worldview, and he expressed that fear often to Winifred. Recalling his feelings upon the occasion of her birth, he wrote revealing words to Winifred on her twentieth birthday. "We fathers haven't as easy a time as it may seem. We are left on the outside. . . . If we venture to act, we usually do it wrong."[26] Rauschenbusch is not only speaking about his emotions in recalling the event of Winifred's birth, but his comments suggest his own inner struggle to be a good father. Even as he found himself disagreeing with many of Winifred's personal and professional aspirations, Rauschenbusch continuously expressed his love and support for his daughter's quest to find her way in the world, even as he hoped that she would advance the cause of American womanhood. As he noted proudly, "I feel very happy and proud about you, and tho I have not the least idea what you will turn out to be, I feel sure you are going to be something fine—provided you keep your health and are not tangled in some moral disaster. You have a strong and rich nature in you, but it must ripen and sweeten."[27]

In many ways, his relationship with Winifred grew closer, and tenser, after she went away to Oberlin College in 1912. What that correspondence between the two reveals is a spirited struggle between a strong-willed young woman trying to find her voice and calling in life and a father who attempts to offer guidance—sometimes against his daughter's desire. Rauschenbusch's letters in this time period ranged from sternness to adoration. His anger could be triggered by many factors—grades, Winifred's sloppy finances, or his daughter's failure to write thank-you notes to family friends. In one letter, he scolded his daughter on her poor grades, making it clear that he held high expectations for her academic work. "I'm glad you feel sore. We need lickings to make us wise," Rauschenbusch noted in response to Winifred's academic woes. "Perhaps by this time you will sympathize a little with the soreness I felt when the daughter whom God and I had fitted out with brains enough to do honor work flunked her freshman work. . . . If you had been stupid I might have learned to be patient and boost you along. . . . Remember I'm your partner in trying to make a great woman of you." He makes it clear that part of becoming a "great woman" had nothing to do with her grades. After admonishing her for her tardiness in writing to him (and scolding her for the fact that when she finally did write, it was to ask for money), Rauschenbusch made it clear to his daughter that she was not living up to the social standards of a cultured young woman. "This is one of the last remnants, I hope, of the unregenerate

Winifred, of whom black fingernails, unsanitary habits, late hours, bad spelling . . . were other symptoms."[28]

From the elder Rauschenbusch's perspective, he had not seen the last of the "unregenerate Winifred," as further correspondences emphasized the father's desire that his daughter conform more to his standards of Victorian womanhood. Not long after she had returned to Oberlin, after Christmas break of her senior year, he castigated Winifred for her failure to turn up for a social gathering while she was home. He sternly wrote, "Just as a soldier subordinates himself to his country, a mother to her baby, a father to the needs of his family, so must a host set the obligations to a guest above his own whims."[29] This anger, however, was usually softened by his vulnerability, often confiding his fear that the two would grow apart. "I think of you oftener than of any of my children. . . . My heart is always crying out for my daughter and I can't find her. I seem to have lost her years ago."[30]

For her part, Winifred struggled in college to live up to her father's hopes for her future. One subject that came up between the two was religion. Although she acknowledged in several letters that she and her siblings lacked the passionate faith of their parents, she also struggled in college to develop her faith. In a revealing letter during her sophomore year, Winifred shared with her father a prayer she had written—a prayer that clearly reflects the theological values of her father.

> Oh God, because it is given to me to sip the cup of the happiness of the future in reality and not merely in dreams, I bring thee praise and thanksgiving from a light-some heart. I would be thrilled to the last fiber of my being by the blazoned gold of autumn, the magic of the moonlight. Outside—in the present—the world to many is not a stimulus, a joy, it is evil. I thank thee, that thou hast lifted the veil for me, so that I may go back to the present and say with a truthful confident spirit that the clear pure joy of living is worth striving for.[31]

As Winifred moved through college, however, it was clear that her major love was sociology, not theology. She read widely in the social sciences, commenting in her letters on the virtues of intellectuals like Havelock Ellis and Sigmund Freud and feminist leaders such as Olive Schreiner, Emma Goldman, and Charlotte Perkins Gilman. She shared with her father her desire to find an appropriate vocation, contemplating at various times careers in writing, social work, and teaching. She looked to her father for advice, and her father willingly gave it to her. At one point in her senior year, Winifred contemplated applying for a teaching position in an African American school. Rauschenbusch's response reveals some of his ambivalence on questions of racism, giving his daughter only a lukewarm affirmation to pursue the opportunity. "If you felt called by God to devote your life to the black race, I might say, 'God bless you, my child,' and should be proud. . . . But if a temporary step is a stairway, it seems to me very unadvisable."[32] Nevertheless, the father did not stand in the way of his daughter's aspirations.

The two discussed many contemporary topics—the merits of socialism and pacifism, the world war, and of course, recent family events. More than to any of his children, Rauschenbusch frequently confided to Winifred on a number of family matters, including his repeated concerns about Hilmar (Stephen), fearing that his oldest son lacked any clear vocational or spiritual direction. Reflecting upon a recent visit with his son, a student at Amherst College, he lamented to Winifred, "The thing that saddens me is the apparent lack of any aim in life, any faith to give relish, any sense of obligation. . . . How I wish he had religious faith as an active ingredient."[33] In several letters to his daughter, Rauschenbusch detailed the divide between himself and his oldest son, noting the similarities in the relationship to his own father. Sadly, Rauschenbusch's letters to Winifred also chronicle the development of the cancer that ultimately took his life in July 1918.[34]

Inevitably, however, the correspondence between the two focused on the struggle over gender and Winifred's growing need to define herself outside the values of her father's generation. While Rauschenbusch alternated between being a stern parent and an adoring father, it is apparent that he made no effort to interfere with Winifred's desire to pursue a vocational path. Indeed after Winifred's college graduation in 1916, it was evident that Rauschenbusch's admonitions about his daughter's behavior had little impact on her decisions about her future. Not long after her graduation from Oberlin, Winifred took a position with the Ohio Suffrage Association, doing fieldwork throughout that state. Rauschenbusch constantly worried about his daughter's safety, especially concerned that she would become a sexual object, preyed upon by lustful men.

Yet Winifred, by this stage of her life, revealed herself as a young woman who was not intimidated by her father's concerns. In fact, with growing frequency, she lectured her father on issues of modern womanhood. Repeatedly, her letters make clear her desire to break free of the gender values associated with her parents' generation, frequently chiding her father for his Victorian views of human sexuality. In October 1916, Winifred wrote a lengthy letter to her father, responding to his worries about her future. "I realize that you are trying to deal tactfully with me in my excursions into friendship and the awakening wonder of the senses. . . . I prefer to be frank; it is my nature. I am diplomatic enough however to tell people only as much of the truth as they can assimilate." Winifred, in a tone reminiscent of her father's frequent admonitions to her in the past, proceeds to castigate him for his overprotectiveness and social conservatism, warning, "the minute you become hard, lay on the heavy hand, and revert to your older and more traditional grooves of that, the moment you are tempted to believe that it is time to throw on the lever of parental authority—I'll quite mechanically close up like a clam." She discusses her desire to engage in sexual experimentation, noting that she went through college "without knowing what it was to have had my sense thrilled by a man." Even as she castigates the values of her father's generation, she also takes on a reconciling tone, acknowledging the differences in generational perspectives separating the two. "There are a number of courses open to us as parents and children. If we were model, docile, unoriginal, finished products there would be no problem. As it is what we do must jar you occasionally, without our realizing it." She continues to lecture her father, however, to allow her to live her life. Winifred's assertions reflect how she shared both the personality and many of the values of her father.

> Of course youth never has all the data and consequently makes blunders. But youth cannot be controlled by fear, adventure, daring and confidence are its familiars [sic], so that the fears of maturity and the experiences of maturity are no good school for youth. It must read life for itself, not from the page of another's book. All parents can do is to build a sure foundation and give children so much training in independent action that they can rely on their steering powers when it comes to a crisis—and then trust that foundation and those steering powers.

The letter's conclusion reflects upon the fact that she also shared much of her father's sense of humor. "Well, Belovedest, I am very much your daughter in many ways: strong, independent, ardent, interested in human affairs, with a streak of humour and another of sanity and another of daring, with a smiling countenance to the world and a deep seriousness inside, so give me your blessing and continue to love me."[35]

The father's response to the letter was one of cautious support, letting Winifred know that as much as he loved his daughter, he still had concerns about her future. "Your straight forward expression of your point of view suits me entirely. I am not . . . trying to impose my authority on you in this, but feel like an old friend trying to make a young and impetuous friend see the wider bearings which she is inclined to overlook." Still worried that his daughter would become snared in an illicit sexual encounter, he warns her not to become entangled in a relationship with a man based solely on sexual passion. "Your tender physical emotions are not strong enough to overcome your critical feelings about the quality of the man next to you. Love even in its faintest beginnings, idealize[s] and pushes you on. That is its nature." Behind his conservatism, however, Rauschenbusch reveals his inner fear that Winifred might fall into a loveless marriage like his own mother, Caroline. Citing the unhappy relationship between his mother and father as one of the "great sorrows in my life," he pleads to his daughter to make the most of her life and the relationships she forms with others. His response reveals the conflicting views that he held toward women, on one hand encouraging Winifred in her personal and public pursuits, but also beseeching her to stand as a moral paragon.

> You have made a splendid beginning in your work, and I see great possibilities open for you. But the greater the treasure in your hands, the more carefully must you walk. For years the main consideration with me . . . that I must not injure you children and must not diminish the moral capitalization which is now contained in my reputation and influence. The Almighty may have great things reserved for you. Don't frustrate the future.[36]

Successive letters between the two indicate that Winifred had the last word. In early March 1917, she wrote a whimsical letter to her father, commenting on a variety of subjects, including the world war, the merits of pacifism—and the latest women's spring fashions. She discusses her purchase of new clothes and flaunts to her father her joy at beginning a subscription to *Vogue* magazine. While clearly attempting to make her father nervous through her assertion of independence, her letter, in a style resembling her father's humor, expressed gratitude for what her father gave to her and her siblings. ". . . your playfulness, tenderness, sympathy, encouragement, your testing of our young wits against your own exuberant youthfulness. I cannot think of you as anything but preposterously young. I guess you're a serious bear sometimes, but, I've never seen much of it." Her conclusion was an appropriate statement of Winifred's love for her father and her independence from many of his values. "Well. Comrade and Beloved, I can just see you reading this at the breakfast table and I hope you'll [forgive] . . . my inability to grow-up. I love you tremendously and I stretch out my arms to you and clinch my hands into joyful abandon—when I'm not trying on my new hat. Be good to yourself and your little red beard."[37]

Even though Rauschenbusch saw little of his eldest daughter in the final year and a half of his life, their correspondence remained frequent. Not long before his death, Rauschenbusch expressed his joy at receiving a letter from Winifred, affirming "everything that has love in it is the heavenly bread that nourishes the soul."[38] As Winifred moved further away from the cultural world of her father, it was nevertheless apparent that both father and daughter fed from the same loaf of heavenly bread.

Conclusion

Pauline Rauschenbusch, in a moving letter to her husband written days before his death, reassured her dying husband that the future of Rauschenbusch's theological vision would survive with their children. "We have five fine children— who are all going to help to make this old world of ours better . . . and you've given them of your spirit—you are their great inspiration and will be more and more."[39] As much as his children, including his cherished eldest daughter, ultimately rejected many of the intellectual underpinnings so crucial to their father's worldview, Pauline's assessment is more than a kind sentiment expressed to a dying man. She reaffirmed the truth expressed frequently in her husband's writings that the ultimate purposes of the kingdom of God are never fully disclosed to a single historical era. The purposes of the kingdom expand and change from generation to generation.

This investigation of Rauschenbusch's family suggests that a more nuanced view needs to be developed in relation to how Rauschenbusch viewed questions of gender. The perception that he blindly followed the precepts of Victorian culture, with regard to his understanding of women, needs to be viewed with some qualification. There is no question that Rauschenbusch defended a conservative cultural view toward women in society, especially showing reticence about women's leadership in the public sphere. However, his willingness to allow his daughter to pursue her own calling in life, even as she moved further away from the values of her parents, possibly suggests that Rauschenbusch's views toward gender were more flexible than previously argued.

Historians, theologians, and ethicists who study the life and thought of Rauschenbusch should not gloss over the paternalistic views that he had toward women (and African Americans) in American culture. One of the great failures of Rauschenbusch (and of many proponents of the social gospel in America) was that he never recognized how the conservative cultural suppositions of his day undermined the transformative social imperatives that he espoused in his public theology. Given the institutional barriers that still serve as boundaries to the full participation of women in the church today, Rauschenbusch's ambivalence, and at times hostility, toward the public gifts of women must be acknowledged and, to a point, chastised.

At the same time, it is a mistake to equate the gender conservatism of Rauschenbusch with that of more theologically conservative incantations of American Protestantism, such as fundamentalism, that emerged at the end of the last century. Unlike fundamentalism, Rauschenbusch's ambivalence toward the public role of women did not rest upon scriptural proof texting, such as those texts that on the surface appear to limit the public role of women in church and society. His ambivalence rested upon the fact that he, like many males of his generation, was limited in his perspective by a culturally bound view of women that did not do justice to the inclusive theological vision that Rauschenbusch, among others, helped introduce to twentieth-century Western theology.[40]

Years after her father's death, Winifred remarked that her father matured on every intellectual question except that of gender, "to which his opinions always remained Victorian."[41] It is conjecture as to whether Rauschenbusch would have changed his views on gender issues, if he had lived into the post–World War I era. It is true that in the years after World War I, many of the heirs to the social gospel legacy in American Protestantism did little to address issues related to gender equality—but there were signs of change. In many respects, the theological heirs of the social gospel tradition became many of the primary advocates that ultimately led to the full ordination of women within several Protestant communions in the later twentieth century. To see Rauschenbusch as a man confined by the cultural suppositions of his time is to acknowledge the limited scope of his theological vision. At the same time, to look closely at his theology is to acknowledge, as Rauschenbusch so often did, that even as theology derives its vitality through an active engagement with the culture of its time, the power of God's love is far greater than the cultural values of a given generation.[42] The human inability to grasp the full extent of God's purposes for humanity was expressed in his final work, *A Theology for the Social Gospel*, when he reminded his readers that the ultimate purposes of faith could never be fully disclosed to a specific historical era. "An eschatology which is expressed in terms of historic development has no final consummation. Its consummations are always the basis for further development. The Kingdom of God is always coming, but we can never say 'Lo here.'"[43]

When Rauschenbusch wrote *Christianity and the Social Crisis*, he hoped that the words of his pen would take on a life of their own—independent of the author's intent. In the early twenty-first century, his vision of a "Christianized" social order, based upon many of the conservative gender suppositions of his lifetime, represents the antiquated vision of a bygone era. On the other hand, Rauschenbusch's theological imperative to work toward the ideal of the kingdom of God within the context of a particular culture has bequeathed to churches in the twenty-first century a challenge to build communities of love, social equality, and justice. As Walter and Winifred Rauschenbusch demonstrated in their relationship, however, love's ultimate purposes can never be confined to any specific time or place: Love must be allowed to grow. For churches that seek to build upon the legacy of the social gospel, faith must be rooted in a belief that what appears improbable in our time will become the basis for new hope and transformation in the future.

5

Women Creating Communities—and Community—in the Name of the Social Gospel

Rosemary Skinner Keller

And it was a glorious age in which to be alive—those years of the eighties—the stirring years of the great social awakening. It is safe to say that more books and articles were written on social problems, more societies started for social reform, more institutions begun in the hope of making the world better in those and the few succeeding years than in any previous period of the world's history. And of those movements Lucy Rider naturally became a part. "Naturally" because she was in its finest sense a world-woman. Not a worldly woman. . . .
—Isabelle Horton, *High Adventure: Life of Lucy Rider Meyer*[1]

Isabelle Horton, one of the early teachers at the Chicago Training School for Home and Foreign Missions, captured the spirit of the women and men who committed their lives to the social gospel at the turn of the twentieth century: "It was a glorious age in which to be alive . . . those stirring years of the great social awakening." The hope of "making the world better" was the idealistic spiritual purpose that spurred their vision, activism, and energy.

Women wrote books. Horton's biography of the "high adventure" of Lucy Rider Meyer, and her founding of the deaconess movement and the Chicago Training School for City, Home, and Foreign Missions in 1885, is an example. However, men wrote most of the books. Women's distinctive contribution to the "stirring years" of the social gospel lay in the creation and day-to-day running of communities, such as the Chicago Training School, founded to confront the social evils and gender exclusions of their day. When women's presence was not welcomed, indeed prohibited, on the governing boards of established church institutions, women formed their own organizations to express their Christian commitment. The Chicago Training School, created for just that purpose, was a separatist, "for women only" society made up of the first professional church women. Its purpose was to train young women who could address the spiritual and social needs of the unchristian, non-Protestant, and underprivileged immigrants pouring into the cities. With modifications and modernization, many of these institutions, particularly women's missionary societies and social settlement and social justice organizations, are still active today.

The creation of communities of voluntary associations to advance the causes of churches and social movements reached its peak during the social gospel period. However, the building of voluntary organizations has been a hallmark of women's participation in public life since early colonial times— and it continues to be so today. When I began my teaching and scholarly research in the early 1980s, my interest in lay women in American church history centered on the building of women's separatist organizations in the churches. I wanted to understand how females first acted beyond the boundaries of their homes, raised vast sums of money for their churches, and sent the earliest single women missionaries into national and foreign mission stations throughout the world. This focus was the emphasis of my work in the three volumes of *Women and Religion in America* and *In Our Own Voices*, which Rosemary Ruether and I edited in the 1980s and 1990s.

Similarly, Anne Firor Scott's major book, *Natural Allies: Women's Associations in American History*, is a broad and inclusive study of the contributions made by women through their separatist reform movements and institutions in religious and secular arenas from colonial times through the mid-twentieth century. The colorful stories and analyses by scholars of women's history over the last two decades have established the significance of women's voluntary associations in changing the landscape of American history over four centuries.

During the past seven years, since becoming academic dean at Garrett-Evangelical Theological Seminary in Evanston, Illinois, and at Union Theological Seminary in New York City, my own interest in community building has taken a different tack. A goal of an academic dean should be to build a community of the faculty within the structure of the larger educational community: to help faculty balance their own academic excellence in teaching and research with their commitment to mutual responsibility and support for the welfare of the corporate group. The purpose is to develop "community" within "the community."

This shift in the vocational understanding of my day-to-day work from teaching, research, and writing to the academic dean's responsibilities has led me to a new angle of vision for the study of women's associations in American religious history. I have looked again at my own work on the creation of women's communities, along with that of Scott and many other writers, and have found another emphasis latent in the materials.

The separatist societies were effective because leaders at the national and local levels built community among the women in their communities. Bringing thousands of women together as team builders and as committed partic- ipants at the grassroots level gave larger purposes to their lives beyond the confines of home, provided ordinary women with networks of support for their daily needs, and offered them education in leadership. All these fruits were crucial to the vision and power of the founders and national leaders of these voluntary organizations. Creating the bonds of sisterhood, of commu- nity within communities, is a major legacy of women's work in American reli- gious history.

The stories of the services performed by these communities of women in the late nineteenth and early twentieth centuries are well told elsewhere. This essay looks at the story within the stories, the ways in which women created community within three types of representative communities during the social gospel period: the deaconess movement, women's missionary societies in Protestant denominations, and social settlement houses. It focuses upon a par- ticular aspect of the meaning of community in each of these types of organi- zations and of the way that the experience of community took effect in the women's lives. Community—within their communities—resulted from the creation of a corporate sense of the members' vocation, and the living out of that commitment in their leadership styles, relations with each other, and daily activities. While addressing the needs of churches and social service and jus- tice agencies, women found individual vocations for their lives and developed bonds of sisterhood that previously had been inconceivable.

The Deaconess Movement

A Deaconess is a woman who is providentially set free from the domestic and social cares that naturally absorb the time of most women, and who is set apart for the special work of the church. The Deaconess is the mother in the "household of faith."
Deaconess Advocate (March 1911)[2]

From 1870 until the turn of the century, more than 140 deaconess homes were opened in the United States. They represented almost every Protestant denomination and some were interdenominational. Deaconesses pioneered as professional female workers in Protestant churches long before the denomi- nations would ordain women. They were young women of strong church background, many daughters of ministers or of women's society leaders, who responded to a call to Christian service, just as their brothers might have chosen to be ministers.

The primary work of deaconesses was to establish and manage charitable institutions, including settlement houses, hospitals, schools, and churches, for the poor in the United States and throughout the world. They interpreted their work as a restoration of the New Testament office of a deacon, or servant. Deaconess orders were the equivalent to those of Roman Catholic nuns, though its members took no lifetime vows. Deaconesses wore plain, dark dresses with white collars—distinctive costumes similar though simpler than those of Roman Catholic sisters.

To create a community of support for the deaconess sisters of the Chicago Training School, Lucy Rider Meyer and her husband, Josiah Shelly Meyer, employed the language and experience of the most basic community: the family. As principal of the school, which opened in 1885, Mrs. Meyer was the designated mother. The Mother House was the residence of the deaconesses, a home for the new family that the young single women formed when they joined the order.

For the most part, the recruits came from farm and small-town backgrounds and were leaving their families of origin for the first time. To venture forth into the world of sin, squalor, and brutishness, the "overgrown social and political tumor" of the burgeoning inner cities of New York, Boston, Cincinnati, Chicago, and San Francisco, was a bold and courageous step, described by Mary Agnes Dougherty in her book *My Calling To Fulfill: Deaconesses in the United Methodist Tradition*.[3] In one district of Chicago alone in the closing years of the nineteenth century, there were estimated to be two Protestant churches, 270 saloons, eighty-five wine houses, seven opium and eight gambling dens, and ninety-two houses of prostitution.[4]

The story of Lucy Rider Meyer interweaves throughout the accounts of all the communities considered in this essay. She herself personified most of the young women who entered the Chicago Training School and became the first deaconesses in Protestant churches. Born in 1849 of devoutly religious parents in the rural village of New Haven, Vermont, she prepared first to join her fiancé as a medical missionary by studying two years at the Woman's Medical College of Pennsylvania. After his premature death, she decided not to become a foreign missionary. As a young single woman searching for a vocation nearer to her family, she entered the field of education, became principal of the Troy Conference Academy in Poultney, Vermont, taught chemistry for a year at the Massachusetts Institute of Technology in Boston, and then accepted a position as professor of chemistry at McKendree College in Lebanon, Illinois. Though gifted as a teacher, she felt drawn to the church and to the direct service of humanity. She stretched her wings farther from home when she became field secretary of the Illinois State Sunday School Association in 1881. Marrying Josiah Shelly Meyer, employed by the YMCA in Chicago and committed to social work within the church, in 1886, they found their vocations together by initiating the Chicago Training School to prepare young women, such as herself, to enter home and foreign missionary work of the churches.

In determining the need for such a community, Lucy Rider Meyer was struck by the rapid pace at which Protestant church members were vacating their churches in the cities to reconstitute them in newly created suburbs in the 1880s. She estimated that 300,000 immigrants, mostly from western and eastern Europe, arrived in Chicago during that decade. The churches needed to reach the masses, both to convert them to Protestant Christianity and to provide them with spiritual and material support. A new kind of consecrated worker was essential to this cause, "not only amateur charity ladies, but an organized force trained in those ministering functions which have their root in woman's nature."[5]

Lucy Rider Meyer and Christian Golder, formative founders of the deaconess movement, captured the double bind created for deaconess recruits in language based upon the image of the family. Meyer described their call in these words: "The world wants mothering. Mother love has its part to do in winning the world for Christ as well as father-wisdom and guidance. The deaconess movement puts the mother into the church. It supplies the feminine element so greatly needed in the Protestant Church, and thus is rooted deep in the very heart of humanity's needs."[6]

This image of womanhood provided the strong mothering and caring qualities essential in the young women who fanned out daily into the streets and alleys to confront the degradation of the city. However, the popular conception also was that a woman's nature was "so fine and delicate" that "a home dwelling in which her personal life and vocation may be grounded" was necessary for her survival. Leaders had to combat the widespread fear within churches that single women were stepping too far out of their places in moving into the public sphere. The Deaconess Home was properly entitled The Mother House, according to Golder, "that form which best suits the substance and objects of the female diaconate, especially for the conditions of the times in which we live. . . . It is the Mother House that obviates all dangers of emancipation which women in public life so easily encounter."[7]

Lucy Rider Meyer also employed the language of family to define the way of life of the deaconesses and to provide them with a safe homelike environment from which to venture out into the new and avowedly dangerous world. She described the deaconesses who resided in The Mother House as "her beloved family of students and deaconesses." Before graduating their second class of fifteen students in 1887, Josiah Shelly Meyer shared this plan with them: Those who wished to stay and continue their field work "could remain as a part of the family, receiving room, board, and their necessary carfare. Further than that they could promise them nothing: but they 'would all work hard and share and share alike.'"[8]

The principle of sharing finances was key to the family system model of the Chicago Training School and of other deaconess orders. No one received an income or a salary. To do so would have degraded the spiritual value of their services. Rather, they received provisions to do the work: room, board, and basic essentials, which primarily meant carfare to and from their places of work for the day. The latter was understood as an allowance, a good family term for small amounts of money doled out to children weekly to provide them the opportunity to buy a few personal items. In exchange for their services over many years, the deaconesses were assured personal care in times of illness or in old age. One of their extended family members of financial supporters, Norman Wait Harris, wealthy philanthropist and president of the Harris Banking House, contributed $100,000 to the retirement fund of the Methodist Deaconess Association to provide better living conditions for elderly deaconesses.

"Mrs. Meyer was pouring her life into the work of the School," wrote Isabelle Horton describing a mothering quality, not the manner of an employer. "She counseled the girls, advised and prayed with them, shared their burdens, and identified herself with their cares. They caught her spirit and their uplifted souls found a way to other hearts."[9] At least initially, she resolved to take her part in the household tasks in which all other family members had to share. Over time she stepped back from some jobs, including washing dishes and windows and bookkeeping, absolving herself of such responsibilities on the basis of the "diversity of gifts" granted to members of God's household!

Lucy Rider Meyer, as principal of the Chicago Training School and mother of The Mother House, had a strong partnership with her husband as the administrator of the school and house. They shared equally in the management and running of the institution. However, it is notable that the language of fatherhood was not associated with Josiah in descriptions of the two and of their work.

Descriptions abound of the sisterhood of women that grew among the students and graduates. A close corps of women stood with the Meyers at the center of a community support network within the communities of the household and school. Horton's description of Elizabeth Holding is representative. "This talented woman," she wrote, returned from missionary work in South Africa, "caught the spirit of self-forgetful adventure and became an invaluable helper in laying the foundations of the new School . . . She was the first of a large number of women that Mrs. Meyer was able to gather around her—women of genius who found in their hearts a response to the splendor of her idealism, and who carried the influence of her dynamic leadership into every part of the homeland, and to continents beyond the sea."[10]

Horton also wrote of a "distinguished quartette" of students at the Chicago Training School, some who stayed to run the Chicago operations and others who were sent out to bring leadership to an extended family of institutions spawned by the school. The quartet included Isabella Thoburn, who became head of the Cincinnati Training School, Mary Jefferson, who took her place as head of the Chicago Home, Isabelle Reeves, who also remained in leadership in Chicago, and May Hilton, who later as May Hilton-Hoover became a missionary to South Africa. This "vanguard of a great movement," in Horton's words, were the first of a large number of women graduates from the Chicago Training School who founded more than forty institutions, figuratively an extended family of The Mother House, including hospitals, orphanages, schools for the homeless, and homes for the elderly.

The "new woman of Protestantism," the single woman who could have a life and a vocation of her own, was a creation of the deaconess family. In 1912, sixteen years before publication of her biography of Lucy Rider Meyer, Isabelle Horton described the significance of Meyer's entry onto the public scene: "It would seem, that the time has come in the history of the world when the unmarried woman no longer needs to excuse or defend her existence, when what she had done for the betterment of humanity should silence all adverse criticism."[11]

As early as 1895, Lucy Rider Meyer stated the significance of these first professional women in the churches in this way:

> A deaconess is often pictured as a goody-goody kind of woman who goes softly up dirty back stairs, reading the bible to poor sick women and patting the heads of dirty-faced children. But there is nothing a woman *can* do in the line of Christian work that a deaconess may not do. Her field is as large as the work of woman, and the need of that work. In deaconess ranks today may be found physicians, editors, stenographers, teachers, nurses, bookkeepers, superintendents of hospitals and orphanages, kitchen-gardeners and kindergartners. In Omaha not only the superintending nurse, but the superintendent of the Methodist Episcopal Hospital, an institution that within two years has cared for 1040 patients, are deaconesses.[12]

By creating a community of women within the community of the Chicago Training School, its members supported, inspired, and trained each other. In turn, the sisterhood opened up new professions for their sisters and released them to venture into "fields of usefulness" previously barred to women of the late nineteenth century.

Women's Societies of Christian
Service and Missionary Outreach

Apart from all considerations of duty to others, it will be profitable
to ourselves to unite together in such associations as are contemplated by this Society.
                            —Editor, *The Heathen Woman's Friend* [13]

Writing in the first issue of the *Woman's Foreign Missionary Society* journal of
the Methodist Episcopal Church, the editor spoke for a far wider community
of women than those of her denomination. After the Civil War, from 1865
until 1894, more women became involved in women's societies of Christian
service and missionary outreach within their local churches than in all areas of
social reform and women's rights movements combined. Foreign missionary
societies were formed in thirty-three white and African American Protestant
denominations, and national missionary societies were begun in seventeen
denominations. Through the communities at the grassroots level of local congregations and the regional and national societies that brought them together,
more than 1,000 women were sent into foreign mission fields during this
twenty-year period.

Societies of Christian service and missionary outreach are grouped together
in this essay. Christian service refers to a wide cluster of work, including
national missions, aid to local congregations, and advocacy of justice issues
beyond the church. Often this work was done in conjunction with foreign missionary work by one society in the congregation while in other congregations
the work was divided between two organizations. Most national and foreign
missionaries were trained in deaconess institutions such as Lucy Rider Meyer's
Chicago Training School. Meyer maintained close relationships with local and
national women's Christian service and missionary society workers. Without
the vision of vocation, the structural implementation of purpose advanced by
the schools, and the community of support developed within the communities, there could have been no corps of single female missionary workers to
send into the national and international fields.

The emphasis here is upon the bonds of vocation and of sisterhood that
were created among women in Christian service and missionary societies in
local congregations. Missionary and Christian service journals, the "mass
media" publications of the women's societies, were a primary means of reaching the large number of women spread across the rural and metropolitan
areas of the United States. By the 1890s, the three largest publications of the
Presbyterian, Methodist Episcopal, and Baptist women's groups alone had
more than 60,000 subscribers. Women who could pay for a copy were urged

to "lend it to the woman who cannot, and thereby arouse and secure prayers."[14]

Leaders who wrote for the journals stated the vocation of women's society members clearly and succinctly. First, the women were commissioned to evangelize the world, to convert all men and women of the world to faith in Christ. Even more important was their commitment to "woman's work for woman." Lucy Williams, writing in *The Woman's Evangel* journal of the United Brethren Church, stated that the Good News of new life in Christ comes to women as a "glad evangel . . . as the name of our paper signifies—an announcement of glad tidings to some of the five hundred millions of women in the degradation and ruin of false religions and oppressive social customs of heathen nations."[15] To bring the Good News meant not only to preach Christian salvation to women but also to work for their release from social and educational oppression.

However, "apart from all considerations of duty to others, it will be *profitable to ourselves to unite together* [italics mine] in such associations as are contemplated by this Society." The national and regional leaders and writers in women's society journals knew that female members and subscribers, isolated in their homes and lacking a larger purpose for their lives, had to be given new purpose, self-understandings that did not limit them to domestic duties. Now they could be laborers in the vineyard themselves. A new status of women at home being missionaries in their own right was inculcated into members of local church foreign and home missionary societies.

A few months later, in the first year of *The Heathen Woman's Friend*, a writer powerfully stated the commission of women's society members on the home front in relation to the deaconesses sent into the field: "A *few* must go forth to teach them, but the *many* must *work* at home. We now especially need the home laborers, ladies who will go to work earnestly to organize praying bands and working circles to earn and raise money to send missionaries abroad and to support native Bible women to teach heathen women." She noted, "How many churches there are in our connection, where the women would gladly do something, if some one would but take the lead, and interest and unite them in some plan of earning or saving a little money." She capped her summons to commitment with these words: "Let every lady, who feels that she *would be a missionary*, go to work at home, and she may, by every dollar raised, teach her heathen sisters."[16] By offering these isolated women a God-given purpose for their lives, the leaders inspired women to raise large sums of money through their penny mite boxes and their nickel campaigns to send sister missionaries abroad.

The community created within the communities of women's Christian service and missionary societies was two-fold in its nature. First, women's organization leaders sought sisterhood within their local churches. Their goal was that every church would have a women's society and that all women in the congregation would become members. Detailed, meticulous instructions were given in the journals for the formation of auxiliaries. The first essay of *The Missionary Helper* of the Free Baptist Woman's Missionary Society in 1878 set forth the process to secure from every woman in each local congregation a pledge of two cents per week or a dollar a year to carry on the work.

Every woman was to write on an envelope "Woman's Work for Woman" and to place two cents or more in it each week. Then, she was to try to get all women in her church to do the same. When even three or four would make this weekly pledge, they were to form a Woman's Christian Service and Missionary Society auxiliary, meet once a month, and report its founding and progress to the district secretary. Finally, each woman was to "ask yourself if it is not your privilege to become a life member. The payment of $20, even if made in installments within one or two years, constitutes a life membership."[17] The hope was that, through this training given in the missionary journals, all grassroots members would contribute their "mite for missions." A picture printed in the January 1891 edition of *The Missionary Link* graphically portrays the purpose. A woman, clearly representing a middle-class member of a woman's missionary society, is holding the left hand of her three-year-old daughter. With her right hand, the young daughter is putting a coin in a mite box, while an older daughter is pointing to a painting on the wall of a large ship, probably carrying missionaries and supplies to those to be evangelized in China or India.

While such activity was clearly a means of creating community among the women in each local congregation, it was also a means of developing bonds of sisterhood with other society members even in the most remote reaches of the United States. "Our Needs," an essay in the July 1878 edition of *The Missionary Helper*, the journal of the Free Baptist Woman's Missionary Society, presents a two-fold need: first, to raise money to support women in far-flung heathen countries and, second, to bring purpose to the lives of women who could supply those resources. Addressing the latter group, the leader wrote: "In the sewing-rooms in our cities, in the far-houses of the prairies, in the kitchens all through our borders, are women who have never thought of life as anything more than a 'bread-winning and bread-bestowing existence. . . .' In blind ignorance of their own individual capabilities, of their passing opportunities, they are wasting their substance, their lives, their all, and the golden harvest all around them are perishing for reapers." Gaining momentum, she continued by bringing together her two purposes of duty to others and duty to selves: "The Free Baptist women of Rhode Island have pledged themselves to the support of one of these young ladies, and it is confidently expected that some part of Maine will assume the support of another. Will not the women of Ohio unite in sustaining the third? If each of the two hundred subscribers to the *Helper* in Ohio give two cents a week and influence another person to do the same, her salary will be secured."[18]

Evelyn Brooks Higginbotham, in her book *Righteous Discontent*, develops a graphic example of the interaction between duty to others and duty to selves on the national scene in the evolution of the Women's Convention of the National Black Baptist Church, 1880 to 1920. Higginbotham takes as her starting point the words of Nannie Helen Burroughs, founder, secretary, and president of the convention, whose leadership extended from 1900 to 1961. Writing in 1900, at the founding of the Women's Convention, the twenty-one-year-old Burroughs summoned her black sisters to form their own female missionary and service society out of the "burning zeal" of women in her denomination to bond together for "collection self-criticism, in order to eradicate inequalities and exclusions within the black community itself." The purpose of bringing together the twenty-six state representatives in 1900 was "to rescue the world for Christ. Women arise. He calleth for thee."[19] Resisting attempts by the male leaders to transform the women's separatist convention into a subsidiary board of the denomination, the women stood firm and established their own independent governing structure.

Community, extending from the local branches to the national society, grew out of carefully nurtured structures at each level. Work of the branches was coordinated and regulated by handbooks that outlined organizational methods and by record books for bookkeeping accountability, all developed to train their members in how to be executive administrators. Annual national meetings of the Women's Convention were held each year at the same time and place of the National Baptist Convention. These gatherings evoked group identity, both to be National Baptists and to be National Baptist Women, and were the high point of the year for the women, resulting both in shared friendships and experiences and in an agenda for fighting Jim Crow laws of segregation and making racial progress. Community was advanced as the black churches responded to the racism in the denial of accommodations in white hotels and restaurants by providing housing and meals in the homes of their members.

The Women's Convention's annual meetings became "schools of methods" for local societies. They featured highly practical topics, such as "How to Increase Attendance at Each Meeting," to address their organizational growth and effectiveness. Further, they pushed their local church ministers and congregations to move from solitary focus on individual salvation to the social gospel emphasis on social reform.

While most of these women's organizations were formally or informally called missionary societies, the work of the Women's Convention of the

National Baptist women demonstrates other kinds of Christian service that these societies saw as their commitments. The practical work of social salvation became the focus of their work after 1900 as they studied issues relating to secular and social betterment: public health, crime prevention, prison reform, sexually transmitted diseases, playground and recreational facilities for children, job placement, and vocational training. "No church should be allowed to stay in a community that does not positively improve community life," Burroughs stated in her 1914 convention address.[20]

Experts in their fields, including physicians, social workers, civic improvement activists, and educators, were brought to the national conventions to share their expertise. Simultaneously, black women themselves were empowered to study and write on social conditions of their own race and not to leave such work to white persons who did not have firsthand knowledge of these conditions. As ideas and expertise were channeled throughout the sisterhood, black women were empowered both to be good mothers and to conceive of higher and wider purposes for their individual and corporate lives.

Simultaneously, as black sisters grew in community within their communities, they championed social reform within their national and local church bodies and were sent out individually to contribute their learning and advocacy in wider communities of secular and social reform. The Woman's Convention was the great preparatory school of women's church societies in the name of the social gospel. By the second decade of the twentieth century, leaders of the convention at local and national levels branched out into secular African American reform societies, including the national League for the Protection of Colored Women and the National Urban League, complementary to their continued church-related activities.

The Social Settlement Movement

> I remember on that exciting day when the house was first promised to us that I looked up my European notebook . . . hoping that I might find a description of what I thought a "Cathedral of Humanity" ought to be. The description was "low and widespreading as to include all men in fellowship and mutual responsibility even as the older pinnacles and spires indicated communion with God." . . . when I read this girlish outbreak it gave me much comfort, for in those days in addition to our other perplexities Hull-House was often called irreligious . . . all higher aims live only by communion and fellowship, [and] are cultivated most easily in the fostering soil of a community life.
>
> —Jane Addams, *Twenty Years at Hull-House* [21]

Jane Addams founded the most famous and one of the first social settlement houses in the United States in 1889. Traveling to Europe a few years before, she visited its predecessor, Toynbee Hall in London, and gained her inspiration from the relief and rehabilitation work done there among the urban poor. A vital cadre of middle-class residents, most of whom were women, formed around Addams. They invested their hope in Hull House that the needs of all people were reciprocal, that the entire society would be improved as classes and races lived and worked together.

Until her death in 1935, Addams remained the leader and a resident of Hull House, though her influence increasingly broadened onto the national and international political and social scene. She became the first woman to receive the Nobel Peace Prize in 1931.

Facing each other on opposite pages of *Twenty Years at Hull-House* are the above statements by Jane Addams about the nature of community. Her words convey the two meanings of community at the heart of Hull House. They also dispel two misconceptions that have lingered about the settlement house over the years.

First, Addams symbolizes Hull House as a cathedral that was an alternative structure to traditional houses of faith, one that did not separate people into communities of particular faiths, sects, or denominations. This cathedral unified people around the wider spiritual principles that all people could affirm of service to each other and to all of humanity. Second, she envisioned Hull House as a way of life based upon communion and fellowship among its members. The bonds of support and nurture cultivated by the mutual service of one to another were meant to lead its members to a deeper vision and higher ideals for their corporate life.

One popular misconception is Jane Addams's supposed opposition to traditional religious faith. Eleanor Stebner discovered and shared in her book *The Women of Hull House: A Study in Spirituality, Vocation, and Friendship* that Addams was a regular attending and contributing member of the Ewing Street Congregational Church down the street from Hull House at least through the mid-1920s. The Ewing Street Church was an outreach congregation of the Chicago City Missionary Society and was an avowedly evangelical congregation.

She also had close ties to Lucy Rider Meyer and the Chicago Training School. According to Isabelle Horton, Meyer and Addams were close friends who personally affirmed both the traditionally religious and the alternative social passions. Meyer invited Addams to become a member of the Board of the Chicago Training School, after she had given a course of lectures to graduating seniors at the school for three consecutive years. Meyer was embarrassed and saddened to withdraw the invitations for teaching and board membership after certain board members objected that Hull House had eliminated direct religious teachings for its curriculum. Hull House simply represented a different expression of religious faith, one not based upon beliefs, creeds, rituals, and forms of worship. Horton defined Addams's faith and Meyer's conviction of why Addams should teach: "It was Mrs. Meyer's desire to give room to any teaching that promised a true interpretation of Christ's mission." And, it was Addams's determination to keep Hull House free from "sectarian religion."[22] Service to address human need—physical, economic, and social as well as religious—represented Christ's mission and Addams's emphasis at Hull House, according to Meyer.

A second widespread misconception is about the kind of leadership that Jane Addams gave to Hull House. According to popular understanding, Addams and Hull House are virtually indistinguishable. The words *Jane Addams* and *Hull House* can hardly be uttered separately from each other. Addams virtually *was* Hull House. Due to this traditional emphasis, the formative role she played in creating and sustaining a female network and structures of support is only recently being recognized. Kathryn Kish Sklar, in her monumental work *Florence Kelley and the Nation's Work: The Rise of Women's Political Culture, 1830–1900*, returns to the evaluation made by Hull House residents and guests at the turn of the century: "Jane Addams's personality and intelligence were the kernel around which the Hull House community took shape." One resident wrote that "Hull House was not an institution over which Miss Addams presided, it was Miss Addams around whom an institution insisted on clustering." Emily Balch, who visited Hull House in 1895 and the only other American woman besides Jane Addams to be awarded the Nobel Peace Prize, said that Addams "did not dominate the group. She, as it were, incorporated it and helped it to be itself."[23]

Stebner wrote *The Women of Hull House* to examine the corporate nature of leadership and life at Hull House. She describes Addams as did Florence Kelley: "the cult figure that tied the Hull House crew together."[24] Addams provided space for companionships of mutual interests and affinities to support the diversity of more intimate communities within the larger corporate group and spiritual vision. The purpose of Stebner's book is to define and describe a community of female support that nurtured and empowered its members out of a spiritual conviction: to redress the dire urban evil of Chicago and the national reforms crucial to the social gospel and to progressivism.

According to Stebner, sisterhood within the Hull House community developed through networks of friendship among the workers that evolved out of their spiritual commitment of service to new immigrants in their neighborhood. In turn, this commitment released the residents to pursue their individual vocations at Hull House and beyond. The in-house residents had both their home and occupational roots in Hull House. They paid room and board out of their salaries from outside work and donated their time and abilities to the inner life of the settlement. "Residency at Hull House was carefully monitored to include only those people believed to exhibit the proper qualities of service, commitment, and tolerance. In this sense, it was a tightly knit community upholding particular ideological and behavioral values . . . to ensure that the spheres of their intended work were compatible with the goals of Hull House."[25]

The "communities within the community" that Stebner describes are exemplified in the friendship among Julia Lathrop, Florence Kelley, and Alice Hamilton. Along with Addams and Hull House cofounder Ellen Gates Starr, Lathrop, Kelley, and Hamilton made up the core of the community. Vocationally, these women were visionary social reformers of the social gospel/progressive movements on the Chicago and national scenes.

Lathrop was the first Hull House resident to be employed in an Illinois State administrative position, appointed to the State Board of Charities by Governor John Altgeld. She was pivotal in founding the first juvenile court in the United States, and was a founder and trustee of the Illinois Immigrants Protection League. Later, she became chief of the Federal Children's Bureau in Washington, D.C., as well as a member of the National Board of the League of Women Voters. Kelley's work led to passage of the Illinois Factory Act in 1893, prohibiting child labor, limiting work hours for women, and setting standards and procedures for inspection of tenement sweatshops. Altgeld appointed her Illinois chief factory inspector. Later she became head of the National Consumers' League, locating herself in New York City for more than twenty-seven years. Hamilton went to Chicago as a Hull House resident when she became professor of pathology at the Women's Medical School of Northwestern University. Spending more than twenty years in Chicago and at Hull House, she worked to eliminate infectious and industrial diseases and the cocaine industry. She later moved to Harvard Medical School as assistant professor of industrial medicine. Hamilton outlived all other Hull House residents, dying in 1970 when she was 101.

The community of Lathrop, Kelley, and Hamilton within the Hull House community was one of mutual support that enabled each woman to deepen her personal vocation. Kelley, wrote Supreme Court Justice and Hull House friend Felix Frankfurter, had "probably the largest single share [of all the Hull House women] in shaping the social history of the United States during the first thirty years of this [the twentieth] century."[26] She widened the vision and pushed Addams and her other sisters into more radical social action. She was high-spirited and impatient, a fighter and a galvanizer. Lathrop, one of her best friends, was known for her pastoral presence, compassion, and patience. Some thought that it was a great waste for such a valuable person to spend so much time and energy seeking to bring Hull House's neighborhood visitors a comfort and companionship that they may not have had in years. Lathrop brought diplomacy and gentleness, never losing her temper, in relating to Kelley.

They shared common traits that also brought them together, according to Frankfurter: "Both were brilliant, imaginative, humorous, and troubled by injustice. . . . When both were at Hull House together, arguing some problem of correcting a social injustice, and disagreeing as they often did on the best method of procedure, it is doubtful if any better talk was to be heard anywhere."[27]

When Hamilton went to Hull House, she felt insecure with some of the residents. She especially experienced Kelley as intimidating when she first met her, while Lathrop was immediately approachable. Kelley and Lathrop were both ten years older than Hamilton, and must have been mentors to her in different ways. In time, Hamilton grew deeply fond of Kelley and found her one of the most vivid, stimulating, and challenging persons she had ever known. Lathrop must have eased the way in bringing Kelley and Hamilton closer together. Hamilton became politicized at Hull House, particularly through Kelley's influence. She found Lathrop, who became a lifelong friend, especially companionable, and soon accompanied her on visits to asylums. The difference in what Kelley and Lathrop brought to Hamilton's life is beautifully complementary. Kelley challenged Hamilton to use her talents to directly confront the most serious social problems of her day, particularly as a doctor to investigate deplorable medical conditions and to become a scientific reformer. On the other hand, she wrote of Lathrop, "Julia Lathrop never roused one to a fighting pitch, but then fighting was not her method. . . .[she] taught me . . . that harmony and peaceful relations with one's adversary were not in themselves of value, but only if they went with a steady pushing of what one was trying to achieve."[28]

Lathrop, Kelley, and Hamilton all were shaped by Hull House, just as they formed it, and all grew from their relationships with Addams, just as they influenced her. Of the communities of coworkers that formed Hull House, none was stronger or deeper than the relationship between Kelley and Addams. Sklar demonstrates the importance of their interaction in forming both the women and the institution.

Kelley came to Hull House in late 1891, just two years after its founding. She felt immediately at home and was trusted by Addams. Within three months, she wrote that "I have cast in my lot with Misses Addams and Starr for as long as they will have me." She remained only seven years, but these seven happy, active years were the most influential of her life in linking her with powerful new means of doing the nation's work. Also, as her son, Nicholas, pointed out, from the time of coming to Hull House until her death in 1932, she counted Addams as her closest friend and confidant.[29]

Addams at once experienced Kelley as a deep friend and a most able surrogate. Kelley always sat beside Addams at dinner and was often in charge of events when Addams could not be present. In both depth and vision, they complemented each other and formed Hull House into its distinctive self. Addams was more personally adept in relating to individual problems and persons that presented themselves, while Kelley pressed her colleague to develop a larger, more structural analysis of society's needs and programs of reform. Lathrop stated that they "understood each other's powers" and joined together in a "wonderfully effective way." Addams, the philosopher, "taught Kelley how to live and have faith in an imperfect world," and Kelley, the politician, "taught Addams how to make demands on the future," Sklar summed up.[30]

Kelley was highly secular in her outlook, and she moved Addams and Starr away from some practices of evangelical Christianity, such as bowing on their knees for prayers and having evening Bible readings. Addams and Kelley both held strong commitments to social justice. Their differences in nature made for a fuller and more embracing approach. "Addams's instinct for peacemaking and conciliating made her see every side of social questions and feel compassion for all the actors, while Kelley's aggressive championing of the exploited usually dealt with stark contrasts behind good and evil. Kelley expressed anger against the causes of social injustice; Addams demonstrated a tragic appreciation of and sympathy with suffering."[31]

Their complementary dispositions undoubtedly provided a needed balance, both for each other and for Hull House. Lathrop described Addams as "serene, dauntless . . . Mrs. Kelley, alight with the resurgent flame of her zeal." Kelley's son, Nicholas, spoke of Addams as "firm beyond all imagining," and stated, "I never saw Miss Addams angry and never heard of her being angry." Frankfurter, on the other hand, termed Kelley "the toughest customer in the reform riot." Another wrote, "By what rare stroke of fortune were they brought together in the days when Chicago was a great focus of our mounting industrialism?"[32]

When Kelley reflected on the connection between gender and class in her own life, she also challenged middle-class women to look at that relationship in theirs and to understand their own culpability as part of the problem. As she asked in her autobiography, "In the great strife of classes, in the life and death struggle that is rending society to its foundations, where do I belong?"[33]

Kelley was reflecting vocationally on her own life, but could have been speaking of Addams, Lathrop, and Hamilton and her other colleagues at Hull

House. They belonged at Hull House and formed its corporate leadership, community and communities, just as they were shaped by Hull House and its members.

Today, one of the spoken or unspoken policies of most professional offices and businesses is that the public and personal areas of one's life should be kept separated. It is paradoxical that many of the abilities that enabled women to create community within communities in their early professional experiences grew out of their lives within their families. Among the contributions that women brought to professional roles at the end of the nineteenth century and continue to bring to the workplace today are distinctive gifts of collaborative leadership, supportive networking, and team building. As their stories demonstrate, women made their own history by naturally exercising these characteristics of leadership. Their experiences within the family gave them power and vision to embark upon larger tasks in the name of the social gospel. It also set them free to develop distinctive vocations.

The language of family and Mother House at the heart of the deaconess movement is undeniably quaint to the ears of feminists at the turn into the twenty-first century. However, the rationale for use of this language is important for us to hear. Advocates of deaconess orders were speaking in a language to make their radical moves as the first professional women in the churches justifiable to national authorities and grassroots members of local congregations, as well as to themselves. Their contribution to raising the status of single women and mothers cannot be underestimated. These single women constituted a community of women themselves. A deaconess may not have known a large number of other sisters in home and world mission stations. However, simply the knowledge of their presence and the letters that some exchanged with each other must have constituted a community of support to her.

Many women were led into women's missionary societies at the end of the nineteenth century because their lives, focused solely within their homes, were isolated, boring, and lacked meaningful purpose. They experienced the limitations of lives narrowly focused within their families. The women's societies in widely spread local congregations became an extended family, an intangible and mighty network of support. Women, conditioned to believe that their duty lay in fulfilling the needs of others, were now told that they also had a rightful duty to seek a broader world of meaning for themselves. An extended family of sisters made it possible for them to be supported in this vision.

In contrast to the women in Christian service and missionary societies, who developed community despite their geographical remoteness from each other, the women of Hull House, like the deaconesses, lived together under one roof. Hull House was not known for intimacy, primarily because of the personality of Addams. Other members, however, brought that experience of community to the household, pointing to the corporate contributions of the group. Addams herself needed support to extend herself within the community. Further, the diversity of personalities and the complementarity of the women's gifts ignited and provided the creative energy of mutual support and wider vision among the Hull House residents.

The result of bonding within communities considered here was that women were not held within the particular communities but were released to venture forth into new vocations of their own. This essay began with the example of Lucy Rider Meyer, and we return to her in conclusion. Her story of Hilda, the abbess of Whitby in England, born in 614 A.D., must have been appealing and inspiring to any of the women who read Meyer's account printed in *The Message and Deaconess Advocate* at the height of the social gospel period in 1895.

> The founder of a double monastery—that is, both for monks and nuns—she became the abbess of each, the head of the training-college from which no less than six bishops went forth.... "The harts [sic] and sciences," says the historian, "were so cultivated by her that Whitby was regarded as one of the best seminaries of learning in the then known world. And more even than this, we find Hilda in the councils and conferences of the church taking part in that Synod of Whitby which determined the form and fate of the church in England. "Her counsel," says J. R. Green, "was sought even by nobles and kings."...
> I closed the life of this noble Abbess of Whitby, wondering if God sent a St. Hilda to Methodism *what should we do with her.*[34]

A host of women have risen to notable leadership in the social revolution of the late twentieth century, yet that leadership is only dubiously accepted in many arenas of the political, business, social, and religious professions. Within the coming decade, those numbers will increase dramatically. In this day, Meyer's concern, which opened this essay, is more pressing than ever. We might restate it for today: Will the world take advantage of the potential that women bring to make this "a glorious age in which to be alive"?

6

Giving Patterns and Practices among Church Women in the Methodist Episcopal and the Colored Methodist Episcopal Churches, 1870–1920: A Social Gospel Perspective

Dianne Reistroffer

Tucked away in a recent two-volume study of twelve American congregations lies Lawrence Mamiya's description of the mutual aid societies' central role in the lives of black people in Baltimore during the opening decades of the social gospel era. One of the leading mutual aid groups was the Ladies Sewing Circle of the historic Bethel African Methodist Episcopal (AME) Church. In one paragraph, Mamiya neatly summarizes the generosity of these women:

> The Reverend John Mufflin Brown, Bethel's pastor, had high praise for the activities of this group. The circle aided the poor of the city by giving them food, clothing and fuel. It had helped about 200 people during the winter by buying 100 cords of wood and in another effort had donated 500 loaves of bread to be distributed to the poor. In the early spring of 1860, Eliza A. Tilgham, George Hackett's daughter, presented a check for $600 on behalf of the Ladies Sewing Circle to the trustees of Bethel Church. The trustees in turn gave a "grand dinner" for the circle with the head table seating about 309 honorees.[1]

The magnitude of this $600 gift by the Ladies Sewing Circle should not be lost on contemporary readers. Bear in mind that the average soldier hired to fill in for a Union conscript received only $300 in annual pay. In addition to in-kind and cash contributions to the poor of the city, the Bethel Ladies Sewing Circle sponsored annual picnics for people in the community, whose numbers had swollen by nearly 30 percent during the 1860s as former slaves made their way into the city. Indeed, by the 1880s, one of every five African Americans living in Baltimore was an ex-slave. Mamiya's study also celebrates the life of John Murphy Sr., a Civil War veteran and famed lay leader of Bethel AME Church, for his many contributions to the intellectual and political life of the city. In 1880 he purchased the *Baltimore Afro-American* newspaper for $200. What is noteworthy, however, is that Murphy, a janitor and a white-washer, borrowed the money from his wife, Martha, who later cofounded the black community's YWCA in 1896.[2] This significant clarification lies buried in one sentence in a lengthy, two-page excursus about John's role in the church and in the Baltimore African American community.

The above example represents a fair amount of the literature on women's roles in financing American religion. In an unpublished study on the history of American Protestant fund-raising, Robert Wood Lynn notes that "much of the tradition produced a literature largely written by and for white men."[3] His own documentary history reveals little of the contribution women have made in financing American religion, a lacuna that begs to be filled. Fortunately, since the late 1970s, several historians have begun to document the history of women's ways of giving and organizing for mission and ministry in the church. The pioneering work of Rosemary Keller, Dana Robert, Anastastia Sims, Carolyn Gifford, Mary Frederickson, Othal Lakey, Betty Stephens, Susan Yohn, and Earl Kent Brown has shaped and guided my own research as I continue to dig in denominational and congregational histories ferreting out the story of women's financial contributions to American church life.

The account of women's ways of giving between 1870 and 1920 fits within a larger financial-historical context. The history of American Protestant giving during the Gilded Age and at the height of the social gospel movement has been dubbed the "Era of the Good Steward."[4] According to Lynn, the prevailing theme of this period was systematization. In imitation of the great secular corporations of the time, denominations were becoming large national organizations. As Lynn points out, "Progress required efficiency, and efficiency required a new kind of church bureaucrat. . . . What was needed were experts who could help churches become truly business-like in fund-raising."[5] The magic words of *system, plan,* and *method* became the *lingua franca* of church leaders. A board of the ME (Methodist Episcopal) Church declared in 1912: "If a well-systematized plan can be presented in the local church, we have confidence that the church will respond in generous measure."[6] The push for education in systematic giving became an all-out effort in various Methodist communities. The Council of Bishops of the ME Church blessed such efforts with these words: "That [systematization] is a tremendous task, but it must be undertaken. And the first step toward it is to find a rational, Scriptural, systematic basis for asking."[7]

During this same period, several new church giving practices appeared. By the end of the nineteenth century, an increasing number of congregations of several denominations asked members to make an annual pledge and pay it in weekly installments. The Sunday collection became a regular feature of worship. The "duplex" envelope for weekly contributions was developed during the closing decades of the nineteenth century. Indeed, in some Protestant congregations, this two-pocketed envelope allowed the giver to divide the offering between the church's operating budget and mission support. It also provided the giver a measure of privacy.[8] Another feature of this period was the use of whirlwind campaigns to raise money for building projects. These short-term, intensive fund-raising projects were dependent on volunteer solicitors who visited every prospective contributor. The YMCA and YWCA made heavy use of this technique.[9]

"Stewardship" became the new motto of this churchwide era of financial activity and systematization. The core message of stewardship invoked three principles:

1. Christians are called to be stewards of what God has given them.
2. The good steward cares for temporary possessions given in trust.
3. The good steward returns to God that portion of money required by scripture.

Lynn believes the metaphor of stewardship appealed to late-nineteenth-century Protestants for several reasons:

> [Stewardship] offered a relatively fresh way of talking about faith and money. Second, it had a biblical lineage. While the previous generation of church leaders had based their giving theology on the slender reed of I Corinthians 16:2, the stewardship enthusiasts could roam through the New Testament parables about stewards. Third, and most important, it blended nicely with the values of white middle-class America. The good steward was an effective manager in addition to being a faithful steward. Stewards, whether of the first century or the twentieth, cherish order, efficiency, planning and taking responsibility.[10]

The interpretation of the third principle of stewardship—returning to God the portion required by scripture—was a subject of some dispute, for there was no common agreement on the amount or fair proportion of what ought to be given by individual Christians. Consequently, by the early 1890s, exhortations to believers "to give as God hath prospered them" gradually gave way to calls for tithing.[11]

This new insistence upon the tithe as a guide to faithful giving disturbed some in the social gospel movement. Leading social gospel figures Washington Gladden and Walter Rauschenbusch supported the belief that devotion to the common good and a sense of justice should move the wealthy to give a far greater proportion than the poor. Gladden worried that moving to a tithe might well "obscure the Christian principle 'every man according to his several ability.'"[12] Rauschenbusch expressed a similar concern, arguing that "it is rare that a rich man gives as much, proportionately, as a laboring man gives habitually."[13]

As the social gospel emerged at home in the closing decades of the nine-teenth century, it echoed abroad in appeals to alleviate social needs in the non-Christian world. The promotion of overseas missions, whether evangelistic or social, emphasized the needs of non-Christian people and the obligations of American Christians to them. A well-known spokesperson for the social gospel and a staff member of the American Home Missionary Society, Josiah Strong, made a case for evangelizing or "Christianizing" America. In his book, *Our Country: Its Possible Future and Present Crisis*, which was published in 1885, Strong declared that Americans were "destined by God to carry the benefits of their superior civilization to less vigorous races and to master them."[14] He argued that a "world emergency" required sacrificial giving that in turn could cure America's obsession with "the money power."[15] Strong became a favorite stumper for home and foreign missions. *Our Country* and his public addresses became extremely popular in Methodist circles, and he frequently lectured at annual gatherings of the Woman's Home and Foreign Missionary Societies of the ME Church and the ME Church, South.

As Lynn notes, Strong was among the first Protestants to advocate "Chris-tianizing" the money power. Later, other social gospel leaders, especially Rauschenbusch, would pursue that same theme but in a more radical fashion. Whatever their differences, Strong and Rauschenbusch both believed that "Christianizing" the money power opened the way to the kingdom of God. For his part, Rauschenbusch foresaw the need to create and ensure economic equity between rich and poor.[16] In contrast, Strong assumed the powerful in American society, particularly the wealthy, could become responsible by giv-ing sacrificially to church-related causes.

Women, as integral members of these communities, were, of course, greatly influenced by these larger movements and the main theological currents in the church. Indeed, several tracts published by women during this period reflect the optimism and the sense of call to evangelize found in materials authored by men.[17] At the same time, there are some noteworthy and important differ-ences in women's ways of giving, in the articulation of their motivations for giving, and in the manner in which they organized themselves for work in and on behalf of the church and toward the kingdom of God.

Nearly twenty years ago, Earl Kent Brown wrote an article for *Methodist History* entitled "Women in Church History: Stereotypes, Archetypes and Operational Modalities." In it, he argued that the stereotypical role of women in the church (women are to be present but silent and excluded from church leadership and decision making) has often been subverted or overcome by cer-tain archetypes of leadership that do not fit the stereotype.[18] He identified five major archetypes of women leaders in church history: the mystic/charismatic woman, the queen regnant, the feminine enclave, members of the community withdrawn, and full ministerial member of the body of Christ. This typology or framework has been useful for me in considering the ways women have organized themselves for mission and ministry and for giving.

Nineteenth-century and early twentieth-century Methodist women adopted the feminine enclave and the community withdrawn as strategies for circumventing certain institutional barriers to their exercise of leadership and ministry. Women's monastic and religious communities, women's missionary societies and councils exemplify the modality of the feminine enclave in a male-dominated church. When women find themselves excluded from leadership roles in the church at large, one solution is for women "to create their own sphere of work and influence," to borrow Rosemary Keller's phrase.[19] In forming their own enclave, women continue to function within the church, while controlling their own destinies and operations. The modality of the community withdrawn arises in situations where women of different religious groups or geographical areas sense a common woman's need or problem to which they might or should minister. The Woman's Christian Temperance Movement, an organization dedicated to social reform and a campaign for individual temperance and civil laws to prohibit the use of alcohol, serves as a classic example of the community withdrawn.

In order to illumine women's ways of giving in this "Era of the Good Steward," I would like to focus on two striking examples of the feminine enclave at work during the social gospel era and examine what they tell us about women's ways of giving: the Woman's Foreign Missionary Society of the ME Church and various women's groups of the then Colored, now Christian, Methodist Episcopal Church (CME Church).

A significant name in the story of the formation of the Woman's Foreign Missionary Society of the ME Church, Lois Stiles Lee Parker and her husband finished their studies at Concord Theological Academy in 1859. In that same year, they set out for India. For Parker, it was the beginning of a sixty-six-year missionary career on the subcontinent. During her first term of service, she founded a school for Indian girls. When she went on furlough after ten years, she was determined to make financial appeals in America on behalf of Indian women and girls and their educational needs. Back in Boston in 1868–69, Parker spoke several times on this topic and discussed it at great length with a number of women, including the wife of the former dean of the seminary she and her husband had attended. Before long, someone suggested gathering the women of Boston Methodism to consult about the process or undertaking that would best address the educational needs of the women and girls of India. This historic meeting took place on March 23, 1869, at the old Tremont Street Methodist Episcopal Church. It was a rainy day, resulting in a turnout of only six women. Nonetheless, Parker made her presentation, and the women assembled decided to do the typical church thing: They formed a committee. The committee proceeded to nominate officers and to prepare a constitution, which was adopted a week later on March 30.

Because these women did not wish to appear to compete with the Missionary Society in New York City, and because they understood the critical importance of the relationship between their new organization and their parent group, they contacted the leaders of the Missionary Society. But while the women were encouraged to raise all the money they could, a nervous New York office made it clear that its own members (the men) would be graciously pleased to spend it. In addition, they would also decide who would go as missionaries—male or female—and what kinds of mission work would be undertaken.

The women had something else in mind. Their intention was to form an autonomous agency committed to a congenial, coexistent relationship with the General Missionary Society.[20] The women believed that male eyes were blind to women's needs in the missionary field. In India, the secluded woman living in the *zenana* was kept inside her husband's house from the time she married until she died. She was particularly inaccessible to male missionaries and to male missionary undertakings. As Earl Kent Brown opines somewhat tongue-in-cheek: "It is not that the leaders of the WFMS thought that the men in New York were of ill will. It is just that they thought they were men and being men, they often did not see some of the issues or problems that women might."[21]

The purpose of the new missionary society was defined as "engaging and uniting the efforts of the women of the Methodist Episcopal Church in sending out and supporting female missionaries, native Christian teachers and Bible readers." The first issue of the society's magazine, bearing the rather unfortunate title *The Heathen Woman's Friend*, came out on May 7, 1869. For the next forty years, *The Heathen Woman's Friend* became one of the most popular missions and women's magazines of its day, shaping key fund-raising appeals of the society and serving as a vehicle for sharing testimonies and letters from the mission field.

Eighteen months after the foundation of the Woman's Foreign Missionary Society, Isabella Thoburn and Clara Swain arrived in India as the first missionaries supported by the WFMS. They were the first single women missionaries sent by the ME Church.[22] During the course of the next fifteen years, similar agencies developed in other denominations that trace their roots to the United Methodist Church: the United Brethren in 1875; the Methodist Episcopal Church, South in 1878; the Methodist Protestants in 1887; and the Evangelical Association in 1884. Dana Robert, noted historian of American

missions, comments on the proliferation of women's missionary societies and
their financial power during this period:

> In 1900, over 40 denominational women's societies existed, with three
> million active women, some despite sustained hostility from the men
> of the church. Publicizing projects through their mission magazines,
> women in local church auxiliaries nickeled and dimed their way into
> building hospitals and schools around the world, paying the salaries of
> indigenous evangelists and sending single women as missionary doc-
> tors, teachers and evangelists.[23]

There was one official effort at the 1876 General Conference to forge a closer
union between the WFMS and the General Missionary Society, but the women
successfully rebuffed it. In a statement made at the time, leaders of the WFMS
declared: "We regard closer financial union as prejudicial to our interests; in short,
a change would be disastrous."[24] With these words, and throughout the history of
this feminist enclave, the women made the society's governing principle clear: *cuia
labor et pecunia, cuia auctoritas,* that is, "She who has the work and the money is she
who has the authority." The General Conference applauded the work of the
WFMS, and the society remained autonomous and free of top-level denominational control. By the 1890s, society members were taking collections for women's
missionary projects during weekly church services. Regular contributions to the
society were also collected at auxiliary meetings, camp meetings, and retreats.

One distinctive feature of ME Church women's fund-raising during this
period was a direct appeal to partnership with other women, both as coworkers and objects of giving. Personal relationships and friendships with non-
Christian women formed the basis for stirring, and at times melodramatic,
appeals to free these pagan sisters from spiritual, economic, social, and intellectual bondage. Jennie Fowler Willing, a laywoman who helped organize the
early Woman's Foreign Missionary Society, spoke eloquently about the plight
of women worldwide. Echoing the great themes of the social gospel, Willing
argued that in order for women to live out God's vision for the world, women
must be able to speak and act on behalf of themselves and their suffering sisters. The following is an excerpt from Willing's exhortation, found in the first
volume of *The Heathen Woman's Friend.* Note the resonance of the message
with the preaching and teaching of Josiah Strong.

> If all men are brothers, all women are sisters. Yes, the wretched widow,
> looking her last upon this beautiful world through the smoke of her
> suttee pyre, driven by public opinion to the suicide's plunge into the
> darkness of the future, and the one throwing her babe to the croco-
> dile—tearing from her heart its only joy, the joy of maternity—these
> women are our sisters. . . . When we look at the domestic, civil and
> religious systems of Pagandom, we sicken at their rottenness. We feel
> greatly moved to give the blessings of Christian civilization.[25]

The familiar refrain, "woman's work for woman," became the case statement for women's missionary fund-raising. The strong maternalistic and imperialistic overtones of these appeals are embarrassing to hear in the twenty-first century, but it is well for us to remember that these heartfelt pleas were rooted in a form of Wesleyan and American idealism that held an optimistic view of human capabilities combined with faith in the democratic potential of educated people.[26] They were above all confident expressions of hope in the power of the present and coming kingdom of God.

Another key element in women's ways of giving was the effective use of testimonies to raise money. One of the society's first missionaries, Isabella Thoburn, mentioned above, spent most of her career in India working on behalf of the educational improvement of women and girls. For thirty years, she worked to establish a girls' secondary school and women's college at Lal Bagh on property located in the region of Lucknow. During 1895 and 1896, at a time when the educational mission was undergoing expansion, the worst floods of the century destroyed the first buildings constructed for the Lucknow Women's College. Undaunted, Thoburn took a furlough to the United States in 1899, mainly to raise money for new buildings. She was accompanied by Lilavanti Singh, a graduate of the Lal Bagh school and the college in Lucknow. Singh spoke at an ecumenical missionary conference in New York attended by former President Benjamin Harrison. After hearing the young woman from India address the crowd, he remarked, "If I had given a million dollars to foreign missions, and was assured that no result had come from it except the evolution of one such woman as that, I should feel amply repaid for my expenditure."[27] A minister writing to a friend told about a similar address by Singh in Detroit: "They listened to her with undisguised pleasure and amazement. The only criticism I could make . . . would be that she is apt to get beyond the depth of the average Methodist pastor."[28] As Thoburn's brother, James, records in his biography of her life, both women returned to India with sufficient money to pay the college's debts.

The Colored Methodist Episcopal Church was one of the churches of the American black Methodist tradition in which women were the principal financial contributors. The CME Church was organized in Jackson, Tennessee, on December 16, 1870, by forty-one black men who had been freed from slavery just five years earlier. At its inception, the CME Church was composed of former slaves who had been members of the ME Church, South, but upon emancipation, wanted to establish their own separate and independent church. The fact that the CME Church arose during the turbulent years of the Reconstruction meant that "mission" was defined largely in domestic terms. Indeed, given the social and economic conditions in which black people lived in the postbellum South, the energies of CME women in the early years were devoted almost exclusively to shaping and maintaining the institutions that would ensure the survival of the African American community.[29]

The women of the CME Church were incredibly resourceful in helping the denomination obtain property and money to support the construction of new churches and the development of church programs. As products of a religious tradition that placed heavy emphasis on the fruits of conversion, CME women believed that the sanctified life and the experience of conversion placed certain moral demands on the individual Christian. One of the church hymns of the period declared the belief in these terms, "If you got good religion, you ought to show some sign."[30]

Perhaps the most tangible expression or sign of "good religion" among these women was their gift for raising money. According to Othal Lakey and Betty Stephens, the fund-raising efforts of CME women "became the major financial resource of the church."[31] Women in the local congregations organized service groups and societies throughout the South. In 1887, *The Christian Index*, the official denominational newspaper for the CME Church, reported that the Ladies Social Circle had raised hundreds of dollars to renovate Israel Metropolitan Church in Washington, D.C. The same report identified a women's group, in Hillsdale Station, known as the Mite Society.[32] Pound suppers, cakewalks, and money-raising clubs for "the good working sisters" generated thousands of dollars for the fledgling denomination.[33] In 1898, in a report published in *The Christian Index*, the "Sisters" Working Club of Bullard's Chapel carefully catalogued club members' efforts:

> Mrs. Mary A. Lane of the Busy Bee Club, $8.90
> Mrs. Rachel Slade of the Willing Workers, $10.35
> Mrs. Sarah A. Grice of the CME Aid Club, $2.50
> Mrs. Rose Wadkins of the Careful Builders, $5.05
> Mrs. Melinda Jones of the Church Builders, $11.60[34]

In addition to collecting money, a number of women proved remarkably skillful in asking white patrons and employers for sizable gifts. The history of Fannie's Chapel in Campbellsville, Kentucky, is an inspiring and poignant case as reported in the congregation's records:

> Following the Civil War, the colored Christians of Campbellsville—Methodists and Baptists—worshiped in the same building on alternate Sundays. After a time, William H. Miles, the first bishop of the CME Church, brought pressure on the Methodists to build their own church. There was a woman member of the CME group by the name of "Fannie" (and no record exists of her last name) who worked for Simon and Martha Hodgen, an aristocratic and fashionable white family of the city—relatives to the Hodgens of Hodgenville, Kentucky, the

birthplace of Abraham Lincoln. She made known to her employers that her church needed some land on which to erect a church edifice. In response, the white people she worked for entered a deed of conveyance to the trustees of the Colored Methodist Episcopal Church. To show their gratitude and appreciation for what Fannie had done, the CME Church was named in her honor: "Fannie Chapel."[35]

Lampkins Chapel in Louisville, Kentucky, provides another example. The original property for this congregation came from a grant from the Vance Land Company. Dilsey Smith, member of Lampkins, happened to mention to her employers at Vance Land Company her church's need for property and added that it would be wonderful if the company would provide "a gift" of land to the church. To her own and others' amazement, the company management agreed and gave the church the property for its first church building.[36]

It was in the mission program that women gained an official role in the various governing structures of the CME Church. In 1890, the Woman's Missionary Society adopted its first constitution and bylaws. Unlike its ME Church and ME Church, South counterparts, the Woman's Missionary Society of the CME Church was totally under the control of the General Missionary Board and the bishops. The constitution stated that the purpose of the WFMS was to "raise money for the advancement of both the local and general mission work of the CME Church."[37] The WFMS was to be organized at all levels—local, district, annual—but all of its operations were subject to the control of the General Missionary Board. Moreover, ten percent of the society dues collected were payable to the parent mission board. Even though it was the "women's" Missionary Society, the group's corresponding secretary was required to be male!

Despite these restrictions, CME women responded enthusiastically to the work of the Woman's Missionary Society at every level. As the denomination entered its fourth decade of ministry, Women's Missionary Societies were active in a number of annual conferences. In 1902, there were 694 missionary societies and 12,660 members.[38] The church's missionary activity focused on home and territorial missions in the United States, primarily in West Texas, the Indian Territory (Oklahoma), and Kansas. The first CME woman to go into the mission field was Lizzie Sweeney. In 1882, she and four ministers were sent by Bishop William Miles to the Indian Territory. Her assignment was to teach at Colbert Station.[39]

Over the next forty years, from 1890 to 1930, women in the Woman's Missionary Society pressed for changes in both the governance and control of funds raised by the various societies. This campaign ran parallel to a movement for laity and women's rights in the denomination as a whole, mirroring the experiences of women in the white Methodist churches a few decades earlier.

By 1918, the Connectional Woman's Missionary Society was formally organized. The new national organization placed authority for use of funds and projects to be supported in the hands of the women. Of course, the Society was subject to the authority of the bishops, but even the male leaders of the denomination realized the financial benefit of putting control of missions in the hands of its most effective fund-raisers. Legislative changes ensured that most of the funds raised by conference missionary societies stayed within individual conferences. The vast majority of causes were home mission projects, including the building of new churches and the support of the church's rural ministry in some of the poorest areas of the South.

The first president of the Connectional Woman's Missionary Society was Dr. Mattie Coleman, a physician from Clarksville, Tennessee. Dr. Coleman's medical practice demonstrated her interest and concern about human problems, and her intense desire to help people in need. She assisted indigent children and gave medical treatment, food, clothing, and shelter to the poor. Dr. Coleman's life and ministry portrayed a theology of mission that began within the context of meeting human need in her own community. It was in meeting the needs of both their home communities and those beyond home that CME women pursued the missionary work of the church.

Another major role women played in their work and giving was that of stewardess. In addition to serving the "table of the Lord," stewardesses in the CME Church were to serve "the table of the poor." When families were destitute and the church assisted them, it was the stewardess who led the effort in providing whatever aid the church was able to give. The stewardesses also tended to "the table of the ministry" by making sure the needs of the pastor and his family were met. Some stewardess boards would "pound" the preachers; that is, they would collect a pound of groceries, meat, vegetables, and other food stuffs from church members and give to the parsonage family.[40]

Women's ways of giving at the height of the social gospel movement exemplified some of the best features of Christian philanthropy. Women in the two traditions examined here drew their strength and motivation to give from a sense of partnership or friendship with the recipient. The women in these churches both delighted and confounded male church leaders with their amazing capacity to organize and sustain fund-raising efforts and mission education programs at all levels of the church. They proved to be creative and resourceful solicitor-managers of cash and material resources for the ministry of the church. These women understood that the power of faith and money was a sacred trust to be exercised within the context of the faith community and on behalf of the "least of these." Finally, within the nurturing communities, or feminine enclaves, these Methodist women—black and white—came to understand that their generous participation in mission was a means by which they were "working out their salvation" and helping to bring about the kingdom of God here on earth as it is in heaven. Dr. Coleman wrote these words in 1909:

> We can lend a helping hand to a fallen brother or sister. We can help the helpless. There are many bright boys and girls in humble homes that need a kind home and need to be brought to Christ. There are many houses that are dark and polluted, that may be light and pure by letting the sunshine of God's love in by a loving word and kind deed. Does that commission ever appeal to us which says, "Go into the hedges and highways, and compel them to come?" The gospel must be preached everywhere, and we must not only send the light, we must carry it.[41]

The enduring legacy of these women and the social gospel upon Christian stewardship has been an abiding sense of the personal and corporate empowerment that comes when faith and money are enlisted as resources in alleviating social needs and overcoming societal injustice. Contemporary research about people's motivations for giving emphasizes reciprocity with God and the religious group, extensions of self and altruism, and thankfulness.[42] Women and men of the social gospel era understood that their giving was an expression of the inseparable relationship between personal faith and a just social order. In a time of private donation and quiet philanthropy, we are reminded today, in the words of Walter Rauschenbusch, that, "To concentrate our efforts on personal salvation . . . comes close to refined selfishness. . . . Our religious individuality must get its interpretation from the supreme fact of social solidarity."[43]

PART II

The Social Gospel Today

7

Social Salvation: The Social Gospel as Theology and Economics

Gary Dorrien

The notion that Christianity has a mission to transform the structures of society is distinctly modern. Near the end of his life, after he belatedly made his peace with the term *social gospel*—the term seemed redundant to him—Walter Rauschenbusch insisted that the social gospel was neither alien nor novel.[1] He protested too much, however; the social gospel was certainly novel. Premodern Christianity had a social conscience and the evangelical movements of the early modern era were rich in antiwar, antislavery, and temperance sentiments, but the social gospel movement was something new in Christian history.

Significantly, it was led by theological liberals; equally important, it promoted social reforms as aspects of what the social gospelers called the church's "Christianizing" mission. The key to the social gospel was not its theological liberalism or its reforms, however. What distinguished the social gospel from other forms of socially engaged Christianity was its idea of "social salvation" and its efforts to fulfill this conception. I believe that this idea, differently imagined and expressed, remains the key to the meaning of the social gospel today.

The faults of the social gospel movement of the Progressive Era are well known. It was sentimental, moralistic, and culturally chauvinist; it spoke the language of triumphalist missionary religion; its various causes were compromised by its middle-class interests and its late-Victorian sensibility; with notable exceptions, it gave tepid support to, and sometimes opposed outright, the struggles for racial justice and women's rights; during the Great War, its antiwar convictions were promptly put aside after a liberal Protestant president committed the United States to making the world safe for democracy; after the war, much of its leadership reduced the social gospel to pacifist idealism. Beginning with Reinhold Niebuhr's icy proto-Marxist assault of 1932, *Moral Man and Immoral Society*, the social gospelers have taken a distinctive pounding for these faults and others for decades. Today we are especially inclined to fault them for their sexism and Anglo-Saxon imperialism. While taking full account of these faults, however, we do well to recognize that the progressive religious legacy of the social gospel surpasses anything produced by Niebuhr's generation and the generations that followed it. Christian realism inspired no hymns and created few lasting progressive institutions; in the United States, the legacy of liberation theology is not much stronger. It was the social gospel movement of the Progressive Era that created the ecumenical and social justice agencies that remain the heart of modern social Christianity.[2]

The theology of the social gospel was usually liberal, but not necessarily so; Josiah Strong and his followers were theologically conservative. At the same time, many theological liberals of the Progressive Era were not social gospelers; notable examples include Borden Parker Bowne, Charles A. Briggs, Phillips Brooks, Frank Hugh Foster, George Harris, Albert C. Knudson, Theodore Munger, and Arthur C. McGiffert. Both of these facts are loaded with ironies worth exploring, but for the present purpose a single point will suffice: The distinguishing feature of the social gospel was not its theological liberalism or its political reformism, but rather its emphasis on social salvation. The figure who best exemplifies the spirit of the social gospel thus defined is Washington Gladden, whose reputation as "the father of the social gospel" is largely warranted. As a cofounder of the movement, he took part in all of its causes; as a preacher, activist, and theologian, he epitomized the optimistic piety and practical idealism of the movement's mainstream.

Political Economy and the Social Gospel

Born in 1836, Gladden began his career as an ill-prepared evangelical preacher. He suffered a nervous breakdown only a few months into his first pastorate, at the outset of the Civil War, and subsequently converted to theological liberalism under the influence of Horace Bushnell. He pastored several churches, took a journalistic stint in-between at the *Independent*, and acquired social ideas. In the mid-1870s, he started writing books that expressed his theologically liberal and mildly social approach to Christianity.[3] A decade later, while serving as a pastor in Columbus, Ohio, he worked with Josiah Strong and Richard Ely to build the first social Christian organizations.[4]

The social gospel began as a gloss on the golden rule; Gladden's ideas of the good society and social salvation were still essentially individualistic during the years that the social gospel founders created the Inter-Denominational Congress, the American Economic Association, and other organizations. If the golden rule of moral conduct was that one should love one's neighbor as oneself, Gladden reasoned, it followed that employers and employees should practice cooperation, disagreements should be negotiated in a spirit of other-regarding fellowship, and society should be organized to serve human welfare rather than profits. In his early career, he preached against business corporations and corporate unionism alike, arguing that the virtues of other-regarding cooperation are practicable only for individuals and small groups. Gladden believed that all individuals combine traits of egotism and altruism, that both are essential to the creation of a good society, and that there is such a thing as self-regarding virtue. Society would have no dynamism without competitive vigor, he allowed. The problem with American society was that its economic basis was based on competitive vigor alone.[5]

This was a structural problem, not merely a moral one, as Gladden gradually recognized. He protested that structurally American capitalism amounted to a form of warfare, "a war in which the strongest will win." In the late 1880s, the conviction deepened in Gladden that this was the heart of the social problem. He responded to it by embracing a cooperativist critique of the wage system. The wage system is antisocial, he argued; for that reason, it is also immoral and anti-Christian. By his lights, there were three fundamental choices in political economy: relations of labor and capital could be based on slavery, wages, or cooperation. The wage system marked a sizable improvement over slavery, but it fell short of anything acceptable to Christian morality. The first stage of industrial progress featured the subjugation of labor by capital; the second stage was essentially a war between labor and capital; the third stage was the social and moral ideal, the cooperative commonwealth in which labor and capital shared a common interest and spirit.[6]

In his early career as a social gospeler, Gladden believed that this ideal was immanently attainable. "It is not a difficult problem," he assured, speaking of the class struggle. "The solution of it is quite within the power of the Christian employer. All he has to do is admit his laborers to an *industrial partnership* with himself *by giving them a fixed share in the profits of production,* to be divided among them, in proportion to their earnings, at the end of the year." Profit sharing was the key to the making of a good society in the realm of political economy. It rewarded productivity and cooperative action; it channeled the virtues of self-regard and self-sacrifice; it socialized the profit motive and abolished the wage system; it promoted mutuality, equality, and community. To the "Christian man," Gladden contended, the strongest argument for cooperative economics was its simple justice: "Experience has shown him that the wage-receiving class are getting no fair share of the enormous increase of wealth; reason teaches that they never will receive an equitable proportion of it under a wage-system that is based on sheer competition; equity demands, therefore, that some modification of the wage-system be made in the interest of the laborer. If it is made, the employer must make it."[7]

To the respected Protestant pastor who preached every Sunday to the business class and very few workers, the crucial hearts and minds belonged to the employers. The ideal solution was to convince the capitalist class to set up profit-sharing enterprises, not to abolish capitalism from above or below. In an age of ascending socialist movements, Gladden repeatedly cautioned that most employers were no less moral than the laborers they employed. It was too soon to give up on a decentralized, cooperative alternative to the wage system. Defining socialism as economic nationalization, he judged that socialism would require an overlarge, overcentralized, and inefficient bureaucracy that placed important freedoms in jeopardy. Socialists proposed to pull down the existing order. They were right to condemn the greed and predatory competitiveness of capitalism, Gladden argued, but they were foolish to suppose that humanity will flourish "under a system which discards or cripples these self-regarding forces." A better system would mobilize good will and channel self-interest to good ends. The reform that was needed was "the Christianization of the present order," not its destruction. The "principal remedy" for the evils of the prevailing system was "the application by individuals of Christian principles and methods to the solution of the social problem."[8]

Gladden was slow to acknowledge the structural limitations on social justice. He sought to appeal to the rationality and moral feelings of a capitalist class increasingly pressured by embittered workers; only gradually did he perceive the irony of his assurances that business executives were at least as moral as their employees. If this assurance was true, it proved that the crisis of the prevailing order was about more than the morality of individuals. As late as 1893, he defended his basic strategy of appealing to the moral feelings of the business class. *Tools and the Man* presented his most developed case for a "third way" profit-sharing model, which he called the industrial partnership model: "I would seek to commend this scheme to the captains of industry by appealing to their humanity and their justice; by asking them to consider the welfare of their workmen as well as their own," he explained. "I believe that these leaders of business are not devoid of chivalry; that they are ready to respond to the summons of good-will." The same book clearly signaled that he was moving to a more explicitly pro-union perspective, however: "I confess that I am strongly inclined to take the workingman's view." Gladden allowed that cooperative ownership represented a plausible and attractive basis for a third way between capitalism and socialism, though he judged that profit-sharing industrial partnerships were better suited to capitalist America. Most importantly, he dropped his assurances that the class struggle could be easily remedied. The deepening chasm between labor and capital that Gladden witnessed in the 1890s drove him to a more realistic, structural view of political economy. His judgment that working people were losing the class war drove him to support unionism more decisively, albeit with a host of criticisms of union violence and featherbedding. By the end of the decade, though he was heartened by the ascendancy of liberal theology and the social gospel, Gladden realized that his hope for a nonsocialist, decentralized economic democracy had less and less of a material basis in a society increasingly divided along class lines.[9]

Like most of the other social gospelers, he took pains to dissociate himself from "socialism," by which he meant centralized state ownership of business enterprises. However, he, like many of his comrades, adopted a politics that combined a "monopoly enterprises" nationalization strategy with an economic democracy model of profit-sharing and cooperativist enterprises. Gladden's critique of state socialism was sensible and prescient. He objected that social-ism denigrated the spirit of individual creativity and invention. "It ignores or depreciates the function of mind in production—the organizing mind and the inventive mind." He rejected the Marxist dogma that labor creates all value: "It is not true that labor is the sole cause of value or wealth. Many substances and possessions have great value on which no labor has ever been expended." He disapproved of the socialist promise to provide meaningful work for every-one. "Socialism takes away the burdens that are necessary for the development of strength," Gladden objected. "It undertakes too much. It removes from the individual the responsibilities and cares by which his mind is awakened and his will invigorated."[10]

Most importantly, he protested that socialism was too grandiose and bureaucratic to work. It required enormous governmental power and virtu-ally infinite bureaucratic wisdom. "The theory that it proposes is too vast for human power," he protested. "It requires the state to take possession of all the lands, the mines, the houses, the stores, the railroads, the furnaces, the factories, the ships—all the capital of the country of every description." Under a socialist order, he noted with incredulity, American government bureaucrats would be vested with the power to set wages, prices, and pro-duction quotas for a sprawling continent of consumers and producers: "What an enormous undertaking it must be to discover all the multiform, the infi-nite variety of wants of sixty millions of people, and to supply all these wants, by governmental machinery! What a tremendous machine a government must be which undertakes, in a country like ours, to perform such a service as this!" Americans were not accustomed to viewing government as an agent of redemption. Gladden linked arms with the socialists in seeking to make American society less stratified and antisocial, but he kept his distance from socialist promises to make centralized government "the medium and minis-ter of all social good."[11]

Gladden-style social gospelism was essentially moralistic, cooperativist, and predisposed to make peace. It was allergic to Marxist rhetoric about smashing the capitalist state. It was skeptical even toward the milder state socialism of European social democracy. The social gospelers sought to Christianize society through further progress, reforms, and evangelization, not through revolutionary schemes to collectivize the economic order. For all of his determination to stand for a third way, however, Gladden drifted to the left in the 1890s. He judged that the greatest threat to his social vision came from a burgeoning corporate capitalism. He counseled that socialists should be respected, and respectfully corrected, as long as they didn't promote unnecessary violence. He called himself "enough of a Socialist" to embrace a foreign policy opposed to war and based on international treaties with all nations. His judgment that working people were losing ground in the class struggle caused him to defend the union movement most of the time. He insisted that the right to property is subordinate to the rights of life and freedom. He also significantly qualified his opposition to state socialism. Gladden persistently rejected state collectivism as an economic strategy, but he made exceptions for the entire class of economic monopolies. In the early 1890s, these included the railroad, telegraph, gas, and electric companies; he later judged that mines, watercourses, water suppliers, and telephone services also belonged to this category. The railroad companies in particular were "gigantic instruments of oppression." In any industry where no effective competition existed, he argued, the only just recourse was state control. The railroad and electric companies did not operate under the law of supply and demand, nor offer their commodities or services in an open market; in effect, they closed the market. "This is not, in any proper sense, trade; this is essentially taxation," Gladden argued. "And, therefore, I think that all virtual monopolies must eventually belong to the state."[12]

His steadily deepening support for trade unionism deepened all of his realist and decentralized-socialist leanings. *Social Facts and Forces* (1897) recognized that unionists had legitimate reasons to intimidate scab laborers, though Gladden still argued that the goal of trade unionism must be human solidarity, not proletarian solidarity. His memoir, *Recollections* (1909), judged that America was probably headed for an imminent plunge "into a Socialistic experiment," though he warned that socialism was inferior to cooperative strategies and that American society was insufficiently educated and socialized for either approach. By the time that he wrote *The Labor Question* (1911), the American social gospel movement was at high tide, but Gladden shared little of Rauschenbusch's faith that the last unchristianized sector of American society—the economy—was in the process of being Christianized. The triumph of corporate capitalism and the rise of aggressive labor organizations such as the National Association of Manufacturers and the revolutionary Industrial Workers of the World ended Gladden's fantasy of a paternalistic share-economy. He realized that his hope for a nonsocialist, decentralized economic democracy had little material basis in a society divided along class lines. Giving up on profit sharing and cooperatives, he took his stand with a flawed labor movement. Unorganized labor was "steadily forced down toward starvation and misery," he observed. Elsewhere he lamented that corporate capitalism was becoming utterly predatory and vengeful toward unions, "maintaining toward them an attitude of almost vindictive opposition." In this context, unionism was the only serious force of resistance against the corporate degradation of labor. If the dream of a cooperative economy was to be redeemed, Gladden argued, it would have to be redeemed as a form of union-gained industrial democracy. The partnership between labor and capital that America needed more desperately than ever would have to be gained through union-organized collective bargaining, gaining for workers their appropriate share of economic control.[13]

Social Salvation: The Social Gospel Difference

The social gospelers were products of the evangelical reform movements that they extended. Social gospel leaders such as Gladden, Rauschenbusch, and Shailer Mathews were raised in evangelical traditions, converted to theological liberalism, and gave liberal Christianity an energizing social mission through their gospel-centered desire to Christianize America. Their movement gained much of its missionary impulse from its connections to the home missions movement. The social gospel theology of social salvation was a product of these influences; in 1893, Gladden described it perfectly, with no glimmer of how perfectly dated its language would become.

He expressed it in the form of a liberal twist on postmillennialism. "The end of Christianity is twofold, a perfect man in a perfect society," he declared. "These purposes are never separated; they cannot be separated. No man can be redeemed and saved alone; no community can be reformed and elevated save as the individuals of which it is composed are regenerated." The message of the gospel is addressed to individuals, he allowed, but the gospel addresses each individual as a member of a social organism, which creates the medium through which individuals respond to the message: "This vital and necessary relation of the individual to society lies at the basis of the Christian conception of life. Christianity would create a perfect society, and to this end it must produce perfect men; it would bring forth perfect men, and to this end it must construct a perfect society." To Gladden the themes of modern social Christianity were the themes of Christ: repentance, regeneration, and the presence of the kingdom. Christ taught, "Be perfect, therefore, as your heavenly Father is perfect" (Matt. 5:48), and "Repent, for the kingdom of heaven has come near" (Matt. 4:17). Gladden admonished that the copula in the latter statement is never to be broken, for repentance is intrinsically connected to the presence of God's kingdom: "The opportunity, the motive, the condition of repentance is the presence of a divine society, of which the penitent, by virtue of his penitence, at once becomes a member."[14]

The social gospelers thus claimed to recover the meaning of Christ's petition, "Thy kingdom come." For Jesus, as for genuine Christianity, Gladden argued, the purpose of God's inbreaking kingdom was to regenerate individuals and society as coordinate interests. Neither form of regeneration is possible without the other: "Whatever the order of logic may be, there can be no difference in time between the two kinds of work; that we are to labor as constantly and as diligently for the improvement of the social order as for the conversion of man." The crucial test of the church's witness is its success in maintaining an equilibrium between active personal and social regeneration. Having grown out of, and beyond, an evangelical tradition fixated on individual salvation, Gladden exhorted, it was time for modern Protestantism to emphasize "the social side of our Christian work." American Christianity needed to dedicate itself to Christianizing America. The church's social mission is to claim the kingdoms of this world for the kingdom of Christ, including "the kingdom of commerce, and the kingdom of industry, and the kingdom of fashion, and the kingdom of learning, and the kingdom of amusement; every great department of society is to be pervaded by the Christian spirit and governed by Christian law."[15]

That was the essence of the novel idea of social salvation. Gladden assured his congregation that applied Christianity contained ample room for personal religion. Throughout his long career, he preached every Sunday morning on personal religion and every Sunday evening on social Christianity. Implicitly in that practice, the old dichotomy still obtained. But the burgeoning movement for applied Christianity put into practice Gladden's assurance that personal and social religion are inseparably linked in the gospel of Christ. Salvation brings the personal and social dimensions together or it is not saving. Social gospelers such as Gladden and Rauschenbusch kept the faith that this was the religion of Jesus; others such as Shailer Mathews and Shirley Jackson Case later judged that the social gospel thus conceived was not the religion of the historical Jesus; all the social gospelers affirmed that in the modern age, the best expression of the spirit of Jesus was the gospel of social salvation.[16] Near the end of Gladden's career, his ministerial successor in Columbus told him that he had two absorbing interests—liberal theology and the social gospel. Gladden looked at the pastor quizzedly and asked, "Well, what else IS there?"[17]

That was a plausible question in 1912; Rauschenbusch might well have asked it. Five years later, the social gospel movement went into an eclipse, though many of its leaders mistook their country's surge of war enthusiasm and national pride for a heightening of social Christian commitment. Rauschenbusch bitterly perceived that the war was a catastrophe for the movement; until April 1917, when the United States intervened, so did Gladden. Like most of the social gospelers, Gladden made a convincing reversal of conviction as soon as America entered the war. The call of country and President Woodrow Wilson's soaring rhetoric about saving the world for democracy were irresistible to them, and to him. Liberal Protestant leader Lyman Abbott, who converted early, called the war "a crusade to make this world a home in which God's children can live in peace and safety, a crusade far more in harmony with the spirit and will of Christ than the crusade to recover from the pagans the tomb in which the body of Christ was buried." University of Chicago Dean Shailer Mathews, who traveled the same path as Gladden, exulted that America at war was proving to be "a glorious super-person, possessed of virtues, power, ideals, daring, and sacrifice."[18]

Gladden was never as jingoistic as Abbott, but he matched Mathews for wartime myth-making. His first pro-war sermon was titled "Making the World Safe for Democracy." He looked forward to a League of Nations and proclaimed that this was, indeed, the war to end all wars. He never doubted that the United States was fighting for democracy. He never doubted that his country was seeking to create a world order based upon the golden rule. "All that is needed to bring permanent peace to earth is that every nation trust all other nations just as it wishes to be trusted by them," he preached to the end. Gladden accepted and preached Wilson's vision of the war as a social gospel cause; he seemed to forget his long-held and often-expressed conviction that war belonged to the jungle phase of human existence. "This war needn't be a curse; it may be the greatest blessing that has ever befallen this land," he declared.[19]

It certainly dramatized his awesome optimism. Gladden and Rauschenbusch both died in 1918, but very differently. For all that they shared as founders and champions of American social Christianity, they were different kinds of social gospelers. Rauschenbusch was a socialist and high-voltage prose stylist who condemned capitalism as unregenerate, supported the ascending trade union movement, and blasted his opponents; Mathews spoke for a sizable social gospel current that avoided political economy, took a moralistic approach to politics, and urged that Christians should try to forget about class; Gladden split the differences between them. He supported trade unionism selectively, but dreaded socialism; he tried to be realistic about the class struggle, but could never say with Rauschenbusch that because idealists have never achieved any great social change on their own, "a great truth must depend on the class which makes that truth its own and fights for it."[20]

Rauschenbusch was inspiring and challenging to pastors, but also dangerous. He called for a radical extension of democracy and a socialist transformation of the economy, and he was devastated by the war, which he saw as the death of social gospel progress. Gladden was never dangerous. He spoke the language of moral progress, cooperation, and peace to the end of his life and claimed to see a renewal of social Christian hope in America's burst of wartime pride. Asked near the end of his life if he knew of any reason not to be hopeful, Gladden replied, "Not one." His entire life had been a miracle, lived through eighty-three years of transforming American progress.[21]

"I have never doubted that the Kingdom I have always prayed for is coming; that the gospel I have always preached is true," he declared in 1912, in a sermon he published six years later, shortly before his death. "I believe that the democracy is getting a new heart, and a new spirit, that the nation is being saved. It is not yet saved and its salvation depends on you and me, but it is being saved. There are signs that a *new way of thinking, a new social consciousness,* are taking possession of the nation." To Gladden, cooperation, democracy, and progress were God-terms; he never lost faith that the kingdom of God was an ongoing American project.[22]

The Social Gospel Today

In his classic history of Christian social thought, Ernst Troeltsch observed that the modern social gospel represents the third major social philosophy established by the Christian church. Medieval Catholicism forged the first Christian social philosophy, he noted, and the Reformed tradition engendered the second, but neither Aquinas nor Calvin could have imagined the claims on Christian conscience that the social gospelers advanced in the name of biblical faith. He further judged that neither of the church's classic social philosophies offered much help in coping with the nationalistic, capitalist, technological, increasingly secular order of modernity. Traditional Catholicism and Calvinism did not speak to what Troeltsch called "all this distress which weighs on our hearts and minds like a perpetual menace." Though Troeltsch's politics were moderate compared to Rauschenbusch's, he heaped singular praise on the Christian socialists, observing that it was the Christian socialists who goaded modern Christianity to face up to "the modern social problem."[23]

Today it is hard to fathom that radicals like Rauschenbusch and even liberals like Gladden and Troeltsch took seriously the social gospel project of saving the world. The distress of the modern social problem has passed to us in globalized postmodern forms that breed self-preoccupation and a cynical resignation to existing socioeconomic structures. Though we are inclined to play up the ways in which our thinking today is more just or advanced than the gendered culturalism of the social gospelers, perhaps the most important difference between the social gospelers and most of us is that they refused to doubt that structural economic change in the direction of justice is possible. Rauschenbusch called on America to redeem the "last completely unregenerate sector of American society." From the social gospel progressivism of Gladden and Mathews to the social gospel socialism of Rauschenbusch and W. D. P. Bliss to the various social democratic and Marxist socialisms of William Temple, Vida Scudder, Paul Tillich, the early Reinhold Niebuhr, and so many others to the present day, Christian thinkers have called for morally defensible alternatives to the prevailing economic system.

But at the end of a century that began with ringing social gospel hopes for a new "cooperative commonwealth," how much is left of the hope of economic democracy? How much of the vision of a democratized economic order can be redeemed in a context in which the word *socialism* mostly conjures up repulsive images of killing fields, prison camps, bureaucratic stagnation, and economic backwardness? Is it possible to reclaim the social gospel vision of democratized economic power at a time when corporate capitalism is turning the entire world into a single market?

Most of the Christian socialist tradition belongs to the democratic socialist tradition that views democracy as the heart of socialism. There is no democracy without democratized economic power and no socialism without democracy. For the most part, Christian socialists from Rauschenbusch to Jürgen Moltmann have sought to fulfill the democratizing promise of liberal democracy. They have sought to renew and extend the liberal democratic revolution. But democratic socialism has its own tradition of overcentralizing state collectivism. Democratic socialists and their Christian socialist allies were wrong to equate socialization with nationalization; they were wrong to reject production for profit; they were wrong to claim that state planners could replicate the pricing decisions of markets; later they were wrong to claim that worker-owned cooperatives could organize an economy not linked by markets. On these key issues, Rauschenbusch looks better today than much of the Christian socialist tradition. His orientation was mainly toward decentralized economic democracy, not state socialism, and he recognized that markets cannot be abolished in a free society. Yet much of Rauschenbusch's work was indistinguishable from the totalizing rhetoric of state socialist ideology; he embraced the Marxist theory of surplus value and often claimed that prices under socialism would be based entirely on services rendered.[24]

I believe it is greatly to their credit that most of the social gospelers firmly opposed state socialism and invested their economic hopes in cooperative ownership, mixed forms of worker and community ownership, and profit-sharing strategies. It is also to their credit that, unlike many of their Marxist and social democratic successors, the social gospelers were not economistic ideologues. They did not treat moral, cultural, and political issues as mere epiphenomena of economic interests. Christian ethicists today are adept at criticizing them, rightly, for their middle-class moralism, sexism, racism, and nationalism, but I think they were better than we tend to be at holding together religious faith and a vision of a more humane economic order. Much of contemporary social ethics doesn't even take a pass at the issue of economic justice.

I assume and strongly affirm that the effort to democratize power today must take place not only at the point of production (as in Marxism), or in the electoral arena (as in liberalism), but also in what Manning Marable calls "the living place"—the postindustrial community where people struggle to create environments that are more diverse and ecological and hospitable. Whatever remains of Christian socialism today requires a multicultural, feminist, ecological consciousness that challenges and transforms its inherited economism. At the same time, it is terribly mistaken to think that any serious challenge to existing relations of power can ignore the factors of production. We cannot significantly advance the cause of social justice by writing off the seemingly hopeless problem of inequality. Those who control the terms, amounts, and direction of credit largely determine the structures of the society in which we live. The question of who controls the process of investment is therefore no less crucial or pressing today than it was when "socialism" seemed an innocent ideal. Gains toward social and economic democracy are needed today for the same fundamental reason that political democracy is necessary: to restrain the abuse of unequal power.

Today we need, and are slowly getting, work that explores the politics and economics of cooperative ownership, the mixed forms of decentralized worker and community ownership, and especially, the possibilities of mutual fund ownership strategies. We need work that takes on the problems of external finance, innovation, and competitiveness that worker-ownership strategies contain. With regard to mutual fund strategies, we need work that spells out the possible functions of the holding companies that would invest collectively owned social capital. Mutual fund models establish holding companies in which ownership of productive capital is vested. How much control should these companies possess over their client enterprises? Is it feasible to separate entrepreneurial and production risks? Is it feasible to expect holding companies to bear capital risks without sharing in the profits they help to generate?

The trend in economic democracy theory is toward the mutual fund approach, which seeks to mitigate the various problems that worker-owned firms confront in the entrepreneurial field.[25] My work in this area has tried to encourage a similar trend within Christian social ethics.[26] A critical problem with the mutual fund approach is that it weakens the democratic power of workers at the firm level. Economic democracy theorists usually try to deal with this problem by placing as much control as possible in decentralized holding companies that work closely with firm managements. This "politically correct" preference has its own problems, however. To the extent that holding companies are kept in a weak position, the entrepreneurial advantages of the mutual fund model are traded off as the client enterprises essentially become cooperatives. There is also the danger that the kinds of holding companies envisioned by theorists such as Saul Estrin, David Miller, Frank Roosevelt, and David Belkin may be too decentralized to compete in markets dominated by large, ruthless, integrated corporations.

The upshot of these problems for me is not that we should forget about democratizing economic power, but that no single scheme should be universalized or enshrined as the next object of faith. Economic democracy is a project that must be built from the ground up, piece by piece, opening new choices, creating new forms of democratic power, seeking to build a new social order that is more egalitarian, cooperative, and ecological than the prevailing order. It is a project that breaks from the universalizing logic of socialism. No political economy worth building would force workers into cooperatives they don't want to join.

The issue of choice, however, is the key to the renewal of the social gospel economic vision that I am advocating. A politics that expands the cooperative and social ownership sectors could give important new choices to workers. The central conceit of neoclassical economics could be turned into a reality if meaningful choices were created. The neoclassical conceit is that capitalism doesn't exploit anyone, because labor employs capital as much as capital employs labor. But in the real world, it's virtually always the owners of capital, and not the owners of labor, who organize the factors of production. To expand the cooperative and mutual fund sectors would give choices to workers that neoclassical theory promises, but doesn't deliver. And that is a quintessential social gospel project.

8

The Reawakening of the Evangelical Social Consciousness

Timothy Tseng and Janet Furness

Much has been made of the recent resurgence of evangelicalism in the United States. The proliferation of scholarly interest in this movement, its reappearance and persistence in public life, and its more recent engagement in conservative politics attest to an evangelical social as well as religious awakening.[1] It can be argued that the presence of evangelicalism in contemporary political discourse and in ministries among marginalized people is as a variant of social Christianity, though most evangelicals and mainline Protestants would shun such an implication. Evangelicals poised now at the threshold of a new millennium embrace numerous opportunities to intervene on behalf of the suffering. The view from the pew has changed for many conservative churches. Youth groups serve weekly in urban soup kitchens. Adults visit prisoners, AIDS patients, and homeless shelters. Ministry teams build Habitat Houses and visit impoverished neighborhoods to fix what is broken and learn from the people there. Denominational benevolence ministries lead congregations on pilgrimages for racial healing and operate hospital services, continuous care communities for the aging, and group homes for troubled youth. Despite the proliferation of social ministries, most evangelicals continue to identify with culturally and politically conservative issues, thus diverging from traditional social gospel concerns.

In this chapter, we will examine the strand of evangelical social consciousness that comes closest to what most church historians refer to as the social gospel. What is responsible for creating this reservoir of social engagement? What contributions made the difference in forming the "new social gospel" of the twenty-first century? We believe that the convergence of several sources over the last forty years has nourished the growth of faith among evangelicals as it relates to meeting human need. Some of these sources will be discussed here. This strand emerged in the late 1960s among a younger generation of intellectuals, although many evangelical urban missions maintained continuity with an earlier prophetic heritage throughout the 1940s and 1950s.[2]

We begin by looking at the historical contexts that shaped contemporary evangelical antipathy toward traditional social gospel concerns. This is followed by an exploration of the efforts to institutionalize a social work program at the Philadelphia College of Bible. We will then follow the attempts of "baby-boomer" evangelical intelligentsia to integrate social justice concerns with their proclamation of a traditional evangelical gospel message. Finally, we'll assess the future of evangelical social consciousness.

The Twentieth-Century Evangelical Quest for Social Consciousness and Respectability

Twentieth-century evangelicalism has become increasingly difficult to define. Some historians root it in an alliance of advocates of Princeton Orthodoxy and dispensationalism prior to and during the Fundamentalist-Modernist conflicts of the 1920s through 1930s. Others view it as a mosaic of diversity from the very beginning.[3] Timothy Weber identifies four distinctive branches: classical, pietistic, fundamentalist, and progressive evangelicalism. He considers the evangelicals discussed in this chapter part of the progressive branch because they "incorporate elements from the other branches but do so with a conscious sense of 'modernity.'"[4] Not all historians are satisfied with simply asserting evangelical diversity. For instance, Donald Dayton critiques the hegemony of the Old School Presbyterian interpretation of American evangelical history by recasting the narrative from the perspective of an Arminian-Wesleyan theology.[5] In fact, the meaning of *evangelicalism* can be stretched so thin and can encompass so many viewpoints that he suggests that the term is no longer useful.[6] For our purposes, we will focus our attention on the evangelicalism represented by Billy Graham, the National Association of Evangelicals, and *Christianity Today*. This tradition has been the dominant voice in American evangelicalism since World War II and is the community from which the individuals in this chapter were raised.

Evangelicalism has often been accused of reducing Christianity to an individualistic ethic and privatizing the faith. Under the sway of premillennial dispensationalism, it has generally located God's transforming activity outside of human history. Thus, twentieth-century evangelicals and their fundamentalist cousins constructed an otherworldly pietism with little relevance to the current social order. As a result, so it is believed, evangelicals have hindered the church from applying the gospel to socioeconomic and political realities. But this criticism does not ring true for all evangelicals. Evangelicals are among the most religiously active groups in America today, particularly within culturally and politically conservative circles.[7] Nevertheless, the charge that evangelicals are politically and socially apathetic no longer applies. Ron Sider, the president of Evangelicals for Social Action, observes that

> The bitter battle between conservative Christians who emphasize evangelism and liberal Christians who stress social action that weak-ened the church for most of this century has largely ended. Increas-ingly, most agree that Christians should combine the Good News with good works and imitate Jesus' special concern for the poor.[8]

Indeed, for all their focus on evangelizing individuals, mainstream Ameri-can evangelicals never really lost the urge to save the American nation. Joel Carpenter suggests that the generation of fundamentalists who preceded the post-World War II evangelical movement expressed "a latent interest in cul-tural politics. Even when fundamentalists have expressed their alienation toward American cultural trends and advocated separation from worldly involvement their words have been more those of wounded lovers than true outsiders. They have seen themselves as the faithful remnant, the true Amer-ican patriot."[9]

Nevertheless, fundamentalists and their evangelical progeny carried with them a strong feeling of marginality. Rejected by modern American society and losers in the battles to control the mainline Protestant denominations in the 1920s, fundamentalists separated themselves from theological liberals and modern culture by creating a distinctive religious subculture. Theologically, fundamentalist preoccupation with demonstrating the rationality of Calvinist affirmations and biblical revelation resulted in a rigid separatism that lost its ability to engage, if not embrace, a changing world.[10]

Thus, by the 1940s, evangelicals of Carl F. H. Henry's generation sought to "reform" fundamentalism and called for a reawakening of the evangelical social consciousness. "The cries of suffering humanity today are many," Henry noted.

> No evangelicalism which ignores the totality of man's condition dares respond in the name of Christianity. Though the modern crisis is not basically political, economic or social, fundamentally it is religious, yet evangelicalism must be armed to declare the implications of its pro-posed religious solution for the politico-economic and sociological context for modern life.[11]

Henry's *The Uneasy Conscience of Modern Fundamentalism* (1947) signaled a resurgence of evangelical interest in the arena of social concern and activism. Written just after World War II ended and before the explosive presence of television in the 1960s made poverty and urban dilemmas popular, Henry charged fundamentalism with failure "to make relevant to the great moral problems in twentieth-century global living the implications of its redemptive message."[12] He challenged evangelicals to serve society by propagating the good news of the gospel and using tangible means to ameliorate human suffering.

Yet, in the middle decades of the twentieth century, the evangelical quest for respectability in American culture and academia was a much stronger impulse than the desire to engage in social change. The success of Billy Graham's "ecumenical" revivals gave evangelicals hope in this quest, as did the tremendous growth in their missionary and parachurch organizations. Fuller Seminary was established, in part, as a desire to win a measure of evangelical intellectual credibility.[13] Though dogged by fundamentalist constituents who viewed these activities as compromises with liberalism, the evangelical quest for respectability was a considerable success.

Confidence in the evangelicals' ability to influence American culture grew in the 1960s, even as the nation underwent a decade of cultural trauma. Billy Graham found himself in the confidence of Presidents Kennedy, Johnson, and Nixon. Several successful evangelical congresses and consultations promised the realization of a united evangelical consensus.[14] At the United States Congress on Evangelism in Minneapolis (1969), prominent political leaders such as U.S. senators Mark Hatfield and George McGovern were in attendance. Evangelicals envisioned building a powerful consensus that would distinguish them from the ecumenical projects of the National and World Council of Churches.

In their efforts to be respected, however, American evangelical leaders tended to support the Vietnam War, oppose Communism and the student protests, feel perturbed by the Supreme Court decision to remove prayer from public school instruction, and feel ambivalent about the Civil Rights movement. Rather than shaping American culture, the evangelical "consensus" in the 1960s tended to identify itself with "the nation and predominant culture."[15]

Charles Yardley Furness, Social Work, and the Philadelphia College of Bible

Just as evangelicalism gained the semblance of respectability and consensus, dissenting voices within the movement would emerge. Dramatic social tensions were hard to overlook when day after day the television news chronicled burning cities, racially incited assassinations, and violent student protests against a foreign war robbing them of their youth. Like their mainline counterparts, many fearful evangelical congregations engaged in white flight, abandoning urban communities for a seductive safe haven in flourishing suburbs. Though this pattern of urban flight was not new, it became much more pronounced in the decades following the Second World War.[16]

For many years, parachurch organizations including rescue missions and urban community outreach ministries expanded to fill the void.[17] The effectiveness of these ministries depended largely on budgeted financial contributions from the few suburban congregations that maintained an urban missionary vision. Successful urban ministry also required a committed team of personnel, not unlike those such as Hudson Taylor and Adoniram Judson, whose dedication and evangelistic fervor introduced foreign missions to the conscience of the church in the nineteenth century. Increasing awareness of poverty in the 1950s prompted respected missionary agencies to assign personnel to America's urban areas hoping to apply their expertise in the increasingly difficult multicultural situations stateside. However, the fundamentalist theological perspectives of evangelical Bible and liberal arts colleges hindered the development of personnel for these ministries. These difficulties were eventually exacerbated by increasingly complex social service delivery systems. Generations of poor had become locked in cycles of poverty that demoralized, depressed, and disempowered them. Public welfare systems had become bureaucratic machines operating to perpetuate their own functions at the expense of the people they were supposed to serve. In order to intervene in these contexts with the gospel message, evangelicals needed more sophisticated tools.

By the 1960s, Henry's *Uneasy Conscience* spoke with greater relevance to evangelical institutions responsible for training young people for ministry. "Many of our Bible institutes, evangelical colleges, and even seminaries, seem blissfully unaware of the new demands upon us," Henry had asserted. He hoped that some ". . . will become concerned before they finish."[18] Soon sociology departments flourished among evangelical institutions. Some began to fashion programs that responded to professional accreditation standards. One surprising approach unfolded when professional social work education was introduced in a Bible college fervently committed to Protestant fundamentalism.

Bible colleges had first appeared as Bible institutes soon after the Civil War. These institutes represented a new kind of training ground in America, a place for the teaching of "the Bible, evangelistic methods and other practical skills useful to students who planned to become missionaries, evangelists, pastors, Sunday school teachers, and Christian workers of other kinds."[19] Practical training was a central emphasis, "demanding that classroom teaching concentrate only on those attainments which students needed for their home and foreign missionary work. Liberal or general education was considered an unwanted extravagance" for students whose single-minded concentration was on the skills and development they needed for a particular religious occupation.[20] By 1920, Bible institutes had become the training grounds for the fundamentalist movement. The Bible institute movement is often described by a complex dispensationalist framework of Bible study that views the end times according to a technical understanding of Old Testament prophecy. This unique persuasion was untouched by the growth of higher education in American society and its influence on Bible institutes to upgrade the quality of students, faculty, facilities, and programs. Curricula expanded, and by 1960 Bible colleges had started to carve out a legitimate place in American higher education, though such schools scarcely paid heed to the social upheaval and crises of America's urban centers.

One of America's leading Bible colleges, however, responded to Henry's challenge. The unique combination of vision, leadership, and personality produced what remains the only accredited social work program in a Bible college in the United States. The Philadelphia College of Bible was born in 1951 when two Bible schools conceived in 1913 and 1914 merged. Degree-granting privilege was secured in 1958 and regional accreditation achieved in 1967. PCB held at its core a commitment to Bible education based on a dispensational worldview that formed the context for all vocational and career decisions.

In 1958, Charles Yardley Furness, a native of Philadelphia, began writing letters to leaders in evangelical higher education. He hoped to encourage schools like Moody Bible Institute, Wheaton College, and the Philadelphia College of Bible to integrate courses in social welfare and social work. On the basis of his studies in American social and church history, he believed Christian colleges and Bible schools were uniquely poised to train students for ministry to the poor and underserved.[21] Furness's personal background pointed to poverty induced by alcoholism and abandonment. His educated and resourceful mother encouraged him to pursue his dream of seminary education, which he completed in 1942 at the Reformed Episcopal Seminary in Philadelphia. Subsequently, after 13 years in pastoral locations facing realities of both rural and urban communities, he earned a baccalaureate degree in American history from Rutgers, the State University of New Jersey. He worked his way through evening classes as superintendent of a downtown rescue mission in Newark, N.J. Soon after graduation, he realized that the growing challenges facing the clients he served at the mission required that he augment his education with a professional degree. He completed the master in social work in 1961. By this time, his vision for professional social work as a tool for ministry was known at Philadelphia College of Bible.

In the same year, Douglas B. MacCorkle assumed the presidency of the college. A graduate of Dallas Theological Seminary, a fiery preacher and charismatic leader, MacCorkle developed a strategy to prepare students for "Careers with Christ."[22] His inaugural address expressed his desire that the college live more responsibly in its setting. "This would include a program for students desirous of knowing how to present the gospel and to also learn the skills and methods to minister to the total person in the community."[23] Compatibility of MacCorkle's institutional goals with Furness's vision worked to the advantage of the college. In 1965, Furness arrived at the college to set up the Bible Social Work Major.

The remarkable nature of this story is lodged in the success with which Furness represented the mission of social work education to the various constituencies of the college. This was no small task. Financial supporters in churches and church agencies often greeted the addition of accreditation measures within Bible colleges with suspicion. Some critics viewed such academic changes as the cause for drifting away from original Bible college missions. One chief academic officer expressed his concern that "a Bible college is a Bible institute on its way to becoming a liberal arts college."[24] Historically, any inclusion of social sciences in a Bible college curriculum mattered most in "their direct application to the tasks of evangelists and teachers."[25] Furness wrote articles in major Christian magazines and brochures for the college that articulated a philosophy of Christian social ministry that satisfied potential detractors. He wrote,

> In this venture the college is in no sense endorsing the "social gospel." Rather it is facing up to the implications of *the* Gospel for society at large. Our Christian schools have long trained foreign missionaries to perform medical and other social service for people and at the same time given them the Gospel; surely the same practice is desirable in our own homeland . . . if Christians meet professional social work standards and use accepted methods in their own agencies and churches, people will be more receptive to the spiritual help they offer.[26]

Furness included his definition of the social gospel in his text *The Christian and Social Action.*[27]

> Evangelicals do not believe in the social gospel as it is so called because they do not believe the gospel needs the prefix of the word *social* before it. The gospel itself is an instrument used in social interaction and has powerful effects in both problematic and normal social situations. Good social action starts with the individual Christian and his influence in the world.

By 1974, the Council on Social Work Education accredited undergraduate social work programs. The Philadelphia College of Bible was among the first to be accredited. Christian liberal arts programs were soon ready to launch prepared social workers into America's social service system. Evangelical social workers went to work with the tools to meet the increasingly stringent regulations of America's human service delivery systems. The impact of these social workers was felt in agencies, rescue missions, churches, and denominationally related services that rose to relate to secular standards as professional programs employing biblical ethics.

Graduate social work education in evangelical contexts emerged slowly, blocked by resistance in the profession to what was perceived as ultraconservative positions on social issues. At last in the mid-1980s, the first accredited master of social work program emerged in the Carver School of Church Social Work at Southern Baptist Theological Seminary. The program owed its existence to the financial support of the Women's Missionary Union and the strong and persistent leadership of its founding dean, C. Anne Davis.[28] A second graduate program was accredited in 1997 at Roberts Wesleyan College, Rochester, New York. The new millennium will see growth in biblically based graduate social work education, largely due to the persistence of evangelical social workers to be recognized as relevant in the context of their profession's commitment to religious diversity. The North American Association of Christians in Social Work, a membership organization founded at Wheaton College in 1950 and requiring members to affirm Jesus Christ as Savior and Lord, has united a critical mass of evangelical social workers committed to the integration of their Christian faith with their professional practice.[29] The association has an increasingly potent role across all segments of the profession.

Furness's successful development of a social work program at the Philadelphia College of Bible and the entrance of a cadre of biblically trained social workers on the scene represent one instance of a small but growing segment within American evangelicalism in the late 1960s that was concerned about social justice. For instance, the Evangelical Foreign Missions Association and the Interdenominational Foreign Mission Association, representing more than 13,000 missionaries, cosponsored The Congress on the Church's Worldwide Mission at Wheaton, Illinois, in April 1966. The Wheaton Declaration called for greater consensus among evangelicals in the face of great social upheaval. The statement also urged all evangelicals "to stand openly and firmly for racial equality, human freedom, and all forms of social justice throughout the world."[30] At the World Congress of Evangelism in Berlin that same year, Henry reiterated the Christian responsibility to evangelism and social justice. "Whenever Christianity has been strong in the life of a nation, it has had an interest in both law and gospel, in the state as well as the church, in jurisprudence and in evangelism."[31]

The Young Evangelicals and Social Action

In addition to growing awareness of social engagement in evangelical colleges and missions in the late 1960s, young intellectuals voiced dissent from the "evangelical establishment's" positions on civil rights and Vietnam. In the mid-1960s, many of these evangelicals were encouraged by the support of older leaders such as Rufus Jones, the general director of the Conservative Baptist Home Mission Society.[32] At the Consultation on Christian Unity in 1965, Jones called for greater attention to urban poverty and the civil rights of black Americans.[33] That same year, evangelical sociologist David O. Moberg published an influential primer entitled *Inasmuch: Christian Social Responsibility in the Twentieth Century*.[34]

While these concerns were being raised, however, the "evangelical establishment," represented by editorials in *Christianity Today*, gravitated in favor of American intervention in Vietnam and opposed student protests. Jones later complained that since 1968, the National Association of Evangelicals "seemed to lose all interest in . . . social issues of a positive nature in their meetings."[35] Billy Graham's refusal to speak out against the Vietnam War despite his personal friendship with President Nixon convinced many of the younger evangelicals that an alternative perspective was necessary.

Historians Robert Clouse, Robert Linder, and Richard Pierard sought to expose "the dangers of the cozy relationships that exist between American evangelicals and political conservatives" in their writings.[36] Donald Dayton, who had felt alienated from his Wesleyan Church upbringing discovered a radical social reform heritage in nineteenth-century evangelicalism.[37] Pierard and several other evangelical professors helped organize "Evangelicals for McGovern" during the 1972 presidential election campaign in order to provide "a counterweight to the unabashed support which was being given to Mr. Nixon by Billy Graham and many other prominent evangelicals."[38] In a fundraising letter, chairman Walden Howard argued that through "the prophets and our Lord . . . God has revealed some fundamental principles about the nature of a just society."

> Social structures which favor the rich displease our God. Policies . . . which are designed to slow down or reverse racial progress grieve the One whose eternal Son became incarnate in the Middle East. If Jesus is to be Lord of our entire life, then he must be Lord of our politics . . . If Amos is right in declaring that God disapproves when the rich live in luxury at the expense of the poor, then surely Christians should help McGovern close the loopholes and make the rich pay their fair share. . . . Electing Senator McGovern won't bring in the Kingdom! . . . But electing McGovern does offer the hope of taking some

significant steps toward greater justice in national and international society.[39]

McGovern's landslide defeat did not appear to faze his evangelical supporters. In a circular letter, Ron Sider, an irenic Mennonite historian and the most active organizer among social action evangelicals, argued that Evangelicals for McGovern achieved some important objectives.

> I believe we helped underlie two basic points: 1) If evangelicals are to take Jesus' Lordship seriously, then He must be King of our politics; and 2) If we are listening to all that Biblical revelation says about justice in society, then our politics must reflect a concern not just about pubs, pot, and pornographic literature, but also about racism, poverty, and the grossly unjust distribution of wealth here and abroad.[40]

Appreciative of the significant press coverage, Sider believed that many had "heard our message that there is a rising tide of theologically orthodox Christians who are not chained to conservative politics." Given the attention they had received in the religious and secular presses, a week after the elections, Sider asked his fellow evangelicals, "Where do we go from here?"[41]

At the same time, Rufus Jones, David Moberg, and Lewis Smedes were in conversation about organizing a conference on Christian social ethics.[42] Most of this socially minded evangelical cohort gathered at an informal conference on "Christianity and Politics" at Calvin College the following April.[43] But by then, there was talk of a working conference of evangelical social activists. Under Sider's leadership, the focus turned toward becoming a "leaven" of social consciousness to evangelicalism rather than a focus on direct political action or theological conferencing.

On Thanksgiving weekend in 1973, fifty evangelicals gathered in Chicago for a workshop on "Evangelicals and Social Concern." From this gathering, Evangelicals for Social Action was born and *The Chicago Declaration* was issued. The *Declaration* repented of evangelical silence in the face of racism, materialism, militarism, sexism, and articulated the strongest statement to date from twentieth-century evangelicals in support of social justice.[44] The Evangelical Women's Caucus was formed soon afterwards to address evangelical sexism. Christians for Biblical Equality was an outgrowth of this effort. Among the original signers of the *Declaration* were many whose careers have taken them into significant arenas of social justice advocacy.[45]

The *Declaration* appeared to have galvanized a significant segment within American evangelicalism in the 1970s. Many who gathered in Chicago ensured that the Lausanne Covenant (1974) incorporated stronger language about social responsibility. Future Lausanne-sponsored deliberations would continue to affirm the social justice dimensions of Christian faith and ministry.[46]

Furthermore, these younger evangelical intellectuals were prolific writers and disseminated their views widely. Magazines like *Sojourners*, *Transformation*, *The Other Side*, and *ESA Prism* reached a broad audience. In 1977 Ron Sider's well-known book, *Rich Christians in an Age of Hunger*, generated much interest among evangelicals. Reprinted three times and translated into six languages, *Rich Christians'* success raised the confidence of social justice evangelicals as they sought to educate and reform American evangelicalism. Like the post-World War II generation of evangelicals who sought to bring respectability to fundamentalism by reforming it, these younger evangelicals also sought to reform mainstream evangelicalism by drawing attention to the impoverished and disempowered in American society.

Recent evangelical thought regarding social justice is characterized by two central arguments: (1) the need to overcome the conservative-liberal dichotomy and (2) the need to balance evangelism with social justice work. Though evangelicals have had difficulty agreeing about who they are, they have always been clear about who they are not. Thus, in the minds of most evangelicals, there is a clear difference between themselves and liberal Christians. Most social-justice-minded evangelicals, however, are more generous toward "liberals" and confess their own shortcomings. "I personally think that during the Fundamentalist-Modernist controversy both liberals and conservatives went to an unbiblical extreme," asserted Rufus Jones. "Both were right in what they affirmed and wrong in what they denied . . . each was guilty of proclaiming a partial gospel."[47] John R. W. Stott probably articulated this point most clearly when he stated that "the evangelical stereotype has been to spiritualize the gospel, and deny its social implications; while the ecumenical stereotype has been to politicize it, and deny its offer of salvation to sinners. This polarization has been a disaster."[48]

Furthermore, social-justice-minded evangelicals are very conscious of maintaining a balance between evangelism and social justice. Always fearful of the slippery slope toward the old "social gospel," which "attempted to identify the kingdom of God with socialized society," social justice evangelicals prefer to live out "the social implications of the biblical gospel."[49] Careful not to supplant evangelism as the church's primary mission, these evangelicals argue that social justice ministry is evangelism's equal partner and that this partnership is mandated in the Bible. But these arguments are directed against those who believe that social involvement is not part of the church's mission. Until recently, the object of evangelical social engagement was for the sake of the powerless, not a desire to support Christian "values" and "norms" in society.[50] But what would happen if evangelicals interpreted social engagement as a defense of "traditional" values?

An Alternative Center?

Few social justice evangelicals anticipated the conservative turn in the 1980s out of which the Moral Majority and the Christian Coalition were formed. Stephen Mott, a professor of social ethics at Gordan-Conwell Theological School in the 1970s and 1980s, observed that "in the 1970s, most [students] came from Bible colleges and struggled against fundamentalists. But the newer students were struggling not against conservative distortion of evangelicalism, but humanism and churches that let them down."[51] This new conservative turn created a financial and ideological crisis for Evangelicals for Social Action and the *Sojourners* community as they faced a diminishing support base and a reinvigorated conservative political philosophy in the late 1980s.

Despite their initial criticism of the Christian Coalition, both *Sojourners* and Evangelicals for Social Action have had to listen and adapt to neo-conservative activism. Both have become more open to neo-conservative public policy proposals such as school vouchers and Charitable Choice (in which federal funding is given directly to religious organizations that engage in social work).[52] Today, Ron Sider refuses to be labeled a "left" wing evangelical. "ESA has been consistently pro-life, pro-family, and pro-poor," he asserts. It has always taken its "social analysis from the Bible."[53] Jim Wallis, *Sojourners* editor, and Sider now argue that faith-based organizations can help the poor make better life decisions. Both affirm the need for strong nuclear families in order to maintain economic sustainability in impoverished communities. Because religion plays such a strong role in character formation, government policies ought to partner with churches not only to change the socioeconomic structure that oppresses the poor, but also to provide the poor with cultural and spiritual resources to survive in America.[54]

The direction in which groups like ESA and *Sojourners* are moving today is an acknowledgment that the evangelical call for social action does not require liberal politics. Indeed, many feel that the political "left" has become increasingly hostile to evangelicals. For instance, the "left's" embrace of a broader view of sexuality has created difficulties for many socially conscious evangelicals whose reading of the Bible will not permit extramarital or homosexual activity. By reconciling with some aspects of cultural conservatism, many socially conscious evangelicals are again seeking an alternative "center" that transcends "right-" *and* "left-wing" accommodations to what they perceive to be the sinful aspects of American culture. While this center can address questions of social justice in binary terms (powerful/disenfranchised, white/black, men/women, rich/poor), it remains to be seen whether it can respond positively to the increasingly complicated religious, sexual, and racial-ethnic diversity in America.

The Social Gospel, Gender, and Homosexuality: Then and Now

Janet Forsythe Fishburn

In 1991, I was a member of a Presbyterian Sexuality Task Force that attracted considerable attention across the country for a report titled "Keeping Body and Soul Together." The intensity of the response to the report in both the denomination and the general public made me wonder how the current inability of Protestant denominations to resolve differences about homosexuality might compare to the way denominations floundered in response to women's issues in the nineteenth and twentieth centuries. That comparison is the subject of this essay. I have analyzed a selection of leaders, documents, and publications of the United Methodist Church and the Presbyterian Church (U.S.A.) then and now. Both were involved in the social gospel movement known to historians for its concern with social issues. In addition, both denominations come from traditions with significant theological commitments to social justice.

The years between 1900 and 1920 were an optimistic time for social gospel advocates. Walter Rauschenbusch, one of the best known social gospel leaders, was convinced that the Social Creed of the Federal Council of Churches, written and adopted between 1908 and 1912, was part of a new social consciousness. The Creed was the culmination of the work of a broad coalition of pastors and professors who agreed that the church had a role to play in social salvation, not just individual salvation. Men like Congregationalist Pastor Washington Gladden were among the earliest social critics to recognize the threatening intensity of an ongoing series of depressions and strikes in the 1880s and to urge church-related men to address social problems created by new industries, labor issues, and living conditions in cities. Even so, denominational acceptance of the Creed owed more than Rauschenbusch knew to a progressive middle-class consensus created by educators, social workers, editors, and suffrage leaders, as well as social gospel leaders.

There was a brief connection between the social gospel and progressive politics in 1912 when Theodore Roosevelt ran for president on a platform

designed to seek the reconstruction of society and social justice through political action. Roosevelt was well aware of the work and writing of social gospel
leaders. For some years, he was a contributing editor to *The Outlook*, a liberal
ecumenical weekly edited by socially conscious pastors like Henry Ward
Beecher and Lyman Abbott. Roosevelt had visited The Labor Temple in New
York City, a rare example of a flourishing church for working people and immigrants, founded by Charles Stelzle of the Presbyterian Department of Church
and Labor. Like other social gospelers, Stelzle enjoyed knowing that Roosevelt
had read his books about labor and industry.[1]

Although woman suffrage was not among the issues of concern to social
gospel advocates, the suffrage movement culminated in the ratification of the
nineteenth amendment in 1920. Between the meeting of the first women's
rights convention in Seneca Falls, New York, in 1848 and passage of the
amendment in 1920, the social gospel movement of the churches came and
went, peaking around 1912. Yet the movement that won legal and political
rights for women set in motion a social revolution that altered the role of
women—and men—in the family, church, and society. Theodore Roosevelt
published an essay in *The Outlook* in January 1912, anticipating the nature of
such a revolution. A similar essay by Rauschenbusch was published in October 1913 in *Biblical World*. While both claimed to support the "woman movement," they welcomed it less with approval than with dread about the social
ramifications of women in politics. A clear dualism is evident in the concern
of social gospel men with social issues in the public domain of men and their
lack of support for the inclusion of women into what were then regarded as
male leadership roles in the church and in society.

During the last three decades of the twentieth century, public acceptance
of gender equality in employment and political participation has increased
from 67 percent to 83.5 percent, even though gender dualism continues wher-
ever people believe that the home is the proper place for women.[2] Some of the
gender dualism of the early twentieth-century social gospel continues, almost
intact, in the twenty-first century. Now, as then, opposition to policies that
would give women—and now, homosexual persons—the same rights and
responsibilities as men is defended in terms of family values. Defenders of
dualism, then and now, say they are protecting the sanctity of marriage and the
stability of the family.

Although sexual orientation and gender are not identical,[3] there are similarities in the way women were ignored or actively opposed in their quest for
equality in the nineteenth century and the way homosexual Christians have
been treated in Protestant denominations since 1970. A close look at what
Methodist Episcopal and Presbyterian social gospel leaders did and did not say
and do regarding woman suffrage reveals a pattern of either benign neglect or

quiet maneuvering at the higher echelons of power to take away what little power women already had or to ensure that they were granted no new powers. The current campaign to bar gay and lesbian Christians from ordination, the refusal to sanction their relationships, is a rerun of the way church women were treated in the nineteenth century with one major exception: Today, the opposition is overt and bereft of shame. Opposition by church members—both women and men—to woman suffrage was usually covert, suggesting that they did not want their position to be a matter of public record.

Denominations and the Social Gospel, 1900–1920

Between 1908 and 1912, five denominations—American Baptist, Congregational, Episcopal, Methodist Episcopal, and Presbyterian—took official action on the Social Creed of the Federal Council of Churches. The meaning of this seemingly progressive action by official bodies varies widely. Episcopalians and Congregationalists had visible social gospel advocates and organizations in the 1880s, while few Methodist or Presbyterian leaders emerged until after the turn of the century.

Although the Department of Church and Labor, a three-man office run by Charles Stelzle between 1903 and 1913, was widely admired for groundbreaking work at the time, it stands almost alone as an example of Presbyterian social gospel activity. There were only a handful of Presbyterian social gospel advocates including Stelzle, his boss Charles L. Thompson, the secretary of the Board of Home Missions, and John McDowell, a colleague in the department. In his autobiography, Stelzle says he resigned primarily because conservatives in the Pittsburgh area became "so determined and so bitter that the Board gradually became very timid" and "[the] budget for my Department was so severely cut by a group of 'financial experts' that the work was greatly crippled."[4]

The story of what went on behind the scenes will never be fully known, but Charles Thompson said the Department of Church and Labor was no longer needed. "By 1911, so much progress had been made that the subject came before the General Assembly, which adopted the report of a special committee, and instructed the Board to establish a 'Bureau of Social Service,' in which the Department of Church and Labor was merged. The principles then announced are much the same as those adopted by the Federal Council."[5] Describing the same events, seminary professor William Adams Brown observed that "the attacks upon the Home Board, like the previous attacks upon Labor Temple, had proved how easy it is to throw suspicion upon even the best-meant efforts."[6] Brown recalled that the Labor Temple was controversial from the beginning because its community programs included events like Sunday evening movies, which many Presbyterians regarded as profaning the Sabbath.[7]

Between 1908 and 1913, the Presbyterian General Assembly, an annual meeting that determines church policy, was pressured by fundamentalists like Charles Erdman and progressives like Stelzle about how—or even if—the church would respond to labor and social issues. It is telling that the 1908 Assembly adopted "the five fundamentals" of orthodox doctrine while the 1910 Assembly adopted a special report, "The Christian Solution of the Social Problem," which constituted ratification of the Federal Council's Social Creed. However, the Federal Council of Churches' report was thoroughly reworked to avoid any appearance of intrusion by the church into the civil or political arena. There was deeply rooted opposition among Presbyterians to the use of legislation for social betterment.[8]

The story of the Methodist Church and the Social Creed stands in marked contrast to that of the Presbyterians. Although there was very little Methodist social gospel activity before 1907, in 1908 Methodist social gospel advocates Frank Mason North and Harry F. Ward cofounded the Methodist Federation for Social Service and wrote a Methodist Social Creed that was later adopted in slightly modified form by the Federal Council. Ward then edited *The Social Creed of the Churches*, a book commissioned by the Federal Council in 1912 to interpret the Creed for study in congregations.

The Social Creed, now known as the Social Principles, has been enlarged and amended as a part of official Methodist polity ever since. The ongoing influence of the Social Principles and the Methodist Federation for Social Service has kept social issues alive among Methodists from 1908 to the present. Yet, as historian Henry F. May points out, "Only in the early twentieth century, when progressive social reform had become the creed of much of the American middle class, did Methodists contribute to the social gospel movement in proportion to their numbers, discipline and fervency."[9]

In the 1914 edition of *The Social Creed of the Churches*, Ward described the role of the church as supporting "every proposal that moves toward distributive justice."[10] The Creed seeks justice for "all men [sic] in all stations of life, for the protection of the family, for the single standard of purity, uniform divorce laws, proper regulation of industry and labor practices affecting women and children in the interest of safeguarding the physical and moral health of the community."[11] The fact that the list contained no reference to woman suffrage is not an oversight. Social gospel leaders advocated limited labor legislation as part of a program to "lift up" the lower class to the living standards and morals of the middle class. Concern about the working conditions and morals of working women and children was real. But it was just a step toward building a Christian America, a society where no woman or child would have to work.

The middle-class values of social gospelers like the writers of the Social Creed were those of "the Christian family," where women were wives and mothers and men supported them. Although evangelical women had been active in social movements like abolition and traditional female moral reform since early in the nineteenth century, the reality of women involved in political activities for most of the century failed to penetrate the consciousness of social gospel men. Instead they took their cues from Horace Bushnell, cited by many social gospel figures as a leading influence in their theology. In 1869, Bushnell wrote *Women's Suffrage: The Reform Against Nature* to oppose both suffrage and ordination for women, saying it would weaken the foundations of the family, the church, and the nation, and would lead eventually to the decline of a Christian America.[12]

This protective stance toward "the Christian family" scarcely differs from that of fundamentalists in the same period. Betty A. DeBerg writes that "Their rhetoric depicted the divinized "Christian" home—the white, middle-class, evangelical, nuclear family, in which husband works and wife remains at home subject to the husband's authority—as the one social institution capable of saving both individuals and the nation from sin and decline. A major part of their agenda—to salvage the gender ideology and conventions of mid-century, thereby defending exclusive male access to the public realm, supporting male domination within the home, and reclaiming the church for men—was radically political and deeply concerned about the maintenance of social institutions."[13] Early fundamentalists, churched conservatives, and social gospel progressives shared the gender ideology that was part of their Christian America agenda for the nation. They differed about how "a Christian America" was to be established.

The Woman Suffrage Movement and the Church

As social progressives, people involved in the temperance and social gospel movements had a lot in common. Many social gospelers were active in the temperance cause along with the great temperance leader Frances Willard. Temperance women and social gospel men were both concerned with living standards and home conditions of the working class, but they differed about the role and status of middle-class women. Unlike men who saw the role of women as primarily domestic, Willard concluded that progress and home protection depended on giving women access to the political process. She argued that the only way to get legislation passed against liquor was to give women the vote. Cognizant of the extent to which women were already active in public roles, she pointed out that in the nineteenth century women had grown in intellectual power and courage through their participation in political processes, occupations, and ruling bodies. In short, women were capable of being voting citizens.

Willard, bitterly disappointed with the failure of social gospel men to support woman suffrage, was blunt in her criticism of their gender dualism. "When all these facts . . . are marshaled into line, how illogical it seems for good men to harangue us as they do about our 'duty to educate public sentiment to the level of better law,' and to exhort true-hearted American mothers to 'train their sons to vote aright.'"[14]

The years between 1885 and 1895 were full of public anxiety about the labor movement and possible class warfare, "the liquor problem," and intemperance of immigrants. The social gospel movement gained adherents through their speaking, preaching, and writing about these issues. After a lull toward the end of the nineteenth century, the suffrage movement emerged again after the turn of the century. Women won the vote in California in 1911 and in Illinois in 1913, the same year they organized marches in major cities around the country to dramatize their cause. Some five-thousand women marched down Pennsylvania Avenue in Washington, D.C., as part of Woodrow Wilson's inaugural parade in March 1913. This initiated a series of pilgrimages to Washington, culminating in an automobile parade to the Capitol where suffrage leaders presented their senators with petitions carrying 200,000 signatures on July 31, 1913.

Willard was a harbinger of things to come. She framed a social argument for woman suffrage more acceptable to church people than the natural rights argument for suffrage. She was one of five women who asked to be seated as voting delegates at the 1888 Methodist General Conference.[15] They were turned away, but several women were seated at the next General Conference. In 1889, Willard published a book titled *Woman in the Pulpit.* It wasn't long before the issues of woman suffrage and full church membership for women fused in the minds of church people, and leading church men began to point out that if women were allowed to preach, the next thing would be ordination.

The fact that women pursued the vote for seventy years before achieving their objective indicates that their victory was eked out in small incremental gains over a long period of time. It also indicates that there was considerable organized opposition as well as a lack of interest in their cause. Well-funded businessmen and the liquor industry waged public antisuffrage campaigns, but there were other less apparent forms of opposition. The curator of the Smithsonian exhibit "From Parlor to Politics" writes that opposition to woman suffrage came from working women who belonged to labor unions and feared losing newly acquired legal gains, and from church women.[16]

Sociologist Steven Buechler observes that although there has been no shortage of antifeminist men to defend their own privileged positions in society, "men are often outnumbered by women in active opposition to women's movements. Thus, women have historically been the only major group to organize against their own emancipation."[17] He has concluded that women with privileged backgrounds identify with class more than gender. Opposition to feminism in both the nineteenth and twentieth centuries came from women whose class or race made them think they had more to lose than to gain from the women's movement. Others opposed suffrage because they experienced the possibility of participating in the public world of men as a frontal attack on identities shaped by dominant societal notions of family, femininity, and motherhood.[18] In the nineteenth century, women who opposed their own suffrage engaged in a "quiet campaign" that was "ladylike and presented itself as an educational effort in keeping with traditional female moral reform rather than a political battle that would provoke conflict and partisan struggle."[19]

Due to the nature of their opposition, hard evidence that church women organized to oppose their own suffrage is scarce. However, the protective stance toward "the Christian home" of both conservative and liberal men repeats the arguments of overt antisuffragists who "believed that the ballot would be a burdensome, destructive influence that would corrupt women and drag them into the unwholesome arena of partisan political struggle. Antisuffragists feared that the vote would unsex women and turn them into the "mannish" suffragists they so strenuously opposed. Perhaps most important, antisuffragists believed that the ballot would undermine true womanhood, the sanctity of marriage, and the stability of the family."[20] Fundamentalist journals were among the most vocal antisuffrage publications of the period.[21]

Social gospel men simply kept quiet about the woman suffrage issue until the vote began to materialize, state by state. When they did write about it, both Roosevelt (1912) and Rauschenbusch (1913) reasoned that since the vote for women was unstoppable, it must be part of the forward movement of civilization. Even so, they doubted that women were ready to be thrust into this role. They belittled suffrage victories, saying that suffrage was a minor issue compared to the conduct of men and women.

Roosevelt had to say something positive about suffrage. He was running on a party platform that included a suffrage plank, as did the Democratic and Republican platforms in 1912. After saying "I believe in woman's suffrage," he immediately added that where women do not want the vote, it should not be forced on them. Like other men writing in church publications, Roosevelt said it was hard to support woman suffrage "when we are assaulted almost daily by the unnatural, unfeminine, almost inhuman blindness of many of its advocates."[22] Rauschenbusch chided suffrage leaders noting that "the resort to physical force was the last thing we should have expected of a woman's movement."[23] Although there was little resort to violence in the United States, the moderate church press was eager to report the violence of Emmeline Pankhurst and other English suffragettes. Otherwise, it, too, was usually silent about the suffrage movement in the United States.

Both men worried that a public role for women would interfere with their primary duty as wives and mothers. Roosevelt said there should be equality of rights and duties but *not* identity of function. Rauschenbusch was irritated by the moral self-righteousness of the social argument for suffrage because it was based on claims about the moral superiority of women. Warning against "half-truths and illusions," he said men should believe that women are morally superior, "but it is a different matter when women think so too. They are not better. They are only made in different ways than men." Men like Roosevelt and Rauschenbusch were caught in a bind; their own dualistic argument about the moral superiority of women was being used against them.[24] They were the kind of men Willard had complained about, more eager to lecture women about their proper sphere than to support their aspirations.

Both men believed that the suffrage movement would succeed in the long run but were concerned with the immediate implications of this momentous revolution. Roosevelt feared that women would delay marriage, thus opposing "the facts of feminine development and psychology." Rauschenbusch, who wrote a more scholarly article, cast aspersions on the leadership ability of women, citing women leaders in Christian Science and Theosophy as signs of regression in religion. He doubted the ability of women to function in the male sphere at all, considering that so many of them seemed incapable of supervising their own domestic help. He said directly what Roosevelt only implied, that women were not morally ready for their "new-found destiny" because of their "semi-seclusion" in the past.[25] Although Frances Willard never explicitly questioned beliefs about the separate spheres of men and women taken for granted at the time, she did this implicitly by pointing out that the ability of women to function in the social and political world of men was already well established.

Woman suffrage was a nontopic in most Methodist and Presbyterian publications. A sampling of Methodist periodicals between 1906 and 1913 gives the impression that a new era is underway. Almost all of the articles in *The Quarterly Review*, a monthly scholarly publication, seem to favor the "social movement." If editors reflect the interests of their readers, woman suffrage was of no interest to readers of *The Quarterly Review*. The only article about women published between 1906 and 1913 was a summary of what Immanuel Kant and Arthur Schopenhauer had to say about the inferiority of "feminine intellect."

During 1912 and 1913, the Methodist Federation *Newsletter*, edited by Harry F. Ward, offered speakers on social topics across the nation. During that period, Ward spoke at 347 meetings and led thirty-six workshops in seventeen states. Only one lecture given between 1912 and 1914 related to women. It was given by Mary McDowell, a colleague of Jane Addams and the only woman listed as a lecturer. In addition to scores of other social issues discussed during these critical years for the suffrage movement, by 1914 there were new concerns about patriotism, "the boy," the war, the nation, and the home. The objectives of the suffrage movement clearly did not fit the Methodist social gospel vision.

The Christian Advocate, a regional weekly covering Methodist and national news, was a different story. Where *The Quarterly Review* and the Federation *Newsletter* were supportive of the social concerns of men, the New York *Christian Advocate*, edited by James Buckley, had a decidedly domestic tone. In addition to columns with resources for groups like the Sunday School and the Epworth League, there were regular articles for women like "The Joy of Housework."[26] Between 1880 and 1912, Buckley ran a series of articles about "woman and the church." His position gradually shifted from arguments against the participation of women in any political arena to implicit opposition to the vote. In the issue for March 13, 1913, a new editor ran one paragraph about the Wilson inauguration without ever mentioning the suffrage parade.

The Outlook, a more progressive church periodical, devoted a full section of its March 15 inauguration issue to the suffrage parade. The writer was critical of local police who failed to protect marchers who were called names and attacked by "street ruffians." He reported that a Senate Committee was formed the day after the inauguration to look into the situation, an event barely mentioned in other church publications.

The Presbyterian church had no equivalent to the *Christian Advocate*, a national publication with regional editions. When Charles Stelzle left the Department of Church and Labor in 1913, he noted that *The Presbyterian*, which had always criticized his work, thought it "wise and manly" of him to resign, while *The Continent*, supportive of the social cause, credited him with having "a wide effect on social thinking."[27] The closest Presbyterian equivalent of the Methodist Federation newsletter was *The Amethyst*, published by the pro-suffrage Temperance and Moral Welfare department. It supported Willard's argument that the women's vote would weigh heavily against drink, saying that voting women would add political clout to the temperance movement.[28]

While there was no groundswell of support by church women for political power in society, some did campaign for full membership rights long before they were able to hold any ordained church office. In the northern Presbyterian church, there was some agitation for female ordination between 1880 and 1920. Powerful leaders like Robert E. Speer responded with a variation of gender dualism, a distinction between public preaching and women's legitimate sphere, "ministration."[29] The General Assembly had almost nothing to say about women's ordination until a committee was formed in 1928 to discuss unrest among church women. An overture recommending the ordination of women as both elders and clergy was part of the committee report. When the ordination of women elders was approved in 1930, Presbyterians hailed it as "progressive," even though ordination to ministry was not approved until 1956. The southern Presbyterian church did not ordain women until 1965.

During the same period, Women's Mission Boards were engaged in a prolonged struggle with the General Assembly over the control of their own finances. Lois Boyd writes that when Charles Thompson was secretary of the Board of Home Missions, he recommended a union of the Women's Board and his board. His proposal for a new board composed of twenty men and ten women "clearly left the control in the hands of men."[30] It was not approved.

Leaders of the Women's Home Missions Board of the southern Methodist Church began to seek laity rights for women in 1910 when they realized they were powerless to stop a merger of the Women's Home and Foreign Boards arranged for them by men. Their proposal won official acceptance in 1918. "The persistence and effectiveness of the women's campaign, buoyed perhaps by the accelerating movement for the state and national political suffrage, resulted in an overwhelming vote in favor of the proposal."[31] Their newly granted status as potential voting delegates to the General Conference had been granted to their northern sisters in 1892. Yet this role gave them far less decision-making power than that of an ordained Presbyterian woman elder who could serve as a member of session, the elected "ruling" body of her congregation. Either way, women were not fully equal church members in either denomination until they were eligible for ordination as clergy. This was approved in the Methodist Episcopal Church in 1956.

From the time that American women won the vote in 1920, it was thirty-six more years before Methodist and northern Presbyterian women achieved full membership rights. Among other half measures approved by the denominations to stave off the full ordination of women, a preaching license was made available to Methodist women in 1920. By contrast, smaller, less middle-class denominations like the United Brethren Church ordained women in the nineteenth century, as did Pentecostal groups like the Assembly of God and Four-Square Gospel congregations. The first United Brethren woman was ordained in 1889. By 1901, there were ninety-seven ordained United Brethren women.[32]

Methodist and Presbyterian social gospel leadership emerged as part of broad middle-class support for selected progressive initiatives after the turn of the century. The leaders' aversion to woman suffrage was rooted in the gender dualism of the widely shared political-religious vision of the family as the foundation of a Christian America. The effort to protect marriage and family as they understood it indicates that white middle-class Protestants were—and still are—content with gender dualism as a way of life.

Women's Rights and the Church, 1970–2000

The author of a paper published by the National Opinion Research Center in 1999 reports that the redefinition of the roles of men and women, husbands and wives, is among the most fundamental changes affecting American society over the last generation, 1970–2000. "A traditional perspective in which women were occupied in the private sphere of life centering around running a home and raising a family while men engaged in the public sphere of earning a living and participation in civic and political events has rapidly been replaced by a modern perspective in which there is much less gender-role specialization and women have increasingly been entering the labor force as well as other areas of public life."[33]

Although church women had just achieved full status as church members by the late 1950s, the Civil Rights movement of the early 1960s inspired women to organize once again on their own behalf. *The Feminine Mystique*, a critique of the empty domesticity of women's lives, was published in 1963. The National Organization for Women was founded in 1966. In a severe setback for the feminist movement, an Equal Rights Amendment passed by Congress in 1972 missed ratification by the states by one vote. Abortion, legalized by the *Roe v. Wade* decision of 1973, has been a target of antifeminist "prolife" forces that have characterized anyone not opposed to abortion as antifamily ever since.

Writing about the restructuring of American religion since World War II, sociologist Robert Wuthnow observes that "gender differences in religious commitment seem remarkably immune to the changing roles that women have begun to play."[34] As the women's liberation movement of the culture gained supporters and opponents, at the grassroots level "many churches were probably better able to mobilize sentiment against feminism than in its favor."[35]

The major difference between the women's movements of the nineteenth and twentieth centuries is that the second women's rights movement— "women's lib"—inspired much more public resistance than the nineteenth-century suffrage movement ever did. Opposition comes from groups like the Eagle Forum, "a national organization of women and men who believe in God, Home, and Country, and are determined to defend the values that have made America the greatest nation in the world."[36] Founded in 1975, the Eagle Forum is just one part of a massive effort by the widely publicized "Religious Right" to defend the values of a Christian America. Confrontations over public and private spheres, the role and status of women, the family, sexuality, and reproduction are still expressed in terms of nineteenth-century gender dualism.

During the 1970s, the enrollment of women in Protestant seminaries increased at a dramatic rate. The number of clergywomen in all denominations has significantly increased, yet they remain a minority in nearly every aspect of church life. A survey conducted in the 1990s revealed that only 10 percent of white clergy were women and that they were underpaid and under-employed, frequently serving in part-time, interim, nonparish, or associate pastor positions.[37]

Inclusive language is a major concern of church-related feminists. The 1970 *Worship Book of the United Presbyterians* had a heavy emphasis on "man" in an effort to be more universal, but its successor, *The Presbyterian Hymnal* (1990), was moderately inclusive. There was noisy objection to changing traditional language despite educational efforts about women, gender, and language. A 1999 poll by the Presbyterian Panel, research commissioned by the Presbyterian Church (U.S.A.), reported that 89 percent of pastors, 84 percent of specialized clergy, and 94 percent of elders and members say they are "extremely likely" or "somewhat likely" to imagine God as "Father." Overtures to the General Assembly recommending a denominational policy on inclusive language are consistently rejected. The United Methodist Church published an inclusive language hymnal in 1989 after considerable opposition.

Among the denominations that adopted the Social Creed of the Churches, there has been continuous resistance to the changing roles of women from the last decades of the nineteenth century into the beginning of the twenty-first century. Mary P. Ryan observes that nothing "strikes terror into the hearts of masses of Americans" quite as much as the link between the role of women and a critique of the family, implicit or explicit.[38] Except for continuing debates about abortion, by the end of the twentieth century the equality of women has once again become a nonissue for most Methodists and Presbyterians. Yet, even as women's issues receded, the same issues were coming up all over again for a different group of disenfranchised church members, gay men and lesbians.

The responses of Methodists and Presbyterians to women's lib and homosexuality reflect mergers by both denominations with smaller, more conservative denominations. The northern and southern Methodist Episcopal denominations reunited in 1939. After merging with the Evangelical United Brethren Church in 1968, the new denomination—the United Methodist Church—was more conservative than the northern Methodist church had been. Two similar Presbyterian mergers in 1958 and 1983 resulted in a denomination also more conservative than the northern church of the mid-twentieth century had been.

The United Methodist Social Principles, 1970–2000

The gay rights movement, like the feminist movement, also emerged from the Civil Rights movement. Unlike the slow response to the membership issues of church women after the Nineteenth Amendment was passed in 1920, overt opposition to the gay rights movement in the church follows a trajectory closer to that of the culture. Where Methodist social gospel leaders Harry F. Ward and Frank Mason North were silent about woman suffrage in the Social Creed adopted in 1909, the document is now used to block any change of status for lesbian and gay Methodists. The Social Principles, long a source of pride to Methodist social justice advocates, is now used to withhold full membership benefits and responsibilities from gay and lesbian Methodists.

Ongoing controversy revolves around the ordination of homosexuals and holy union ceremonies to celebrate committed gay or lesbian relationships. Special-interest groups on both sides work prodigiously to dominate church policies. The Good News Movement, a well-funded conservative lobbying effort, publishes a magazine sometimes sent free to nonsubscribers. On the other side, the Reconciling Congregation Program consists of congregations that have publically declared themselves "welcoming" of all people, including gays and lesbians.

The two positions have been defined and redefined ever since 1972, when a phrase saying, "We do not recommend marriage between two persons of the same sex" was added to the Social Principles.[39] In 1980, that was replaced with a statement saying, "We affirm the sanctity of the marriage covenant which is expressed in love, mutual support, personal commitment, and shared fidelity between a man and a woman." The issue of gay "marriage" continued to fester until the 1996 General Conference declared that "ceremonies that celebrate homosexual unions shall not be conducted by United Methodist clergy or in United Methodist churches." Since then, several nationally publicized holy union ceremonies have been conducted in Nebraska, Illinois, and California on grounds that the Social Principles are advisory and not binding. When a judicial commission ruled that the Social Principles are binding, one pastor was defrocked and another suspended until he agrees to recant. In January 1998, ninety-two Methodist ministers jointly blessed the holy union of a lesbian couple in California, issuing an even more dramatic challenge to church policy. A Committee of Investigation decided to take no action.

While official policy says that God's grace is available to all and that homosexual persons are persons of sacred worth, it also says that Methodists do not condone the practice of homosexuality. In a major statement to that effect, the 1976 General Conference mandated that "no agency shall give United Methodist funds to any 'gay organization' or use any such funds to promote the acceptance of homosexuality." Even as the ongoing conflict commands detailed coverage in the public press, this means that no United Methodist publication, board, agency, committee, council, or commission can publish or say anything positive about homosexuality.

The United Methodist Church supports "certain basic rights and civil liberties" for homosexual persons, as well as "efforts to stop violence and other forms of coercion against gays and lesbians." Yet, church membership privileges for gays and lesbians are entirely different, based on a belief that the Bible clearly rules out any expression of homosexuality. The contradictions in policy represent the same double-bind found in social gospel writing about women as equal but different from men. The different rights accorded women—and now, homosexual persons—in the public and private spheres implicitly identifies the church with the private, domestic sphere associated with women.

Although there had been strong opposition to the ordination of homosexuals since the 1970s, it was not an official policy until 1984. The issue was forced by a 1983 judicial ruling that the *Book of Discipline* did not prohibit the ordination of homosexual persons. In 1984, after a long and complicated debate, the General Conference adopted a statement saying that commitment to "fidelity in marriage and celibacy in singleness" is the standard for ordained clergy. This was further clarified, saying that "since the practice of homosexuality is incompatible with Christian teaching, self-avowed practicing homosexuals are not to be accepted as candidates, ordained as ministers or appointed to serve in the United Methodist Church."

Since the 1970s, there has been a downward trend in membership and threats of a denominational split. In November 1999, the Council of Bishops sent out a pastoral letter to be read in all congregations. Its theme was the unity of the church. Noting the unrest caused by "the many issues surrounding homosexuality" during the past twenty-eight years, the bishops encouraged delegates to the 2000 General Conference to "move beyond legislative solutions." Since this plea was immediately followed by a statement pledging adherence to the official policies of the church, the letter creates the impression that the bishops were backing the profamily, antigay forces of both church and culture.

In the nineteenth century, the most progressive social gospel denominations were the Congregationalists and the Episcopalians. They still are. In November 1998, Paul H. Sherry, president of the United Church of Christ (formerly Congregational), sent out a pastoral letter to be read in all congregations. He reminded them that their denomination never approved any antigay legislation and encouraged members of congregations to stand fast against antigay forces in church and society. He closed the letter saying, "I believe our voice among the churches and within our society is urgently needed, bearing witness to the belief that God cherishes all and dignifies all, and to our experience of gay, lesbian, and bisexual persons as gifts of God, called with us by their baptism into the fullest participation in God's mission of reconciliation in the world."[40]

Presbyterians and Homosexuality

There is a persistent belief that the Presbyterian Church is a liberal denomination. This assertion, used by conservative Presbyterians to explain serious membership loss over the last thirty years, was correct up to about 1960. Since then, conflicts about abortion and homosexuality suggest that the denomination can no longer be characterized as liberal. Like the Methodists, this is partly due to unions of the northern Presbyterian church with more conservative denominations. The southern Presbyterians and United Presbyterians were both slower than the northern Presbyterians to approve and act on the ordination of women.

Like those of the Methodists, Presbyterian special-interest groups formed around holy union ceremonies and ordination. Since 1990, these issues have been prominently featured in conservative newsletters like *The Presbyterian Layman* and *reNEWS*, and in the progressive publications of Presbyterians for Lesbian/Gay Concerns and More Light congregations, a movement similar to the Reconciling Congregations of the Methodists. The well-funded Presbyterian Layman organization, which sends free newsletters to nonsubscribers when major votes are pending, represents a theological position close to that of the politically active religious right.

Presbyterian polity is made through General Assembly approved legislation and is clarified through appeals to denominational courts. Although Presbyterians experience the ongoing animosity as divisive and disturbing, the denomination has approved less legislation than the Methodists and has been slower to do so. There is a clear public sphere-private sphere dualism in the denomination's practice of filing court briefs in support of civil rights for homosexuals while opposing full church membership for gay and lesbian members. The church has consistently supported the legal rights of gays and lesbians. In 1987, the General Assembly called for the elimination of laws governing private sexual behavior between consenting adults and for the passage of laws forbidding discrimination based on sexual orientation in employment, housing, and public accommodations.[41]

The ordination of homosexual Presbyterians is another matter. In 1976, a Task Force on Homosexuality was mandated to lead the church in a study of homosexuality and ordination. In a study paper prepared for the 1978 General Assembly, the Task Force recommended that the church affirm that homosexuality is no bar to ordination. This was offered not as binding legislation but as a guideline to be administered on a case-by-case basis by governing bodies. It also implied that the church would not go on record to oppose the ordination of homosexuals.

The recommendation was rejected by the General Assembly, which approved a report written with the assistance of four dissidents from the Task Force. The report, saying that homosexuals could not be ordained, was approved by overwhelming majority by the General Assembly. The same Assembly approved an addition to the *Book of Order* saying that "unrepentant homosexual practice does not accord with the requirements for ordination." After annual challenges to this policy by Presbyteries and by another Task Force in 1991, the 1993 General Assembly strengthened the 1978 statement by adding an amendment to the *Book of Order,* saying that "current constitutional law in the Presbyterian Church (U.S.A.) is that self-affirming practicing homosexual persons may not be ordained as ministers of the Word and Sacrament, elders, or deacons."

The 1991 report of the Task Force on Human Sexuality created controversy across the country. Members were interviewed on late-night television, rumors about the contents of their report were spread through radio talk shows before the report was published, and major newspapers like the *Washington Post* ran articles with inflammatory headlines such as "Church Shaken by Report Endorsing the Joy of Sex." This article was influenced by a critique of the Task Force report published in the newsletter of a Presbyterian special-interest group. The author had argued that the report was nonbiblical and confused sexual rights with civil rights. Some of her points were reproduced almost verbatim in several national news magazines and newspapers.[42] The report included a theological critique of gender dualism that attracted ridicule from critics who also said the report had no theology. The church's overwhelming rejection of the controversial report was voted the top religion story of 1991 by religion news reporters.

In addition to refusing to change the denomination's stance on the ordination of homosexual Presbyterians, the 1991 Assembly stated its policy on "the institution of marriage." An addition to the *Book of Order* that year also advised session members that they should not allow the use of church facilities for a "same sex union ceremony" if they determined it to be the same as a marriage ceremony. Likewise, it would not be proper for a minister to perform a "same sex union ceremony" the minister determined to be the same as a marriage ceremony.

It was not until 1997 that a connection was made between ordination and marriage in language reminiscent of Methodist legislation of 1984. "Those who are called to office in the church are to lead a life in obedience to Scripture and in conformity to the historic confessional standards of the church. Among these standards is the requirement to live either in fidelity within the covenant of marriage between a man and a woman, or chastity in singleness. Persons refusing to repent of any self-acknowledged practice which the confessions call sin shall not be ordained and/or installed as deacons, elders, or ministers of the Word and Sacrament." This implies that a "chaste"—celibate—homosexual can be ordained. Just as some Presbyterians regarded the ordination of women as elders in 1930 as a progressive policy, some Presbyterians today believe that the ordination of "chaste" homosexuals is a liberal policy.

Like the suffrage movement women, gays and lesbians experience slow incremental gains in civil rights through social legislation. Laws to that effect are being considered by legislatures in a number of states. In 2000, Vermont passed legislation giving homosexual couples civil rights similar to those of heterosexual couples, including the benefits of a civil ceremony to recognize the relationship. Opponents of liberalizing measures continue to repeat arguments originating in American culture before the Civil War. As the twenty-first century begins, conservatives in both church and society continue to see the end of the family, the decline of society, and the loss of American power and prestige around the world in every small gain of persons they regard as less than equal because of gender or sexual orientation.

In a study of the social gospel between 1919 and 1939, Robert Moats Miller documented a gap between precept and practice in the mainline denominations. "The churches often permitted their words to outrun their deeds. Fine sounding utterances somehow never materialized in action. The old parson who termed denominational resolutions the most harmless form of amusement ever devised by the human mind was issuing more than a pleasantry." His point of reference was progressive policies where there was indeed a division between precept and practice.[43]

Since 1970, there has been no lack of Methodist or Presbyterian enforcement of policies concerning gay and lesbian members. Watchdog groups have been vigilant in filing charges in church courts against any pastor, congregation, or judicatory that may have violated policy. Little has changed in the intervening years, except that both denominations have become ever more specific in their intention to treat some of their members as less than fully responsible adults even though both say that homosexual members are persons of sacred worth.

Researchers from the Institute for Democracy Studies, writing about the crisis in mainstream Presbyterianism, say they chose the denomination because it is the most endangered of the mainstream denominations since the conser-

vative takeover of the Southern Baptist Convention. They note that the radical right inside and outside the churches "has benefitted from the absence of
strong and effective counter movements."[44] Although the United Methodist
Church and the Presbyterian Church (U.S.A.) both come from theological traditions with strong social justice components, concerns regarded as progressive or liberal in the modern church have had few proponents whose vision was
free of the gender ideology that undergirds denominational preoccupation
with "the sanctity of marriage and stability of the family."

The Social Gospel Movement in Cultural Context

The term *social gospel* can refer to either a theology or a movement. Historians
sometimes distinguish the two by capitalizing social gospel when referring to
a movement, its social philosophy and activities. The social gospel movement
was a form of an impulse found across the centuries in the Christian tradition
whenever theology was sensitive to the social context of the church, as was the
case with both John Wesley in eighteenth-century England and John Calvin
in sixteenth-century Geneva.

It took Calvin fourteen years of jousting with the town council of Geneva
to establish the kind of Christian commonwealth he envisioned. Unlike Martin Luther, his predecessor in Reformation history, he regarded the civil and
ecclesiastical realms as complementary and not exclusive of each other. As a
pastor in Geneva, he labored for a just society and practiced his own teaching
that pastors should advise local rulers, in his case the magistrates of Geneva.
Calvin did not hesitate to introduce legislation concerning refugee relief and
resettlement, work for the unemployed, health care for all, or to speak out
against unfair business practices and public policies that ignored the needs of
the poor.[45]

The separation of church and state in the United States creates a different
political context for Christians. Because of that separation and because most
Americans at the turn of the twentieth century believed in moral progress in
history, social gospel leaders opposed the use of legislation as a tool of social
change. They believed that legislation should express an already existing public consensus. While suffrage movement women lobbied legislators, collected
signatures for petitions, and engaged in public demonstrations in their quest
for suffrage legislation, social gospel men put their energy into shaping public opinion. When they wrote of their work as labor arbitrators, it was to
encourage others to follow their example as Christians and citizens addressing social problems—not an argument for church participation in politics. In
his autobiography, Charles Stelzle described his activities as an arbitrator in
labor-management disputes in New York City. He added that he did this, not

as a representative of any organization, but as an individual familiar with unions.[46] While many social gospelers participated in civic activities, these apolitical progressives publicly supported Theodore Roosevelt in 1912 because he was part of their movement.

Social gospel leaders concentrated their efforts on public sentiment in order to build a public consensus for legislation they favored. Rauschenbusch was excited by the Social Principles because he assumed it represented an existing consensus of Protestant opinion. When he acknowledged the suffrage movement as an unstoppable force, it was because he could see the consensus building, state by state. When Roosevelt cautioned that the vote should not be forced on women who did not want it, it was a way to hold out hope that the ratification of suffrage in a few states was not necessarily a sign of a national consensus.

Although Presbyterians have a history of sending social pronouncements to government officials and encouraging members to engage in civic activities as individuals, they have also displayed a reticence about the political activism of clergy or congregations similar to social gospel progressives.[47] When Stelzle left the church in 1913, he was disillusioned with the failure of both the Federal Council and the Presbyterian Church to engage in any significant action other than the approval of impressive sounding documents. The gap between word and deed, deplored by Stelzle, comes from a progressive social philosophy wed to a conservative political strategy.

The willingness of the religious right today to raise money for political candidates, tell people how to vote, and to support or oppose specific legislation is evidence of how much times have changed. Yet, they do this in pursuit of a Christian America. Now, as then, official policy reveals that Methodists and Presbyterians differ very little from conservative and fundamentalist views about "the family," women, and now, homosexuality. On these issues, people who otherwise differ radically about Christian belief and practices all still espouse beliefs about family, marriage, and sexuality elaborated in the dualistic worldview of nineteenth-century American culture.[48]

In the twentieth century, from beginning to end, historic Protestant beliefs have been constantly challenged by new knowledge, social change, and changing worldviews. Rauschenbusch was accurate in anticipating the revolutionary nature of new roles for women, although it took almost seventy years for public acceptance of those roles to emerge. Church women still do not enjoy parity with church men, but very few regard gender dualism or exclusionary language as a problem.

It remains to be seen whether Methodists and Presbyterians will follow recent cultural trends indicating a slight increase in acceptance of homosexual persons.[49] Social concerns come and go with changing times, but one constant remains: the resistance of Methodists and Presbyterians to any change in polity that violates the gender dualism in the old vision of a Christian America. Their constancy reflects a historic gender bias in Christian theology that has been defended in the nineteenth and twentieth centuries by white middle-class men and women who are convinced that the family values of American culture are biblical. It is both tragic and ironic that the social gospel, long regarded as the most liberal progressive movement in American church history, contributed so much to spreading and defending the values of "the Christian family" in "a Christian America."

10

The Fifth Social Gospel and
the Global Mission of the Church

Max L. Stackhouse

The American social gospel, I believe, was not and is not a fixed set of doctrines, a single social program, or a passé period piece, so much as it is a set of particular expressions of an enduring recognition that a biblically grounded faith requires an engagement with the social and political issues of the age, a view that was given fresh articulation at the end of the nineteenth century and the start of the twentieth. It is the demand that we acknowledge that the dynamics of the common life need the moral and spiritual guidance of a discerning theology, that Christian theology can amply meet that need, and that the internal impetus of that theology drives the truly faithful to engage public issues.

The periodic recovery and restatement of this dimension of what Christianity is about is necessary because of the fact that the inevitably fluctuating variables of social change and the always dynamic developments of doctrine, both with many false starts, detours, and occasional disasters, can easily obscure any sense of a stable ethical architecture for human life together. The experience of rapid social change as we have come to experience it in the last two centuries can, in fact, render a radical sense of moral relativism on the one hand or a militant sense of fundamentalist reaction against the relativism on the other. And the development of doctrine can become an end in itself, a dogmatic unfolding of the inner meanings of the faith that focuses so intently on those meanings that the dogmas neither learn from any wider wisdom nor inform the wider world. Moreover, the fact that the Christian faith has profound meaning for the individual human soul and for the life of the worshiping community can invite a private piety or an enclave fideism that can easily obscure the wider implications of the faith. The genius of the American social gospel at the beginning of the last century was that it drew from the depths of the biblical and theological traditions in a way that prompted simultaneously a reconstruction of the guiding themes of that heritage so that they could speak normatively to the burning, dynamic issues of the day.

It had been done before, to be sure, although it seems like slow motion, long ago, and far away. Who can deny that Moses and the Hebrew prophets shaped ancient Israel, drawing on traditions that went before them as they faced new conditions? The Fathers of the Church did the same in the context of the Roman Empire. The Scholastics did so at the height of late medieval civilization. The Reformers did the same in the context of the rising cities and the new humanism of early modernity. And the Puritans, Pietists, and Evangelicals did likewise in the New World's frontiers and later in the world missionary movements. Indeed, it is doubtful that it is possible to understand the history of Christianity, the course of Western civilizational history, or the simultaneous continuity and repeated novelty of Christian social ethics if this is not recognized.

As the American social gospel movement began to take conscious responsibility for the earlier indirect and unintended effects of the Christian faith in its impact on society in the last quarter of the nineteenth century, so its heirs developed their contributions and modulated them by attending to the deeper legacy and newer conditions in the twentieth. The founders of the American social gospel movement were, of course, most notable for the ways in which they faced the crises of the Industrial Revolution, especially as it had a major impact on labor. That revolution had been prompted by the Civil War, which accelerated America's late entry into the industrial age, and even more by the Spanish-American War, which made the United States something of a world power for the first time. This is the period in which Francis Greenwood Peabody, Washington Gladden, Shailer Mathews, and Walter Rauschenbusch, among others, developed their enduring convictions.

The message as these "fathers" of the movement developed it (with some variations) continued to be a formative influence from World War I to the Great Depression. They strongly supported the growing labor movements and advocated both voluntary and government programs to aid those whose lives were shattered by the transition from an agricultural-rural to an industrial-urban society.[1] The fruits of this movement arguably generated the moral and spiritual ethos that legitimated if it did not generate the New Deal policies of the 1930s, when the Depression hit full force and it appeared that more materialist, antireligious, and more authoritarian movements might capture the loyalties of the working classes. After all, that is what happened with the rise of both a neo-pagan, premodernist, racially oriented national socialist and a militantly secular, hypermodernist, class-oriented proletarian socialist movement in Europe.

The social gospel leaders were alert to international issues in a way. They believed in the universality of their message. Many came from or ministered to immigrant churches and thus were allergic to the temptations of "Americanist nativism"—the view that those European Protestants born in America had a special destiny to preserve "White, Christian" culture from both the degradations to which it had fallen in Europe and from the corruptions of misogyny to which it was tempted in the multiracial United States.[2] Those who were rooted in the ancient Catholic traditions had a sense of the wholeness of humanity, and those who became deeply engaged in the Evangelical mission movements sought to reach out to all peoples and also resisted that "nativism."

Yet it must also be said that a decided inclination to pacifism borne out of their idealism and optimism made many unable to deal with the terrors on the international front that the National Socialist movements took under the ideologies of fascism, and the Proletarian Socialist movements took under the influence of Soviet Communism after World War I. The pathetic and seemingly pointless sacrifice of hundreds in the trenches of Germany between 1914 and 1918 for only a few yards reinforced the pacifist tendencies. Thus both conviction and experience disarmed the movement from its capacity to face more devastating perils that were soon to follow. In both cases, one on the radical right, the other on the radical left, the state sought to use its military prowess to control the world. The depths of human identity, of freedom, and of justice were threatened. To preserve them, the pacifist impulses of the social gospel had to be modulated by the deeper and longer Christian teachings about the depths of sin in human affairs and the sometimes justifiable use of coercive force in a just war that would have as its aim the establishment of a more lasting just peace.

Thus, a second, modified embodiment of the social gospel, Christian realism, carried much of the burden of Christian witness from World War II through the Cold War. In spite of the often sharp critique of the social gospel by advocates of Christian realism on matters of the depth of sin and the immorality of irresponsible pacifism,[3] there is more continuity than discontinuity in what they were about. Both saw modern constitutional democracy, the protection of the rights of the exploited, and the reformation of the dominant institutions of society as demands of the gospel and the legacy of Christian influence as it interacted with social realities and philosophical reason.[4]

Neither the primary nor this second form of the American social gospel was oblivious to the oppressed status of minority groups and women in Western society, but they did not make these issues their central focus, and have sometimes been criticized for that lack of emphasis. Still, in the first social gospel, several leaders openly supported women's suffrage, more advocated laws to protect women and children in factories, and a number saw Prohibition as a way of defending women by upholding Christian "family values" (as they were understood in that Victorian age), even if other priorities seemed more immediate. The biases of that period have been much corrected by more recent feminist thought. Still, it is not wrong to say that the social gospelers were among the first public "authorities" who became advocates of the early feminist movements. And their heirs, the Christian realists, were deeply involved in defending American blacks, Jews, and, later, Hispanics and Asians. Moreover, the racism and classism of those who opposed them made their disciples more alert to other evils lurking below the surface of American life and Euro-American thought. Thus, as World War II wound down, the descendants of both early forms of the social gospel joined hands in supporting the movements for civil rights and, more widely, for human rights. They were among the first to support the movement headed by Martin Luther King Jr. Whatever their other disagreements, they jointly and eagerly embraced this new phase of the American social gospel. Indeed, they both reappropriated a modified form of the earlier social gospel's pacifist instincts, augmented by Gandhian ideas of "active nonviolence," some for principle's sake, some for strategic reasons. Both also adopted a realist reading of class and race relations in America.[5] The result was the civil and human rights movement that turned out to be the third incarnation of the social gospel in America—one that expanded to include not only women but other groups who were discriminated against.

This development was paralleled by decolonialization movements around the world, backed heavily by missionaries who had themselves been motivated to undertake their vocations by the influence of such representative figures as Walter Rauschenbusch, Reinhold Niebuhr, and Martin Luther King Jr., and their colleagues, heirs, and disciples. It made many who did not go abroad sympathetic to liberation theology as it developed among the indigenous anticolonial movements, often using many of the categories of Marxist-Leninist social analysis. One way or another, under various names (Dalit theology in India, Minjung theology in Korea, Black theology in South Africa, etc.), this became the major form of the social gospel in the "Third World." They did not doubt the depths of social sin or eschew the use of coercive power in revolutionary movements. Indeed, some saw revolution as the only cure for social sin. This became the fourth form of the social gospel of the twentieth century, and, like Christian realism and the human rights movement, made the social gospel less a peculiarly American phenomenon than a worldwide development.[6]

Indeed, American Protestants became also more and more aware not only of the contributions of voices long silent, but of the Roman Catholic "Social Encyclicals," which paralleled many of these developments. By the Second Vatican Council of the mid-60s, Protestant and Catholic thought increasingly converged on many of these issues of public moment. The earlier, harsh polemics between Catholics and Protestants were muted and cooperative programs and conversations were expanded, even if profound disagreements remained in regard to authority in the church, teachings about birth control, and the nature and character of sacraments.

Each of these incarnations of the social gospel had its great successes and failures. All called for a renewal of the heart and a new relationship to God through Christ, each also sought the revitalization of the mission of the church at the hands of the Holy Spirit manifest in the renewal of the prophetic and priestly offices of the church. Each identified the struggles they saw as part of the ongoing manifestation of a kingdom ethic in the common life of humanity. Moreover, in many ways, these movements accomplished their goals—they helped bring about a greater dignity for labor, former slaves, and women. They contributed to the defeat of Nazism, the collapse of Communism, to the expansion of constitutional democracy under more just laws around the world, and to the decolonialization of subject peoples. We can surely rejoice at what they left as a legacy to the faith, to the church, and to society, even if they did not solve these problems once and for all.

In fact, as we enter the first decade of a new century, we find a continuation of all the issues with which the social gospel, in its various forms, struggled. Economic inequality and manifest suffering among those caught up in urbanizing, industrializing, and now globalizing processes are notable in every region—and are devastating for those left out of these developments, even if the middle classes are expanding in most lands. The viciousness of ethnic conflict and discrimination is present on every continent, even if it is not of the same scope as the twentieth-century wars. Violations of civil rights and both theoretical and practical resistance to human rights are present among every people, even if more countries have adopted rights constitutionally than ever before. The residues of neo-pagan nationalist violence and of militant secular revolutionism explode at the margins of civility in the North and South, the East and the West, even if their main international centers are gone. Women and minorities have not yet found full acceptance, whatever gains they have made; and both old forms of tyranny and new fantasies of grandeur appear out of the disarray of broken societies and shattered dreams, however much the world seems to have sobered. The "super-personal forces of evil," as Rauschenbusch called them, are with us still—even if they have changed their masks and lurk only as the side-eddies of life.

Indeed, in some ways, several social problems have become more threatening precisely because they have become global in scope and are related to great and complex civilizations. What we do not have is either a social analysis or a theology large enough to match the dilemmas we face. Many of the institutions on which we relied in the past—the ecumenical churches and councils, the alliances of religion and labor, the missionary agencies, the "programs" for this and against that, continue to struggle with these issues, for they rightly know that they are not solved; but they often seem tired, using ideological frameworks to interpret what is going on, and exhausted slogans without compelling visions, precisely because they do not grasp the wider context in which we face such issues. Many seem fixated on an essentially liberationist view of the world, not recognizing that it was but one expression of a much wider and deeper heritage. Indeed, it tends to isolate the church from public discourse because it has not and perhaps cannot become a genuinely public theology. The particular incarnation of the social gospel that pertained to the decolonializing period could help deconstruct some oppressive and corrupt old orders under some conditions; but it cannot reconstruct just and viable new ones any more than the Marxist-Leninist social analysis, on which it largely depended, could.

Our New Global Situation[7]

Today, the world cannot so simply be divided into first, second, and third worlds, or into a new version of the old class struggle, "the West and the Rest," "the North and the South," or "the East and the West." It is at once a more integrated and a more variegated historical interaction of people and societies undergoing a dynamic transformation that is called globalization, one that has many implications also for the world as biophysical planet and for the world as a philosophical-theological realm of meaning, precisely because it is creating a new public that surpasses the one addressed by previous forms of the social gospel. While sometimes seen as essentially, or only, an economic development, globalization is in fact a vast social, technological, communications, and structural change laden with ethical perils and promises as great as those brought about by the ancient rise, and subsequent fall, of the ancient empires, the later development and then demise of feudalism, the still later rise of modernity with its nationalisms and recent industrial revolutions, and their decline.[8] While it is true, as some fear, that the multinational corporation is a chief vehicle of many of these changes and is particularly suited to take advantage of the processes that make globalization viable (in part because it is less politically accountable than other institutions), the extent of the wider process is so monumental that no area of life will be untouched. Globalization in the broader sense invites, almost demands, a reassessment of those traditions that have not only contributed to the dynamics now reshaping what we have, but may enhance or inhibit the capacity to participate in, avoid victimization by, and constructively guide what appears to be the creation of a new encompassing and highly complex civilization. Some Roman Catholic scholars working with the idea of "subsidiarity," some Reformed and Evangelical scholars working with the concepts of "sphere sovereignty," some Jewish and Protestant scholars working with federal-covenantal theory, and some secular scholars advocating communitarian ideas of the "common good" are already seeking fresh ways of drawing on and recasting classical traditions to guide our future.[9]

Many, of course, take up these questions from more limited points of view. Many public protests against globalization in the United States and around the world are quite strident, fully convinced that the data is clear and that globalization is having devastating effects everywhere. But in a summary of current social scientific literature on the changes brought by globalization, Giovanni Arrighi and Beverly Silver review the current state of research with an eye to the effects on politics, national economies, working peoples, and minorities. They write:

> [There is] little consensus on anything but the fact that an era of history has ended. There is no consensus on which state, if any, benefitted most from the confrontation of the Cold War and is now poised to replace the United States as the dominant player in the global political economy. There is no consensus on whether the proliferation in the variety and number of multinational corporations and the formation of global financial markets is undermining state capacities and, if so, how generally and permanently. There is no consensus on whether the world's working class is an endangered species or simply changing color and the countries of its residence. There is no consensus on whether modernization is shoring up civilizational divides, melting them down, or restoring the inter-civilizational balance of power of modern times. Above all, there is no consensus on what kind of world order, if any, we can expect to emerge from the combination of whatever changes are actually occurring in the global configuration of power.[10]

In spite of the lack of consensus, people have very strong views about these issues. Many are locally affected by the changes and are not unwilling to project local experiences and interests onto a global screen. Kofi Annan, secretary-general of the United Nations, recently pointed out that many see globalization less as "a term describing objective reality" about the creation of a new social or civilizational possibility than as "an ideology of predatory capitalism," which they experience as a kind of "siege." Against it, they join a "backlash" that takes at least three major forms.[11] One is a growing nationalism, sometimes threatening multiethnic-states. The second, more troubling in view of the history of the twentieth century, is the call for strong leaders—seldom democratic, often overtly antidemocratic—who seek to mobilize these national interests against internationalism. And the third is the attempt to use globalization as a scapegoat for all the ills that in fact "have domestic roots" of a political and social nature.[12] To many, globalization has nothing to do with religion, theology, or ethics except the changing of the way they used to live. They do not know how to control it or to join it. Appeals to religion, religious ethics, or religiously shaped cultural attitudes are then used to mobilize sentiment against global trends. Local elites who find themselves swamped by developments they do not understand and cannot negotiate are particularly negative.[13]

Such views, however, seldom help understanding even if they are understandable, and even if they do point to some necessary reforms and cautions in a number of areas. It is more likely that globalization has promising as well as threatening possibilities—possibilities that cannot be clearly seen without attention to the larger picture and to certain kinds of "public theological" matters. Thus, one of our responsibilities is to assess the degree to which various reactions are justifiable, and to chart responses that are more likely to address the realities we face. In doing so, we must remember the realistic forms of the social gospel legacy.

We must not obscure the fact that globalization is disrupting many aspects of traditional religion, ethics, culture, economics, politics, and society, but we must do so from that side of the social gospel that does not see religion only as a force to mobilize against things as they are, but as a force capable of aiding and guiding the transformation of things as they are changing. Indeed, we shall repeatedly find that a deeper analysis demands that we acknowledge that people do, or can, know something about what is holy, and can recognize that holy possibilities are not entirely absent from globalization. Neither part of this hypothesis is universally accepted or decisively proven. However, they have not been decisively refuted or universally rejected either. In spite of a widely held view that the future is inevitably and increasingly secular, the resurgence of religious vitality has puzzled various secularizers to no end, and it is again becoming clear to a great number of scholars that religious insights and traditions are a permanent feature of human life, clearly evident in global trends, and the locus where questions of righteousness—of truth, justice, and holiness—take their most intense forms.[14]

However, since not all religious insights are in agreement, and all cannot be equally valid, the various claims that are made about truth, justice, and holiness must be subjected to critical examination. Thus, comparative philosophical theology, comparative ethics, and comparative social analyses, and not only appeals to this or that particular religion, are indispensable in investigating the relative validity of various religious claims about how we should live in this life and the role in this life of that which transcends it. Issues of justice and responsibility, righteousness and compassion, truth and holiness are thus intrinsic to this assessment, for no one can authentically give loyalty or credence to a view or lifestyle that does not evoke, ground, manifest, or sustain these qualities. In an emerging global civilization, theological ethical issues are thus again unavoidable. Insofar as we can know these things with any degree of confidence, we must come to an informed judgment, as many traditions would put it, about how God wants us to live in it, respond to it, and shape it.

We are faced with a complex question in a complex situation. Obviously, the question demands the joining of ethics and theology. In concert with most classical traditions and in contrast to many modern trends that divorced or even opposed the two, we hold that theology and ethics are mutually supportive, even necessary to each other. Still, we must acknowledge the validity of the modern insight that the two are analytically distinct in a way that allows them to correct one another. Thus, we may use ethics critically to inquire into and assess the assumptions and implications of every theologically approved practice and every dogmatic claim. We may demand further that valid ethical criteria must find their ultimate sanctions in what is truly universal and enduring and not only in what is religiously and temporarily "mine" or "ours" at the moment. This is one of the characteristics of public theology, which works with, but also beyond, confessional dogmatics.[15] Without these critical principles, theological ethics is tempted to be little more than another species of idiosyncratic subcultural folkways and taboos, and theology is tempted to be simply the ideological megaphone for what this or that group wants to believe or practice.[16] It must be said that, like the gaps in social gospel thinking filled by the Christian realist, civil and human rights, and liberation movements, public theology may well be required in our global era as the fifth incarnation of the social gospel—drawing on, expanding, and modifying what has gone before.

The theological ethical questions can be pressed by inquiring not only into the inner mechanics of the spiritual life, but also into the decisive issues that have been pressed into contemporary consciousness by the emergence of global business, technologies, ecological awareness, the struggles for universal human rights, and a host of related developments after the defeat of militant nationalism in World War II, and the collapse of international socialism at the end of the Cold War. These developments are rooted in long, historic trends that seem to many to now be leading humanity toward the possible creation of a global civilization that will alter every community and tradition.[17] Of particular interest to theological ethics as it inquires into such issues are the often implicit key moral assumptions and metaphysical convictions that form the moral ecology, the "ethos" of the worldwide social environment in which we increasingly live. The ethos conditions the minds of ordinary people more than they know, as well as the thinking of the theologian and ethicist more than they often admit. Further, since every viable social context is constituted by a network of interactive, interdependent spheres of activity, organized into various practices and institutions, we must pay attention to the various spheres of activity that shape life, and to the question of what holds these various spheres into identifiable units of common action. Thus, theological ethics tries to understand, evaluate, and help guide the various spheres of the common life in which the social ecology is manifest as ethos, and to discern how theological ethics should interact with various nontheological forces and fields of study beyond ethics that also influence these spheres of life, for these "other" areas are always also bearers of values and norms.

The Special Problem of the World Religions

The social gospel authors knew that those perennial institutions of the common life—family, politics, economy, and culture—were always necessary and necessarily influenced by religion.[18] Indeed, that was their essential program— to make the religion they knew and loved an effective influence to reform the institutions of the common life. They also knew that how they were held together was fateful for the well-being of persons and civilizations as a whole. That is why they resisted the Roman Catholic tradition of their time, which seemed to them to be based on the coercion of belief and on the forms of conservative, evangelical piety that celebrated the conversion of souls but resisted the conversion of society. Thus, they sought to use religious resources to reform these perennial areas of life. Moreover, they suspected and sometimes commented on the distinctively modern spheres of activity, particularly the classical professions of education, medicine, and law, and occasionally touched on the marvels of modern technology as well. But they rarely saw how these too were framed by religion, although they were frequently much engaged in establishing schools and colleges for education, hospitals and clinics for health care, and more just laws for the protection of workers and children.[19]

In our day, migration, travel, the media, and education have brought everyone into contact with the various world religions. People in the West may not know a single Hindu, but they have heard not only of Gandhi, but of karma, yoga, and transcendental meditation. They may not know a Buddhist, but they have heard of the Dalai Lama, and possibly of Aung San Suu Kyi, and of the concepts of compassion and nirvana. Most people in the West know Jews, and increasingly they have come to know Muslims, or at least bits and pieces about Islam, and know that they do not eat pork and they have a profound sense of religious law. They also know something about various forms of spiritual healing, Native American practices, and new-age religions, most of which are retro-fitted versions of ancient cults. In brief, the world religions are not only long ago, far away, or beyond our horizons as options, they are present in the mix of the common life.

There is enormous historical evidence that religion always has been a decisive influence on the shape of social life. Can Africa be understood without some knowledge of tribal life, loyalties, and traditions? Can the Mideast be understood without reference to Islam? Can the social-political shape of South Asia be analyzed without dealing with Hinduism? Can East Asia be understood without noting the various syntheses of Tao, Buddhism, and Confucianism? And if it is also true that we are forming a global civilization in which everything in the West will be influenced by everything in the East, and vice versa, and those in the South will find their destiny tied to those in the North, and vice versa, the question of what kinds of religion will become more or less influential will be fateful. No civilization has ever survived without a religion at its core, although in the twentieth century the programmatic atheism of Marxism and the functional agnosticism of liberalism in politics, libertarianism in economics, modernism in the arts, and postmodernism in cultural analysis have been the most extended efforts to test whether that is a possibility. Still, behind these developments, religious or secular, most versions of the social gospel have presumed an essentially Christian theological perspective and conducted most intellectual and organizational battles on an intramural basis.

In a global environment, however, it is not simply a question of whether the Baptists or the Catholics, the Reformed or the Anabaptist versions of the Christian faith would be the most influential, or how they might relate to Jews, it is a question of what religions are in contention to define the moral and spiritual center of the global common life. After all, the primal religions, which we sometimes identify as "tribalism" in Africa, Hinduism in India, Buddhism in Southeast Asia, Confucianism in East Asia, and Islam, from North Africa through the Mideast to Indonesia, have, with local variations not unlike the branches of Christianity in various regions, distinctively stamped whole civilizations. Indeed, the various cultures of the world can easily be treated as the outward and visible signs of various inward spirits. This has been recognized by Samuel Huntington in his much discussed *The Clash of Civilizations and the Remaking of World Order*, which has the virtue of acknowledging the formative role of religion in society and culture, and the vice of not asking whether deeper unifying moral and spiritual realities are possible to discover and cultivate.[20] When we, if we, move toward a global civilization, how shall these religions relate, and, more importantly, how does each of the great world religions shape the social, political, legal, and cultural environment it stamps with its moral and spiritual genetic code in regard to the treatment of other religions, the basic human rights of all, the possibilities of intermarriage, conversion, economic opportunity, and so forth? This is an area that the social gospel and most of its heirs simply did not face.

During the twentieth century, the earlier versions of the social gospel faced the acids of the laissez-faire capitalism of the robber baron era and the rising power of the neo-paganism of the Nazis and the secular materialism of the Communists. Then the more recent versions attempted to confront the deep legacies of racism, sexism, classism, as we have seen. In all of these, the question of the relationship of Christian thought as public theology to the other religions was not on the agenda—except for the occasional recognition of the fact that religions might cooperate to overcome certain recognized evils. Thus, from the Parliament of Religions of 1893 through the formulation of the United Nations Charter and Bill of Rights, the religions of the world cooperated (more or less) against various forms of grotesque barbarism.

Still, a certain view, derived from the Enlightenment, tended to reign—that ethics, especially as they dealt with public issues, could be separated from any and all religious and theological grounding. Various doctrines and dogmas may be held by anyone and freely taught by various religious groups; but people could know right and wrong, good and evil, without any need of religious appeal. God was essentially irrelevant to public morality. Indeed, religion, especially in an "orthodox" form, was often seen as the cause of violence, discrimination, hate, ecological damage, and war. Not only must we have the institutional separation of church and state, but religiously grounded ethics and theologically warranted morality had no place in public discourse. This, of course, tended to silence both the religious bigots of the world and to disenfranchise the multiple heirs of the social gospel. The very idea of a public theology, especially one capable of critically and comparatively evaluating various religions, was considered dubious.

It was in this context that the concerns of the various versions of the social gospel began to converge with certain other developments. The Christian foreign missionary movements, both Protestant and Catholic, were at their heights precisely during the early years of the American social gospel, and, indeed, two of the great leaders of the early social gospel, Washington Gladden and Shailer Mathews, were presidents of the American Board of Commissioners for Foreign Missions. Walter Rauschenbusch himself wanted to become a missionary, but was turned down because of his "unorthodox" interpretation of the message of the biblical prophets. The experience of other religions and cultures by missionaries abroad and the struggles to redefine social ethics in the face of industrializing and urbanizing developments at home mutually influenced each other.[21] Further, the children of missionaries became the founders of the new discipline of anthropology, just as the children of the social gospel pastors became the founders of the new discipline of sociology, and these too informed each other—both with an alertness, at least for several generations, of the decisive role that religion does and can play in shaping society.[22] All this was deeply disrupted by the world wars, hot and cold, that dominated attention from World War I until the Fall of the Wall, and predictions of inevitable secularization dominated the field for many years; but with the new global openness, it turns out that religions are not fading from view, but reasserting their vigor. Islam is obviously reasserting itself in many ways throughout North Africa, the Mideast, to Indonesia, and is a major voice in the African American community. Hinduism has captured the government of India, and a missionizing form of Hinduism has influenced many in the West. Buddhism has reestablished itself in several countries of Southeast Asia, and is sending missionaries into China, even if Tibetan Buddhism is under threat. A rebirth of Confucian studies is taking place especially among "overseas Chinese." Evangelical and Pentecostal forms of Christianity are reshaping the Americas, Africa, and Korea, as the pope calls for a reinvigoration of Catholic missions and the "reevangelization of Europe."

It is in this context that several have recognized that we need, above all, a "theology of religions." This is presently taking three forms. The first is most clearly represented by Wilfrid Cantwell Smith, a child of the missionary movement, who argues that faith is a universal feature of human existence, and that the various religions and theologies are expressions of this underlying reality.[23] What is interesting to him, however, as an historian of religion, is the variety by which this is articulated and the multiplicity of forms by which it is expressed. A second approach is best represented by the former Catholic missionary Paul Knitter, who artfully surveys the current Christian attitudes toward other religions and argues for a nonexclusive pluralism of religions, all of which have a validity, even if each may be assessed accordingly as it does or does not promote a liberating movement against social oppression—a criterion, of course, that sets one incarnation of the social gospel as the universal standard for both Christianity and all the world religions.[24] The third form, the one that is most likely to converge with the public theology promise of the social gospel in a global era is best represented by the renegade Catholic theologian Hans Küng, the maverick Protestant social theorist Francis Fukuyama, and the highly independent Jewish political scientist Daniel Elazar.[25] What these scholars share is a deep commitment to comparative and historical studies, a recognition of the role of religion in the formation of a social ethic, and the necessity of evaluating various religious traditions according to their capacity to form and sustain a viable, just, pluralist, open, and culturally and economically flourishing civilization. They know that any encounter with the world religions involves a social, cultural, and intellectual encounter, and the possible reconstruction of every institution in civil society. In my view, they could each include aspects of the views of Smith and Knitter in what they offer, but they will not only affirm a deep common humanity or an inevitable pluralism, they will invite the many members of the emerging global civilization to participate in the reformation of the common life, and will do so on the basis of what is, ultimately, a biblical view of justice, righteousness, and holiness.[26]

I am, in brief, proposing a fifth incarnation for the social gospel, one that will substantially deprovincialize it of its Americanist roots, bring it more clearly into dialogue with the world's religions, and risk the attempt to construct a biblically based and theologically rooted, but broadly ecumenical social ethic, one intentionally open to interfaith influences and able to give guidance in and to the emerging global civilization. Of course, other voices with other roots will also be involved; but at least those who find meaning and encouragement from the social gospel traditions will be prepared to participate in one of the most important missions to the human future.

11

The Social Gospel and Pastoral Care Today

Pamela D. Couture

"Is American Romance Too Risky?" reads the center, large-font headline this morning on the Microsoft News Service (MSN) newspage that I must pull up to check my e-mail. I can't miss this headline even if I want to avoid it. With some effort, I can find headlines in smaller font, hidden in a less obvious section of the page. "Leaders Head to High Stakes Summit" anticipates the fragile Middle East peace summit with President Clinton, Israeli Prime Minister Ehud Barak, and Palestinian leader Yasser Arafat. "AIDS to Reduce African Population" reports that life expectancy will be halved in African countries where the AIDS pandemic is the worst. This morning's headlines follow the usual pattern: The international stories report with detachment on situations and interventions that may determine the literal survival of nations and millions of people, while the lead story hooks the reader's fears about the quality of life in the United States.

The problem I face each morning as I pull up my e-mail is similar to the problem that haunted the social gospelers a hundred or so years ago and liberation theologians after them. The public power is focused on creating a better quality life for people already flourishing, while it relegates to its peripheral vision those persons whose survival is in question and whose basic needs go unmet. In contrast, in the realm of God, the persons of greatest need receive the most immediate attention. How can life on earth mirror the realm of God?

Is Christian ministry, especially pastoral care, strengthening the world's priorities, or is it actively participating in creating a world that reflects the realm of God? Some critics would say that pastoral care education after World War II has contributed significantly to the creation of the kind of "culture of the therapeutic" that is drawn to MSN-type headlines. "The relationship" itself has become the content of pastoral care—whether it is relationship of self with self, of self with lover, or self with family—rather than the content of pastoral care being ministry for the sake of bringing about the realm of God and enabling people to live the Great Commandment. I would argue that

160

twentieth-century education in pastoral care had its roots in the social gospel and, after intense work on various forms of personal relationships in the decades after World War II, has made natural strides toward returning to that heritage in a later twentieth-century form.

Is there a future for pastoral care that is based in something like a social gospel? The social gospel, as a theological school of thought developed in the first two decades of the twentieth century, is most known for its theological criticism of the capitalist system that developed in the early years of that century. The social gospel, as a movement that continued in importance well into the Cold War era, is most associated with social ethics, the academic discipline that emerged in conjunction with sociology.[1] However, its initial flurry of activism and ministry emerged from interpersonal encounters as ministers responded to the dire urban poverty that marked turn-of-the-century capitalism. Walter Rauschenbusch's personal transformation in New York City's Hell's Kitchen is well known. Other face-to-face relationships with persons in extreme suffering in New York, Boston, and Chicago provided social gospelers with the motivation for cultural and social analysis. However, the link between interpersonal encounters and the social and cultural systems within which interpersonal relationships occur was all but severed as pastoral care and counseling and social ethics developed into discrete academic disciplines. As pastoral care lost its social context, social ethics also lost sight of the persons whose lives were so deeply changed by the social institutions that social ethics analyzed. Over the last decade, theologians of care have made distinct attempts to reconnect the suffering of people with the social and cultural conditions that create that suffering, and some social ethicists, most notably feminist and womanist social ethicists, have reconnected people with systems. In that sense, the theology that supports pastoral care has already prepared a significant amount of theoretical work that articulates "pastoral care and the social gospel today." However, more work remains.

Through education in pastoral care and counseling, ministers can learn to respond to individuals and families who are actively suffering; they can learn the theological presuppositions for doing so; they can learn much about the cultural and social conditions in which present-day suffering occurs. However, education in pastoral care and counseling faces two challenges if it is to truly reflect a social gospel for the twenty-first century. It must learn to teach a set of interventions that relieve suffering at cultural and social levels that parallel the interventions it knows so well for individuals and families. It must also learn to communicate its vision for theological wholeness to a society whose rules for communication depend upon fragmentation.

In brief, what were the conditions of society that produced the social gospel and twentieth-century pastoral care at the turn of the last century, and what analogies might be drawn to society and pastoral care at the beginning of the twenty-first century? What conditions in today's society call for new kinds of caring intervention and teaching? How can pastoral care communicate a vision of holistic care that identifies with the theological aim of the social gospel, the promotion of the realm of God on earth?

Pastoral Care and the Social Gospel in the Twentieth Century

The idea of "the social gospel" was articulated for the twentieth century by Washington Gladden and Walter Rauschenbusch, theologians who had direct ministerial experience with persons suffering from the social and cultural changes in the United States at the beginning of the twentieth century. To these names we can add Elwood Worchester and Samuel McComb, founders of the "Emmanuel Movement," clergy whose names are significant in the history of pastoral care.[2] Laity are now understood to exercise pastoral care ministries; so we can add the names of women such as Frances Willard and Ida B. Wells-Barnett, whose work on behalf of the care of families and individuals would today be considered a ministry of pastoral care.[3] These religious leaders have in common a social consciousness that resulted from their direct experience of the suffering of persons displaced by the social and cultural currents of the late nineteenth and early twentieth centuries. They intervened to relieve the suffering of individuals and families, but they also sought social and cultural solutions that would prevent extreme suffering from repeating itself.

What suffering did these religious leaders seek to alleviate? Industrialization and capitalism brought with it a growing disparity between those who grew rich from the new economy and those whose lives were used up by its demands. The new economy brought a heavy influx of immigrants from foreign countries and a migration of poor persons within the United States. Competition for lower-paying jobs became intense among the lower classes, including poor whites and persons who could be stigmatized by race or ethnicity. Within this economy, the emerging classes conflicted with one another over their perceptions of gender roles: Working-class women often sought the Victorian ideal of highly differentiated gender roles, just as middle-class and professional women began to disdain the idea of separate spheres for women and men. In the midst of these social changes, leaders such as Worchester and McComb reconstructed churches so that they included parlors and gymnasiums and could become community centers; Willard and others challenged the domestic violence that was present in families and communities; and leaders Wells-Barnett and others sought to expose and reduce the class and racial violence that resulted in the lynchings of mostly black men. Many lesser-known and nameless ministers assisted these causes and shaped their understanding of pastoral care; for example, pastoral theologian Charles Gerkin has an early memory of the Ku Klux Klan's burning a cross in his family's yard as a result of his father's ministry. Gerkin later created the first integrated worship service at the segregated "Gradies," or Grady Hospital, which served African American and white populations through parallel sets of services in Atlanta.[4]

As activists and communities attempted to relieve suffering, social science emerged as a powerful intellectual construct. Worchester and McComb and many other religious leaders specifically concerned themselves with the urban mental and physical health problems and the ways that the psychological sciences could relieve distress. Although in early days psychology informed a general ministry, within a short time ministry, like other professions in the United States, formed its own specialty branch of experts. As psychology became a cultural power, its adherents sought to differentiate those who were trained and credentialed in this work and those who were not. As a sense of expertise in psychology arose, it became generally believed the work of care in this new society might be best guided and done by professionals who specialized in the caring activities that had previously been the domain of women, families, and communities. Since women and ministers were already adept at caring activities, professionalizing care brought new employment opportunities in private psychological practice and in public social work employment within the developing welfare state.

As care professionalized in the first half of the twentieth century, the earlier organic relationship between activities of care and displacements within the social system disintegrated. By the late 1950s, pastoral care had become most creatively focused upon intrapsychic and interpersonal relationships that were understood acontextually. Pastoral care and pastoral theology were quite differentiated as a discipline from social ethics. The tide turned quickly, however, bringing pastoral care reflection into conversation with increasingly complex systems: families, congregations, communities, and culture. In the 1990s, the idea that the "context" of care significantly alters the course of care had firm hold.

The 1990s produced a significant number of pastoral care publications that analyzed the contexts in which care occurs. In most cases, the publications involve an analysis of the assumptions within a culture related to the social variables that are attributable to persons: genders, races, mental and physical disability, age, class, and sexual orientation. More generalized aspects of contemporary culture, such as postmodernism and multiculturalism, have also been explored. Some limited attention has been given to environmental, economic, political, and international conditions, although more work is in progress. Specific actions that arise as a result of the conditions of culture and society, including domestic violence, clergy sexual misconduct, and incest have gained special attention, as has the use and abuse of power. Theological reflection has highlighted themes such as despair and hope, lament, mutuality, advocacy, the image of God, and the Great Commandment. These themes in the pastoral care and pastoral theology texts of the late twentieth century continue the general trajectory set by the social gospel in the earlier part of the century.[5]

Pastoral Care and the Social Gospel Today

In the early twenty-first century, many social and cultural contexts for care resonate with those of the early twentieth century. In the United States, a new economy is creating greater distance between the very rich and the very poor. The rapid expansion of medical and information technology creates boundaries that mark who is within and who is outside this economy. A multicultural population simmers and at times boils with racial and ethnic tension. Multiculturalism also brings interfaith communities that may or may not understand each other. Even within Christianity, and all the more when one adds interfaith dimensions, gender and family ideals are in conflict with one another. U.S. society is perhaps most unified in its expectations of class: Society expects employment, not stay-at-home parenting, of poor mothers and parental involvement of poor fathers, and it expects parents to provide regular and adequate supervision for children. Children, especially those under six, are the most materially poor population in the United States, but many children of all classes have tenuous connections with adult networks within their communities. Among all classes, rapid economic change has created an insecure and driven workforce. Among all classes, the use and abuse of legal and illegal drugs supports webs of mental illness, criminality, and violence; these, in turn, support an expanding prison industry and the prison industry supports the economy of communities in decline. These and other social conditions reflect the deep suffering of individuals and families. If the imitation of the compassion of Jesus is the model for pastoral care, and bringing about the kingdom of God is its eschatological vision, then each of the situations has embedded within it claims on the pastoral care ministries of the church.

In the late twentieth century, pastoral care and counseling has been one of the "specialities" of practical theology that has been routinely taught in ministerial education. Other specialties have included worship and liturgy, preaching, education, and administration. Professors in the practical theology areas are aware that congregations face conditions that call for training in emerging ministries. Professors of practical theology gathered at the Wabash Center for Teaching in Theology and Religion in June 2000 identified emerging practices that may need to be taught: faith-based sustainable economic development, community organizing, interfaith collaboration, artistic expression, spiritual formation, technological communications, peacemaking (including community and domestic conflict resolution, victim-offender reconciliation, and non-violent living), ethical guidance around biomedical technology, postmodern worship styles, bivocational ministry, and the cultivation of public square leadership when the congregation's place in the local community is changing.[6] Some of these emerging practices of ministry are directly related to pastoral care ministries; all involve components of care that must be addressed in order to create adequate ministerial training. Many of these ministries, especially economic development and community organizing, have direct relations to the ministries of social gospel congregations of the past.

The new contour to this old story, however, is internationalization. The disparity between rich and poor persons is evident in the United States, but the gap between rich and poor nations and the conditions in which their populations live is even more stark. Although generally, wealthier nations are in a position to create better systems of care and social welfare, wealthier nations do not necessarily use their wealth for social welfare, and national wealth does not determine the welfare of persons within countries. Immigration, multiculturalism, and racism continue to create tension in the United States, especially as the population becomes more aware of the United States' transition from its Euro-American white majority to a genuinely multicultural majority. Internationally, the poverty of nations is also directly related to violence and war between ethnic groups within races. In the United States, class issues intersect with issues of race and family as rates of poverty, especially among families headed by single mothers, are significantly higher among nonwhites. Internationally, gender and poverty are significantly related, and discrimination against women in many countries means that women and the children they bear lack adequate nutrition and medical care, often because the best food and medicine are saved for men. Children in the United States are poorer than in any industrialized nation, but children in Sub-Saharan Africa are destitute. Children are increasingly likely to be orphaned as a result of war and AIDS; their future is bleak. As the world economy and world aid become increasingly globalized, the use of economic and political power by wealthy nations directly influences the care and welfare that persons in destitute parts of the world receive. At the heart of these issues is the suffering of individuals and families, and therefore, issues of pastoral care are directly embedded in these conditions. Methods of care and healing related to these conditions are beginning to be addressed by theoreticians of pastoral care and its theological literature. Pastoral care and the social gospel today must be placed within an international perspective to be truly up-to-date.[7]

An internationalized pastoral care rooted in the concerns of the social gospel is at once simple and complex. The simplicity is this: The love and justice of the Great Commandment and the realm of God require that ministries of care attend to their peripheral vision, where those in greatest need and suffering are often found. Attending to our peripheral vision, we find those who are suffering and whose basic needs are not met in our local communities and in other nations. Thought of in this way, pastoral care and mission are directly connected. The complexity of acting in a caring, gospel-oriented manner is one of ecclesial transition. The common wisdom now is that mission agencies that have provided church work primarily as arms of denominations are necessary as relief agencies but need additional relational strategies. First, the global development of Christianity in poorer nations needs to be guided by the people of those nations rather than by persons who represent former colonial powers. Second, persons in local congregations in the United States are motivated to support international relief efforts by direct, personal, religious experience in their mission work. They are interested in "practicing" such values and qualities such as hope, compassion, and hospitality.[8] These kinds of personal experiences in local and international ministries, where personal and social implications are evident, can be as transformative for Christians today as Rauschenbusch's experiences in Hell's Kitchen were for him a hundred years ago.

Communicating Pastoral Care and the Social Gospel

What are people searching for in religious experience when they claim the power to construct their own lives and communities and seek direct personal experience with persons of other communities? They are seeking a connection with God and humanity that counteracts the psychological, social, political, and economic fragmentation of the postmodern world.[9] The fragmentation that individuals feel is mirrored in their experience in the church, especially when private religious needs and public social issues seem distanced from one another. 1 Corinthians 12:26 reminds us of a great truth: When one part of the body suffers, the whole of the body suffers. People feel fragmented by the sense that they are helpless in the face of the extreme suffering of the world. Personal religious experience that empowers individuals to improve communal and social conditions provides a sense of reality and authority in a world of fragmented appearances. Though the church seems fragmented, it can transform its basic building blocks so that it can provide a social, ecclesial context in which people can find the sense of personal cohesion they seek. Helping people gain a sense of cohesion in their lives through their religious experience is a basic pastoral care function.

How can a social gospel-based pastoral care help people gain cohesion in a fragmented, postmodern culture? How can it help people develop a sense that their lives are grounded in reality, a reality that coheres with conditions in the world and with their hope for love, justice, and the realm of God? The church has two kinds of knowledge, says Keith Clements in the recent book *Learning to Speak: The Church's Voice in Public Affairs.*[10] One kind of knowledge is on-the-ground, real-world knowledge of people's lives. The knowledge is gained through the church's extensive network of people throughout the world who work shoulder-to-shoulder with people in local communities. It is the kind of knowledge about the human condition that pastoral counselors gain when they listen for hours on end to the minute details of real-life situations, a real-world knowledge that is similar to the knowledge of the missionary who listens and works with people in life-threatening, war-torn countries. The other kind of knowledge is the knowledge that God cares for the suffering, that God is working to bring about the reign of God. It is the knowledge of eschatological hope. These two kinds of knowledge ground the church's reality.

Clements contrasts the church's knowledge with the media culture that creates a distorted sense of reality.[11] The social witness of the church is often seduced into the mores of the media culture, thereby rendering the church's social witness ineffective at best and alienating at worst. His proposals for effective ecclesial witness suggest that in a media-driven culture such as our own, social witness and pastoral care work hand in hand to ground people in a world and kingdom-based reality.

Clements suggests that contemporary culture is characterized by three features: reality/publicity, problem/solution, and instant/value. Each of these features creates smooth appearances that contribute to the sense of postmodern fragmentation. First, reality/publicity: Publicity creates the appearance of reality. Few criteria are applied to discern what situation deserves publicity more than the next. Therefore, all situations, regardless of importance, must compete for publicity in order to become part of reality. Yet the actual publicity they receive may obscure the reality (as witnessed in the television coverage of the Gulf War in 1991). When church pronouncements on social issues compete for publicity in this "chattering culture," they lose connection with the experienced reality they try to represent. People need support to prevent collapsing the dissonance between what they experientially know and the images that are presented to them, a kind of pastoral care that supports a sense of cohesive reality and social witness.

Second, problem/solution: Situations are deemed important and effective, and are given publicity if they involve problems to be solved. The emphasis on solving problems reflects a society dominated by engineering and technology, in which reality is a problem to be solved. The problem-solving emphasis in society suggests that we should be able to remove all pain and threat, and when we cannot do that, we should distance ourselves from the instability around us. The overemphasis on problem solving in all areas of life seduces human beings to believe that they can transcend finitude. The reality may require that human beings develop the resilience to continue to work to reduce suffering even though the problems of the situation cannot be fully solved. Helping people develop resilience and steadiness in the presence of ambiguity is a task of social witness and pastoral care.

Third, instant/value: News gains importance when it has a quality of suddenness and can be communicated with speed. Images of those efforts that require hard, steady, incremental work are much more difficult to create. Such work is rarely considered "news," does not seem "solvable," and does not become part of "reality." Yet such work is what is often called for in both enduring social witness and in pastoral care.

In contrast to the exhibitionism of the media culture, unreality is the church's knowledge that is often profoundly rooted in the hiddenness of God. The church's knowledge of the real world and the work of the realm of God imitates not the media culture but the way that Jesus turned the center-stage visibility away from himself, toward those he found in his peripheral vision, who have no business being there at all.[12]

Clements describes an example of a ministry of the ecumenical international community that is grounded in real-world knowledge and eschatological hope. The ministry is a day school for handicapped children that was begun in the Bekaa valley in Lebanon. It was founded after civil war in Lebanon, fueled by interfaith enmity between Christians, Muslims, and Druze, and it came to an end in 1990. Amid a myriad of needs, the ecumenical ministry in Lebanon asked itself

> . . . what would most clearly indicate the values of the kingdom at this particular point in the history of Lebanon. The question therefore became still more concrete. Which communities in Lebanon are tending to be most forgotten? . . . Answer: the people in remote villages such as in the upper Bekaa. And who, in such places, are the most vulnerable and under-resourced people? Answer: children with mental and physical handicap. And how, given the tragedy of the recent past, might such service witness to hope? Answer: by being open to, serving, staffed by, managed by, people from both Christian and Muslim communities. To serve the weakest, in the furthest and most hidden places, and to do so in a way which transcended the walls of enmity, was considered the most adequate kind of response to the challenge and promise of the gospel of hope and reconciliation.[13]

Such a ministry illustrates the power of a social gospel-based pastoral care. It is designed as a place where the realm of God can be partially realized: The most vulnerable are cared for and grounds for peacemaking are established. It is the kind of ministry that has the power to ground and reconnect the persons involved in the care-giving ministries. It is an example of the way that pastoral care, as an interpersonal ministry, is deeply connected to social witness. And yet, as remarkable as it is, it is not a far departure from social gospel ministries of the past.

Conclusion

Toward a New Social Gospel?

Christopher H. Evans

Imagine someone living in the early twenty-second century who is trying to come to a fuller understanding of the nature of Christianity in the United States in the late twentieth and early twenty-first centuries. She is interested in this topic not simply for the sake of learning about the history of our time, but to see if it is possible to connect the events of our era with the issues she faces as a Christian living in the early twenty-second century. In the midst of that person's quest to find out about faith at the beginning of the twenty-first century, she does a search on her era's equivalent of the Internet and, on a site dealing with religion in the early twenty-first century, she downloads a volume with the intriguing title *The Social Gospel Today*.

As the person flips through the table of contents and skims through the chapters, we can only conjecture what, if any, of the visions espoused in this book's pages will resonate with her worldview. Will the arguments in this book strike the reader as a series of anomalies, a collection of eclectic arguments that serve to corroborate her preconceived notions about the confused state of mainline Christianity at the dawn of the twenty-first century? Or will the reader of these pages recognize something of her own time through the book's voices? Will she discern in this book a cogent narrative that reflects upon the issues facing the church of her day, suggesting to her the nascent origin of what could be called a "new social gospel"?

This book represents an effort to relate a particular movement of church history to the unique circumstances facing Christians living at the beginning of the twenty-first century. It is hoped that the virtue of this approach will enable contemporary readers to relate an important historical tradition to contemporary questions of Christian faith and practice. The danger of such an approach, however, is that one runs the very real possibility of presenting a worldview that can become quickly antiquated. Just as many of the seminal writings of the social gospel era often sound antiquated to our ears, we must confess that our efforts to articulate issues for the twenty-first-century church can easily become usurped by social, cultural, and theological currents that we, as yet, cannot even envision. Consequently, the usefulness of this book in twenty-five, or fifty, or a hundred years from the "present" may very well be reserved for the relatively small number of people who are committed to study the past solely for intellectual, not practical, reasons.

If, in some way, I could speak to the person of the early twenty-second century who has rescued this volume from the abyss of cyberspace, I'd want to say this to her about why she should read this book. First, I believe the social gospel legacy will speak to her era because it serves as a powerful reminder that the most lasting theological traditions are often the most historically dated. At first this sounds like an oxymoron; however, it is merely a reflection upon a simple truth: Any theological movement is rooted in the contextual suppositions of persons living in a specific time and place. The social gospel, especially in the history of American Protestantism, served as the prototypical model for twentieth-century churches that believed that working toward the goal of social transformation was the primary imperative for Christianity. Even as historical circumstances over the past one hundred years have changed, the social gospel's insistence that Christian faith must engage contemporary social issues in order to utilize the full force of the gospel remains a central, and taken-for-granted, principle among many denominations at the opening of the twenty-first century.

At the same time, I would tell this future person to read this volume because she will likely live in an era, as did the social gospelers, as we do today, where many people of faith will challenge and reject this basic theological supposition of the social gospel as anathema to an authentic Christianity. The history of twentieth-century Christianity has been frequently divided into two wings: one "evangelical" that stresses personal conversion, and one "liberal" that stresses social justice. These labels do an injustice to the diversity of theological and historical perspectives that highlight the multifaceted nature of twentieth-century American religion, a tapestry that will likely become even more diverse by the early twenty-second century. However, the fact that contemporary theological discussions still recognize some sort of polarity between two factions, dubbed as "evangelical" and "liberal," reflects that there is an indisputable division among Christians over fundamental theological matters related to revelation, biblical authority, the nature of salvation, and a host of other issues. My guess is our friend in the future will still be wrestling in some fashion with this theological divide, and perhaps sharing the lament of many of us today who observe that Christianity is often characterized more by fragmentation than by unity.

It is my hope, however, that as this person laments the reality of a fragmented church, she will recognize the importance of tying her faith to an active engagement with the social issues of her era, seeing that engagement as an integral part of her faith. The social gospel often failed miserably in its effort to relate historical events of that era to the divine will of God. The result, like that for many who represented the emerging Fundamentalist movement, was often a dogmatic and monolithic view of society that allowed little room for theological and cultural diversity. Indeed, an irony of the social gospel was the fact that in the effort of many of the movement's leaders to "free" God from the moorings of more traditional theological doctrine, their under-standing of the church often remained culturally bound to a narrowly con-ceived Protestant vision of Christian unity.

Yet, the person of the future needs to know that the social gospel legacy, at its best, reflects a powerful synthesis tying together individual and collective social witness that takes a positive view of the future. The social gospel move-ment was represented by women and men who believed that their actions in this life manifested a larger foundation that future generations could build upon. While emerging out of a unique historical context, the social gospel embodied a theological tradition that believed that social conditions of the future would outstrip those of the past.

Since the era of Reinhold Niebuhr, it has become commonplace to belittle the possibility of sustained social progress in any tangible form. The late social theorist Christopher Lasch, although praiseworthy of how the social gospel lifted up the prophetic ideal, believed the movement's great failing was how it confused the eschatological imperative of hope with the predominantly secu-lar ideal of social progress. Echoing Niebuhrian sentiments, Lasch warned of the dangers of associating God's will with specific desirable social outcomes, noting, "The hope that heals depends less on the expectation of social improvement in the future than on an underlying conviction of the goodness of being. The first is easily shattered by untoward events, reverses, defeats; the second endures. It cannot be shaken by the discovery that rain falls alike on the just and the unjust; precisely this impartiality of life-giving force, for the truly hopeful, constitutes the most important intimation of its benevolent character."[1]

It is true that social gospelers, like other theological liberals of their gener-ation, were guilty at times of relying on a naive progressivism, often seeing the hand of God at work through just about every aspect of contemporary culture. And yet a vital question for our time, as will be a vital question for the future, is how do we create and sustain a vision of hope unless that vision is grounded somehow in the social realities we face in the present? No one would dispute the violent and tragic character of the twentieth century, marked by two world wars, the Holocaust, countless incidences of war and genocide, racism, grow-ing economic disparities between rich and poor nations, and the suffering generated by the AIDS epidemic. Many within the social gospel movement believed that scientific knowledge was a panacea leading to the kingdom of God. Instead of being a gateway to the new Jerusalem, however, history has revealed the passing of a century where science often served as the handmaiden to some of the worst systematic evils in human history. There is indeed ample evidence from twentieth-century history (the so-called Christian century) that the story of humanity is not, to paraphrase Reinhold Niebuhr, a success story.

At the same time, I believe we make a grievous error to negate both the ideal and, at times, the realization of progress, consigning ourselves to a view that sees social struggle as a vain effort to achieve any sort of earthly incantation of God's "kingdom." Twentieth-century battles against racism and for gender equality, advances in health care, countless measures of economic reform, and movements of political revolt against the dominant suppositions of Western colonial power do not suggest a final victory in any one social arena. However, these struggles do give credence to the view espoused by many social gospelers that to labor on behalf of the kingdom is never marked by a belief in final victory, but is marked by a sustained faith that visions of social transformation will not only endure, but will, in some way, have their earthly realization—even amidst signs of worldly failure.

Like those in our era, our twenty-second-century friend has a choice. If she sides with a more orthodox interpretation of Christianity, then one must continuously muster a great deal of energy to justify a struggle against the forces of societal injustice. It would be an understandable choice (because it has been the choice made by many faithful Christians throughout the course of modern church history) for this person to view the world as hopelessly evil, instead opting to stake her future upon a faith that Christ's second coming will save her from her worldly sin. On the other hand, if she chooses to believe that her efforts of social engagement offer her a foretaste of a new heaven and a new earth, she has in some way placed herself within the legacy of the social gospel tradition. The question we need to wrestle, as will the person in the early twenty-second century, is a simple and timeless one: Is there any explicit connection between our earthly struggle to build a better society to the ultimate intentions of God for creation? If one is inclined to answer no to this question, then there is little basis for a recovery of the social gospel legacy in the future. If one is inclined to answer yes to the question, then one cannot avoid a serious wrestling with the issues discussed in this book. Historical circumstances will change a great deal; the imperative to call upon God's name to challenge injustice and to envision a transformed society, however, is a timeless and sacred heritage.

Finally, I would say to that reader of the future that no matter how captivating a theological heritage may be to a specific generation, for it to endure, it must be allowed to grow and adapt to emergent circumstances. In a very biblical sense, sometimes a tradition needs to die in order to be born again and speak to each new generation with renewed vitality and power. As we look one more time at the question of the social gospel's legacy, we can see many illustrations of how the movement was a by-product of its historical era. The theological triumphalism of many social gospel exponents, the often narrow parochialism of its Western Protestant worldview, and the Victorian suppositions of that time often cloud over its more visionary and transcendent qualities. Like every theological tradition in church history, the social gospel shared one fatal flaw: a limited vision. In the early 1930s, *Christian Century* editor Charles Clayton Morrison noted that one of the failures of the social gospel was that it never penetrated beyond the domain of the clergy.[2] He was accurate in terms of noting that the social gospel often erected its denominational and ecumenical power bases through a relatively small cadre of denominational leaders (of which Morrison was a part). By the same token, it never apparently crossed his mind that many of the women's movements and lay leaders discussed in this book's pages constituted part of the social gospel heritage. The problem with Morrison's statement was not so much that he was making an incorrect assessment; the problem was that he, like the representatives of the social gospel, like all of us who live in the present, and like the church to which our friend in the future will belong, carried an incomplete vision of God's activity in the world.

What I would suggest to that future reader is that the theological legacy of the social gospel touches her life, even if she doesn't call it by that name. Perhaps she will be inspired by the ministries of individuals like Washington Gladden and Walter Rauschenbusch. Or perhaps her experiences will draw her to understand the historical struggles of women to define their ministries in the church, or the ongoing struggle of churches against racism and the quest of Christians to articulate a compelling vision for a just economic order. Perhaps she will be fascinated by the Christian struggle to engage issues of theological, cultural, and interfaith diversity, or the quest to work for a society in which all citizens receive quality health care, regardless of income. In some way, as this person seeks to recover her past for the sake of the future, she will be compelled to embrace part of the legacy of the social gospel. If such a spark is ignited in our twenty-second-century reader, then perhaps this book represents a tentative step toward articulating for the church of our time a compelling vision for a new social gospel.

Notes

Introduction. Historical Integrity and Theological Recovery:
A Reintroduction to the Social Gospel

1. Some of the prominent church leaders who gave the Rauschenbusch lectures in the first decade of the series included Justin Wroe Nixon, Charles Clayton Morrison, Henry Van Dusen, and Reinhold Niebuhr.

2. F. Ernest Johnson, *The Social Gospel Re-Examined* (New York and London: Harper & Brothers, 1940).

3. Ibid., 12–13.

4. Charles Howard Hopkins, *The Rise of the Social Gospel in American Protestantism, 1865–1915* (New Haven: Yale University Press, 1940), 3.

5. Johnson, 12.

6. Quoted in Hopkins, 3. The ambiguity of defining the social gospel as a historical and theological movement is noted in Susan Lindley's opening chapter in this book. For an excellent overview on the development of social gospel scholarship, see Ralph E. Luker, "Interpreting the Social Gospel: Reflections on Two Generations of Historiography," in *Perspectives on the Social Gospel: Papers from the Inaugural Social Gospel Conference at Colgate Rochester Divinity School*, ed. Christopher H. Evans (Lewiston, N.Y.: Edwin Mellen Press, 1999), 1–13.

7. Johnson, 10.

8. Sidney E. Mead, *The Lively Experiment: The Shaping of Christianity in America* (New York: Harper & Row, 1963), 178.

9. Susan Curtis, *A Consuming Faith: The Social Gospel and Modern American Culture* (Baltimore: Johns Hopkins University Press, 1991), 277.

10. See Dennis N. Voskuil, "Reaching Out: Mainline Protestantism and the Media," in *Between the Times: The Travail of the Protestant Establishment*, ed. William R. Hutchison (Cambridge: Cambridge University Press, 1989), 72–92; Mark Silk, "The Rise of the 'New Evangelicalism': Shock and Adjustment," in Hutchison, 278–299.

11. William McGuire King, "'History as Revelation,' in the Theology of the Social Gospel," *Harvard Theological Review* 76:1 (1983): 110–111.

12. At the same time, it is critical to reiterate an important point: *Liberalism* and *social gospel* are not interchangeable terms. Theological liberalism must be viewed as a larger movement in which the social gospel arose. See, for example, Kenneth Cauthen, *The Impact of American Religious Liberalism* (New York and Evanston: Harper & Row, 1963), William R. Hutchison, *The Modernist Impulse in American Protestantism* (Cambridge: Harvard University Press, 1976), and Gary Dorrien, *Soul in Society: The Making and Renewal of Social Christianity* (Minneapolis: Fortress, 1995).

13. King, "An Enthusiasm for Humanity: the Social Emphasis in Religion and its Accommodation in Protestant Theology," in *Religion and 20th-Century American Intellectual Life*, ed. Michael J. Lacey (Cambridge: Cambridge University Press), 51.

14. Walter Rauschenbusch, "The New Evangelism," *The Independent* (1904). Reprint pamphlet in the Rauschenbusch papers, the American Baptist Historical Society, Rochester, New York.

15. H. Richard Niebuhr, "The Attack upon the Social Gospel," in *The Social Gospel: Religion and Reform in Changing America*, ed. Ronald C. White Jr. and C. Howard Hopkins (Philadelphia: Temple University Press, 1976), 264.

16. In fact, Robert William Fogel has recently argued that the social gospel was a significant component of what he calls a "Third Great Awakening" in American religious history. Fogel argues that the reform ethos of the social gospel was a significant factor in facilitating the rise of the modern egalitarian political ideals that were enacted by the federal government in the 1930s and 1940s. See Fogel, *The Fourth Great Awakening & The Future of Egalitarianism* (Chicago and London: University of Chicago Press, 2000).

17. See Donald Meyer, *The Protestant Search for Political Realism, 1919–1940* (Berkeley: University of California Press, 1960); Eldon Eisenach, *The Lost Promise of Progressivism* (Lawrence: University of Kansas Press, 1994); Paul T. Phillips, *A Kingdom on Earth: Anglo-American Social Christianity, 1880–1940* (University Park, Pa.: Pennsylvania State University Press, 1996).

18. For examples of the scholarship dealing with the wider impact of the social gospel in the twentieth century, see Martin Luther King Jr. *Stride Toward Freedom* (New York: Harper, 1958); Ralph Luker, *The Social Gospel in Black and White: American Racial Reform, 1885–1912* (Chapel Hill: University of North Carolina Press, 1991); James Tracy, *Direct Action: Radical Pacifism from the Union Eight to the Chicago Seven* (Chicago: University of Chicago Press, 1996).

19. These secular social theorists stress, in particular, the pragmatist thought of John Dewey, whose idealism emphasized the necessity to reform social institutions, not necessarily individual values. See, for example, Todd Gitlin, *The Twilight of Common Dreams: Why America Is Wracked by Culture Wars* (New York: Henry Holt & Company, 1995); Richard Rorty, *Achieving Our Country: Leftist Thought in Twentieth-Century America* (Cambridge: Harvard University Press, 1998), and John Pettegrew, ed., *A Pragmatist's Progress?: Richard Rorty and American Intellectual History* (Lanham, Md.: Rowman & Littlefield, 2000).

20. King, "History as Revelation," 129.

21. Martin Luther King Jr. "Remaining Awake Through a Great Revolution," in *A Testament of Hope: The Essential Writings of Martin Luther King, Jr.*, ed. James Melvin Washington (San Francisco: Harper & Row, 1986), 274.

22. Robert T. Handy, *A Christian America: Protestant Hopes and Historical Realities*, 2nd ed. (New York: Oxford University Press, 1984).

23. Rauschenbusch, *Christianizing the Social Order* (New York: Macmillan, 1912), 464–465.

24. The explosion of published literature in the field of church growth highlights that this is not a monolithic movement. Its adherents often share different suppositions surrounding evangelistic styles, pastoral care and social organizational models, and the desired institutional ends of local congregations. For a small sampling of literature in this field, see William Easum, *The Church Growth Handbook* (Nashville: Abingdon, 1990), George Barna, *User Friendly Churches: What Christians Need To Know About The Churches People Love To Go To* (Ventura: Regal Books, 1991), Lyle Schaller, *21 Bridges to the 21st Century* (Nashville: Abingdon, 1994), and Thomas Bandy, *Kicking Habits: Welcome Relief for Addicted Churches* (Nashville: Abingdon, 1997).

25. The use of the term *confessing* has been adapted by a number of contemporary church movements and denominational caucuses, which frequently employ early church patristic models in support of conservative political agendas (such as the call for "family values" and concerted opposition to the ordination of homosexuals). For an overview of some of the theological debates surrounding the confessing movement within the United Methodist Church, see Henry H. Knight and Don E. Saliers, *The Conversation Matters: Why United Methodists Should Talk with One Another* (Nashville: Abingdon, 1999).

26. J. Philip Wogaman, *Faith and Fragmentation: Christianity for a New Age* (Philadelphia: Fortress, 1985), 12–14.

27. Johnson, 12.

28. Jaroslav Pelikan, *The Vindication of Tradition* (New Haven and London: Yale University Press, 1984), 65.

29. Johnson, 10–11.

30. Max L. Stackhouse, Preface from *Perspectives on the Social Gospel*, xii.

31. Rauschenbusch, *A Theology for the Social Gospel* (New York: Macmillan, 1917; reprint, Nashville: Abingdon, 1978), 1.

PART I: HISTORICAL AND THEOLOGICAL LEGACY
Chapter 1. Deciding Who Counts:
Toward a Revised Definition of the Social Gospel

1. Charles Howard Hopkins, *The Rise of the Social Gospel in American Protestantism, 1865–1915* (New Haven: Yale University Press, 1940), 3; Shailer Mathews, "Social Gospel," *A Dictionary of Religion and Ethics*, eds. Shailer Mathews and Gerald Birney Smith (New York: Macmillan, 1921), 416.

2. For a helpful survey of social gospel historiography, see Ralph Luker's essay, "Interpreting the Social Gospel: Reflections on Two Generations of Historiography," in *Perspectives on the Social Gospel: Papers from the Inaugural Social Gospel Conference at Colgate Rochester Divinity School*, ed. Christopher H. Evans (Lewiston, N.Y.: Edwin Mellen, 1999), 1–13.

3. Among the classic studies of this first generation are Hopkins, *Rise of the Social Gospel*; Aaron I. Abell, *The Urban Impact on American Protestantism* (Cambridge: Harvard University Press, 1943); and Henry F. May, *Protestant Churches and Industrial America* (New York: Harper & Row, 1949).

4. See, for example, Timothy L. Smith, *Revivalism and Social Reform in Mid-Nineteenth Century America* (Nashville: Abingdon, 1957).

5. See, for example, William R. Hutchison, "The Americanness of the Social Gospel; An Inquiry in Comparative History," *Church History* 44 (September 1975): 367–381; Richard Allen, *The Social Passion: Religion and Social Reform in Canada 1914–28* (Toronto: University of Toronto Press, 1971); Paul T. Phillips, *A Kingdom on Earth: Anglo-American Social Christianity, 1880–1940* (University Park, Pa.: Pennsylvania State University Press, 1996).

6. In *The Modernist Impulse in American Protestantism* (Cambridge: Harvard University Press, 1976), 165, William R. Hutchison asserted that not only was the concept of social salvation the critical key to social gospel theology, but it took precedence over individual salvation.

7. See, for example, John Lee Eighmy, "Religious Liberalism in the South during the Progressive Era," *Church History* 38 (September 1969): 359–372; Herbert G. Gutman, "Protestantism and the American Labor Movement: The Christian Spirit in the Gilded Age," in *Work, Culture and Society in Industrializing America: Essays in American*

Working-Class and Social History (New York: Knopf, 1976): 79–117; Ronald C. White Jr., *Liberty and Justice for All: Racial Reform and the Social Gospel (1875–1925)* (San Francisco: Harper & Row, 1990); Ralph E. Luker, *The Social Gospel in Black and White: American Racial Reform, 1885–1912* (Chapel Hill: University of North Carolina Press, 1991); John Patrick McDowell, *The Social Gospel in the South: The Woman's Home Mission Movement in the Methodist Episcopal Church, South, 1886–1939* (Baton Rouge: Louisiana State University Press, 1982); Susan Hill Lindley, "The Social Gospel," in *"You Have Stept Out of Your Place": A History of Women and Religion in America* (Louisville, Ky.: Westminster John Knox, 1996), 135–147.

8. Ronald C. White Jr. and C. Howard Hopkins, *The Social Gospel: Religion and Reform in Changing America* (Philadelphia: Temple University Press, 1976), 87.

9. For an argument on why Burroughs should be considered a part of the social gospel, see Susan Lindley, "'Neglected Voices' and *Praxis* in the Social Gospel," *Journal of Religious Ethics* 18 (spring 1990): 91–98.

10. Paul T. Phillips, *A Kingdom on Earth: Anglo-American Social Christianity, 1880–1940*, xxiii, 201.

11. See, for example, Janet Forsythe Fishburn, *The Fatherhood of God and the Victorian Family: The Social Gospel in America* (Philadelphia: Fortress, 1981.)

12. For example, Luker demonstrates in *The Social Gospel in Black and White* that even among African Americans and those white social gospelers who gave attention to racial issues there was a significant variation in specific goals and methods.

13. Christopher H. Evans, ed., *Perspectives on the Social Gospel: Papers from the Inaugural Social Gospel Conference at Colgate Rochester Divinity School*, xi.

14. Isabelle Horton, *The Burden of the City* (New York: Fleming H. Revell, 1904); reprinted, Carolyn De Swarte Gifford, ed., *The American Deaconess Movement in the Early Twentieth Century* (New York and London: Garland, 1987), 151–193. See also, for example, Mary Agnes Dougherty, "The Social Gospel According to Phoebe: Methodist Deaconesses in the Metropolis, 1885–1918," in Hilah F. Thomas and Rosemary Skinner Keller, eds., *Women in New Worlds: Historical Perspectives on the Wesleyan Tradition* (Nashville: Abingdon, 1981), 200–216.

Chapter 2. The Social Gospel Movement and the Question of Race

1. W. E.B. Du Bois, foreword to *The Souls of Black Folk* (New York: New American Library, 1969).

2. By white supremacy, I do not mean the common current usage of this term to describe violent, hate-filled, white-rights movements such as the Ku Klux Klan or the Aryan Nation. Instead, white supremacy merely means the adherence of a group or organization to the maintenance of a white-dominated society in which the primary actors—morally, politically, religiously, socially, and economically—are exclusively "white people." In particular, a white supremacist organization lacks the moral imagination to contemplate, let alone create a beloved community as conceived by Martin Luther King Jr., in which opportunities for all are normative and in which relationships between individuals and groups are not limited and facilitated solely by the groups' or individuals' racial identity.

3. The documentation of the racism of white social gospelers is so extensive as to be irrefutable. See Preston N. Williams, "The Social Gospel and Race Relations: A Case Study of a Social Movement," *Toward a Discipline of Social Ethics: Essays in Honor of Walter George Muelder*, ed. Paul Deats (Boston: Boston University Press, 1972) 232–256; Susan Lindley, "Neglected Voices and Praxis in the Social Gospel," *Journal of Religious Ethics*, vol. 18:

75–102; Calvin Morris, "Reverdy Ransom, the Social Gospel and Race," *Journal of Religious Thought*, vol. 41: 7–21, spring-summer, 1984. For a highly unpersuasive and contrary view, see Ralph E. Luker, "Social Gospel and the Failure of Racial Reform, 1877–1898," *Church History*, vol. 46: 80–99, March 1977.

4. H. Richard Niebuhr writes of this phenomenon as follows: "But, on the whole, the sufficient reason for the frankness with which the color line has been drawn in the church is the fact that race discrimination is so respectable an attitude in America that it could be accepted by the church without subterfuge of any sort." From *The Social Sources of Denominationalism* (New York: New American Library, 1957) 236.

5. All of the efforts of racial reform that are cited in Luker's article are attempts to maintain a white-dominated society. If they had succeeded, that is the only society they could have created. Accordingly, the failure of such reforms is fairly irrelevant in that their success would have, at best, simply created a different white-dominated society than the one that was historically achieved. As Luker notes, "This conception of the origins and nature of the social gospel also refocuses the whole approach to the social gospel to the three surviving traditions of nineteenth-century racial reform: the home missions movement, the post-abolition tradition of civil equity, and the colonization movement. Finally, it sheds light on and is re-enforced by the response of the social gospel prophets to the problem of lynching in the 1890s." All three reforms were designed to create a new white-dominated society in the South and hence were by definition, white supremacist. In addition, the work of social gospelers in the nineteenth and twentieth centuries was never actively effective in opposing lynching, in contrast to the work of a genuine anti-lynching Christian, Ida B. Wells-Barnett.

6. Promise Keepers, for example, have had very limited success in opposing racism and engendering genuine far-reaching race relations among American fathers.

7. Ransom in particular fought for social gospel initiatives. Calvin Morris writes of Ransom's endeavors in "Reverdy Ransom, the Social Gospel and Race": Ransom stressed that, "The battles of socialism are not to be fought by white men, for the benefit of white men. It is not, we have said, a question of race, it is a question of men. . . . When millions of toilers are degraded, labor is degraded, man is degraded. While one class of toilers is outraged and oppressed, no man is free."

8. Jack Dempsey, for example, was noted for not defending his title against black opponents.

9. See Lindley, "Neglected Voices," 94.

10. See Emilie Townes, "Because God Gave Her Vision: The Religious Impulse of Ida B. Wells-Barnett," in *Spirituality & Social Responsibility*, ed. Rosemary S. Kelley (Nashville: Abingdon, 1993) 149.

11. Ibid.

12. Martin Luther King Jr., *Strength To Love* (Philadelphia: Fortress, 1981) 101.

13. The influence of Walter Rauschenbusch on King's thought is most comprehensively examined in Smith and Zepp's *Search for the Beloved Community: The Thinking of Martin Luther King, Jr.* (Valley Forge: Judson Press, 1974). See chapter 2, "Walter Rauschenbusch and the Social Gospel Movement." What is interesting about their work, however, is in the second chapter and their concluding chapter, "Vision of the Beloved Community," where they point out King's complete commitment to the realization of the beloved community and its shared ideas with Rauschenbusch's kingdom of God, without ever addressing the enormous difference between the two: King was fighting to realize a community free from white domination, in which power is shared by all; Rauschenbusch's conception never contemplates or dreams of any human order in the kingdom of God that is not first white hegemonic. This systematic association

of the two concepts, coupled with the systematic glossing over of the opposing views of race, allow some writers to characterize King mistakenly as a carrier of the social gospel tradition.

14. King writes, "I was immediately influenced by the social gospel. In the early 1950s I read Walter Rauschenbusch's *Christianity and the Social Crisis,* a book which left an indelible imprint on my thinking. . . . Rauschenbusch gave to American Protestantism a sense of social responsibility that it should never lose. The gospel at its best deals with the whole man, not only his soul but also his body, not only his spiritual well-being but also his material well-being. A religion that professes a concern for the souls of men and is not equally concerned about the slums that damn them, the economic conditions that strangle them, and the social conditions that cripple them, is a spiritually moribund religion." *Strength To Love* (Philadelphia: Fortress, 1981) 150.

15. Vincent Harding, a noted King scholar, writes of him on this point: "So he moved and sent his staff among the Native Americans, Hispanics, Appalachian whites, returned to the young black gang members of Chicago and Cleveland, attempting to recruit a courageous band of rainbow warriors for the still inadequately defined, but deeply felt, nonviolent army of hope. So he began to consider making connections with Latin American sisters and brothers who believed in the possibilities of nonviolent revolution, for he knew that our hope and our pain were organically connected to their own." From *Martin Luther King: The Inconvenient Hero* (Maryknoll: Orbis, 1997) 108.

16. Williams, "The Social Gospel and Race Relations: A Case Study of a Social Movement," in *Toward a Discipline of Social Ethics: Essays in Honor of Walter George Muelder,* 246.

17. Ibid., 247.

18. Ibid.

19. Ibid.

Chapter 3. The Kingdom of God, the Church, and the World: The Social Gospel and the Making of Theology in the Twentieth-Century Ecumenical Movement

1. Walter Rauschenbusch, *A Theology for the Social Gospel* (Nashville and New York: Abingdon, 1945), 131. Originally published in 1917.

2. Ibid., 146.

3. One of Rauschenbusch's early and influential books was *Christianizing the Social Order* (New York: Macmillan, 1912).

4. While many ecumenical histories identify the World Missionary Conference of 1910, held in Edinburgh, as the first major ecumenical conference of the twentieth century, I consider the 1910 conference to have been the culmination of a series of missionary conferences held in the nineteenth century. These conferences began with gatherings in London and New York in 1854, continued in Liverpool in 1860, in London in 1878 and 1888, and in New York in 1900. The purpose of these conferences was to enable Protestants to cooperate more helpfully on various fields of mission. Ecumenical conferences have aimed to bring the churches into agreement or unity, the nature of which has itself been debated.

5. Rauschenbusch, *A Theology for the Social Gospel,* 129–130.

6. Edward Shillito, *Life and Work: The Universal Christian Conference on Life and Work Held in Stockholm, 1925* (London: Longmans, Green & Co., 1926), 3. See also, for example, Charles Henry Brent, *Understanding Being, an Interpretation of the Universal Christian Conference on Life and Work, Held in Stockholm, August 15–30, 1925* (London: Longmans, Green & Co., 1925).

7. G. K. A. Bell, ed., *The Stockholm Conference 1925: The Official Report of the Universal Christian Conference on Life and Work held in Stockholm, 19–30 August, 1925* (Oxford: Oxford University Press; London: Humphrey Milford, 1926), 4.

8. Ibid.

9. Ibid., 5.

10. The World Alliance for Promoting International Friendship through the Churches was formally founded on August 2, 1914, the day after World War I erupted. On August 3, delegates who had gathered in Constance (Switzerland) quickly left for their homes. The Alliance came in to being in response to the conviction of church leaders, already in the early years of the twentieth century, that Christian principles ought to help shape international relations and, most particularly, to promote mutual understanding among nations toward the strengthening of international law. Charles S. Macfarland, general secretary of the Federal Council of Churches of Christ in the USA, took the lead in work for closer relationships between U.S. and European churches. In 1914, Andrew Carnegie contributed $2 million to finance the activities of the World Alliance, which held its first postwar conference in 1919.

11. Christian socialism was a movement for social reform initiated in mid-nineteenth century primarily by members of the Church of England. Among its best-known leaders in England were F. D. Maurice, Charles Kingsley, and J. M. F. Ludlow. Archbishop William Temple, a pioneering ecumenical figure in the 1920s and 1930s, stood in the lineage of this tradition. See M. B. Reckitt, *Maurice to Temple: A Century of Social Movement in the Church of England* (1947).

12. For his statement of working guidelines bringing together Christian theology, legislation, and industrial problems, see William Temple, *Christianity and the Social Order* (Harmondsworth, Shepheard-Wolwyn & SPCK, 1942).

13. Bell, ed., *The Stockholm Conference 1925*, 18.

14. Ibid., 38–45.

15. Ibid., 38.

16. In 1917, the Roman Catholic code of canon law forbade Catholics from attending meetings, particularly public meetings, with non-Catholics, and most particularly if they were for discussion of faith, unless they received permission from the apostolic see or their local bishop. This canon law was confirmed in 1928 by an encyclical from Pope Pius XI, *Mortalium Animos:* "There are those who nurture hope that it would be easy to lead people, despite their religious differences, to unite in the profession of certain doctrines accepted as a common basis of spiritual life. . . . Such efforts have no right to the approval of Catholics, since they are based on their erroneous opinion that all religions are more or less good and laudable. . . . The Apostolic See has never allowed Catholics to attend meetings of non-Catholics; the union of Christians can only go forward by encouraging the dissidents to return to the one true church." Cited in *Rome Has Spoken*, ed., Maureen Fiedler and Linda Rabben (New York: Crossroad, 1998), 106.

17. Bell, ed., *The Stockholm Conference 1925*, 56.

18. Ibid.

19. Ibid., 59.

20. Ibid., 76.

21. Ibid., 78.

22. Ibid., 140. See also Shailer Mathews, *The Church and the Changing Order* (New York: Macmillan, 1907), esp. chap. VI.

23. Ibid., 162.

24. Ibid., 186.

25. Ibid., 108.

26. At a 1933 meeting of the Universal Christian Council of Life and Work, the continuation committee of the conference, a German delegate declared, with regard to the Stockholm conference: "Its message is obsolete . . . the offspring of humanitarian ideas of the Enlightenment and the French Revolution. . . . The rising Reformation theology today would put a question-mark at almost every sentence in it." Cited in Edward Duff, S.J., *The Social Thought of the World Council of Churches* (London: Longmans, Green & Co., 1956), 33, n. 1.

27. Bell, ed., *The Stockholm Conference 1925*, 18.

28. Edward S. Woods, *Lausanne 1927: An Interpretation of the World Conference on Faith and Order Held in Lausanne, August 3–21, 1927* (New York: George H. Doran, 1927), 38.

29. Ibid., 68.

30. See H. N. Bates, ed., *Faith and Order: Proceedings of the World Conference, Lausanne, August 3–21, 1927* (New York: George H. Doran, 1927).

31. Nathan Söderblom, key architect and leader of the Stockholm conference, left the Lausanne conference early to fulfill other obligations. Later, he heard about the difficult debate on the report of Section VII, the section he had co-chaired. The debate was initiated by some delegates who strenuously objected to a proposal that Faith and Order collaborate with Life and Work and the World Alliance for Promoting Friendship through the Churches. Söderblom reflected that, if he had foreseen the difficulties, "I would have done my utmost to stay through the last day." Whether Söderblom would have been able to forestall what came to be ongoing tension between Faith and Order and Life and Work ecumenism can, of course, only be a matter for speculation. Söderblom quotation from Marlin VanElderen, "Editorial," *The Ecumenical Review* 1 (1996), 1.

32. See, for example, "Non-theological Factors that May Hinder or Accelerate the Church's Unity," in *The Ecumenical Movement: An Anthology of Key Texts and Voices*, ed. Michael Kinnamon and Brian E. Cope (Geneva: World Council of Churches; Grand Rapids: Wm. B. Eerdmans, 1997), 212–216. This text, written by scholars such as C. H. Dodd, George Cragg, and Jacques Ellul, is actually quite ambiguous. On one hand, the text insists that "all too human factors, for example, language, forms of government and civilization, and . . . economic and social structures," have and may indeed "threaten the unity of the Church." On another hand, these factors are clearly set apart, "for want of a better term," as "non-theological."

33. Anna-Marie Aagaard, "The Present Status of the Ecumenical Movement," in *Ecumenism: Present Realities and Future Prospects*, ed. Lawrence S. Cunningham (Notre Dame: University of Notre Dame, 1998), 70.

34. "Report of the Section on Church, Community and State in Relation to Economic Power," in *The Oxford Conference: Official Report* (Chicago and New York: Willett, Clark & Co., 1938), 76.

35. See Klaus Scholder, *The Churches and the Third Reich*, vol. 2: *The Year of Disillusionment: 1934 Barmen and Rome*, trans. John Bowden (Philadelphia: Fortress, 1988), 122ff.

36. *The Oxford Conference*, 76.

37. Ibid., 79, 155, for example.

38. Ibid., 187–188.

39. Ibid., 45.

40. The topics of the conference's four sections alone confirm this: 1) the grace of our Lord Jesus Christ; 2) the church of Christ and the Word of God; 3) the church of Christ: ministry and sacraments; and 4) the church's unity in life and worship. See *The Second World Conference on Faith and Order, Edinburgh 1937*, ed. Leonard Hodgson (London: SCM Press, 1938).

41. Ibid., 275. See, for example, the very influential text, "Affirmation of Union in Allegiance to Our Lord Jesus Christ," which began: "We are one in faith in our Lord Jesus Christ, the incarnate Word of God."

42. Vatican II was inspired theologically by the work of the so-called *theologie nouvelle*, a Roman Catholic theological "movement" centered in France during the 1940s and 1950s. Among its key figures were M. D. Chenu, Yves Congar, Jean Danielou, and Henri de Lubac.

43. "The Dogmatic Constitution on the Church" (*Lumen Gentium*), in *The Documents of Vatican II*, ed. Walter M. Abbott, S. J. (New York: Guild Press, American Press, Association Press, 1966), 15.

44. "Report of Section I: The Holy Spirit and the Catholicity of the Church," in *The Ecumenical Movement: An Anthology of Key Texts and Voices*, eds. Michael Kinnamon and Brian Cope, 96. See also *The Uppsala Report 1968*, ed. Norman Goodall (Geneva: World Council of Churches, 1968), 13–18.

45. This study initiative was influenced by a second Vatican II document, the "Pastoral Constitution on the Church in the Modern World" (*Gaudium et Spes*). See *The Documents of Vatican II*, 183ff.

46. *Unity in Today's World*. The Faith and Order Studies on "Unity of the Church— Unity of Humankind," ed. Geiko Muller-Fahrenholz (Geneva: World Council of Churches, 1978), 26. Five aspects of the "unity of mankind" theme were explored: the struggle for justice; the encounter with living faiths; the struggle against racism; the handicapped in society; differences in culture.

47. The Joint Working Group was established in 1968, just after Vatican II, to be the official consultative forum of the Roman Catholic Church and the World Council of Churches. It was charged with the tasks of initiating, evaluating, and sustaining collaboration among their various organizations and programs.

48. *Your Kingdom Come: Mission Perspectives*. Report on the World Conference on Mission and Evangelism, Melbourne, Australia, 12–15 May 1980 (Geneva: World Council of Churches, 1980), 235–236.

49. Ibid., 184. See also *Witnessing to the Kingdom: Melbourne and Beyond*, ed. Gerald H. Anderson (Maryknoll: Orbis Books, 1982).

50. In this way, Melbourne resounded the Second Assembly of the World Council of Churches, held in Evanston, Illinois, in 1954: "The Church's visible structure passes away with age, but as the chosen people of God it will enter into the glory of the Kingdom of God that is to come." Cited in *Witnessing to the Kingdom*, 22.

51. *Church and World: The Unity of the Church and the Renewed Human Community*. A Faith and Order Study Document (Geneva: World Council of Churches, 1990), 4. This study focused on two major problems as obstacles to the unity of the church—the community of women and men, and the search for justice. See also, Thomas F. Best, ed., *Beyond Unity-in-Tension: Unity, Renewal and the Community of Women and Men* (Geneva: World Council of Churches, 1988) and Gennadios Limouris, ed., *Church, Kingdom, World: The Church as Mystery and Prophetic Sign* (Geneva: World Council of Churches, 1986).

52. Ibid., 23–24.

53. See *Baptism, Eucharist and Ministry* (Geneva: World Council of Churches, 1982), para. 20.

54. *Costly Unity: Koinonia and Justice, Peace and Creation*, eds. Thomas F. Best and Wesley Granberg-Michaelson (Geneva: World Council of Churches, 1993), 86.

55. *Costly Commitment: Ecclesiology and Ethics*, eds. Thomas F. Best and Martin Robra (Geneva: World Council of Churches, 1995), 74–75.

56. Ibid.

57. "Costly Obedience," in *Ecclesiology and Ethics: Ecumenical Ethical Engagement, Moral Formation and the Nature of the Church*, eds. Thomas F. Best and Martin Robra (Geneva: World Council of Churches, 1997), 61–63.

58. See, for example, reports of international assemblies of the Ecumenical Association of Third-World Theologians. These are all published by Orbis Books and include *African Theology en Route* (1979), *Asia's Struggle for Full Humanity* (1980), *The Challenge of Basic Christian Communities* (1981), *Irruption of the Third World: Challenge to Theology* (1983), *Doing Theology in a Divided World* (1985), and *With Passion and Compassion: Third World Women Doing Theology* (1986). See also *Theology By the People: Reflections on Doing Theology in Community*, eds. Samuel Amirtham and John S. Pobee (Geneva: World Council of Churches, 1986).

59. Mark Ellingsen, *The Cutting Edge: How Churches Speak on Social Issues* (Geneva: World Council of Churches; Grand Rapids: Wm. B. Eerdmans, 1993), 136–137.

60. At the First Assembly of the World Council of Churches in Amsterdam 1948, the Orthodox churches of the four ancient Patriarchates of Alexandria, Antioch, Constantinople, and Jerusalem, together with the Church of Greece, the Orthodox Church in the United States, and the Russian Exarchate in Western Europe, were represented and became members. The Eastern European Orthodox churches of Bulgaria, Poland, Romania, and the USSR became members of the World Council of Churches at the Third Assembly in New Delhi in 1961.

61. See "Patriarchal and Synodical Encyclical of 1902," in *Orthodox Visions of Ecumenism: Statements, Messages and Reports on the Ecumenical Movement 1902–1922*, compiled by Gennadios Limouris (Geneva: World Council of Churches, 1994), 1–5. For a recent discussion of a common date for Easter, see Dagmar Heller, "A Common Date for Easter—a Reality in the New Millennium?" in *Ecumenical Trends*, vol. 29, no. 3 (March 2000), 8/40–12/44.

62. "Encyclical of the Ecumenical Patriarchate, 1920," in *Orthodox Visions of Ecumenism*, 10.

63. Ibid., 11.

64. See W. A. Visser't Hooft, *The Genesis and Formation of the World Council of Churches* (Geneva: World Council of Churches, 1982), 4.

65. "Encyclical of the Ecumenical Patriarchate, 1920," 10.

66. Ibid., 9–10.

67. Rauschenbusch, *A Theology for the Social Gospel*, 129, 146.

Chapter 4. Gender and the Kingdom of God: The Family Values of Walter Rauschenbusch

1. I am grateful to Naomi Annandale, Colgate Rochester Master of Divinity student, for her valuable research assistance in writing this chapter.

2. Letter Walter Rauschenbusch (WR) to "Mr. Lyon," 10 January 1908, Walter Rauschenbusch Papers (WRP), box 108, American Baptist Historical Society, Rochester, New York.

3. Janet Forsythe Fishburn, *The Fatherhood of God and the Victorian Family: The Social Gospel in America* (Philadelphia: Fortress, 1981), 122. For an overview of how social gospel men viewed questions of gender, see also William D. Lindsey, "The Social Gospel and Feminism," *American Journal of Theology and Philosophy* 13 (1992): 194–210; Susan Hill Lindley, *You Have Stept Out of Your Place: A History of Women and Religion in America* (Louisville, Ky.: Westminster/John Knox Press, 1996), 136–138. The historiography related to the role of women in propagating the social gospel will be examined

in an upcoming volume edited by Wendy J. Deichmann Edwards, *Women, Gender and the Social Gospel.*

4. Betty A. DeBerg, *Ungodly Women: Gender and the First Wave of American Fundamentalism* (Minneapolis: Fortress, 1990), 151–152.

5. Walter Rauschenbusch, *Christianizing the Social Order* (New York: Macmillan, 1912), 263.

6. Walter Rauschenbusch, *Dare We Be Christians? A Classic Treatise on Love* (Cleveland: Pilgrim Press, 1914; reprint, Cleveland: Pilgrim, 1993), 23.

7. Donovan E. Smucker, *The Origins of Walter Rauschenbusch's Social Ethics* (Montreal & Kingston: McGill-Queen's University Press, 1994), 62.

8. Walter Rauschenbusch, *Christianizing the Social Order*, 131.

9. See Rosalind Rosenberg, *Beyond Separate Spheres: Intellectual Roots of Modern Feminism* (New Haven and London: Yale University Press, 1982), and Nancy F. Cott, *The Grounding of Modern Feminism* (New Haven and London: Yale University Press, 1987).

10. Very little attention is paid to the Rauschenbusch children in the two standard biographies of Walter Rauschenbusch. See Dores Robinson Sharpe, *Walter Rauschenbusch* (New York: Macmillan, 1942), and Paul Minus, *Walter Rauschenbusch: American Reformer* (New York: Macmillan, 1988). Hilmar (Stephen), Rauschenbusch's oldest son, was an economist, an author, and a staff member of the U.S. Department of the Interior during the New Deal administrations of Franklin Roosevelt. The middle son, Paul, was a student of the famed liberal economist John R. Commons, and pioneered in the development of America's earliest unemployment compensation legislation. The youngest son, Carl, was a longtime member of the New York State Department of Labor. Elizabeth (Lisa), the youngest child, became a fine arts and drama professor at the University of Rochester. All five children adopted the spelling *Rauschenbush* for their last name after their father's death. The Walter Rauschenbusch Papers in Rochester, New York, contains an extensive collection of the children's papers.

11. Biographical information on Winifred was found in the WRP, box 167.

12. Letter Winifred Rauschenbusch to WR, no date. WRP, box 144. Ironically, later in life Winifred identified herself, like her father, as a pacifist and socialist. She did not consider herself a feminist, as the term came to be used in the 1960s. See WRP, box 167.

13. In a recently published essay, Casey Nelson Blake examines how the relationship between Walter and Winifred Rauschenbusch influenced the thought of Winifred's son, philosopher Richard Rorty. Blake argues that the father-daughter correspondence "reveal a tragic story, in which father and daughter sought desperately to find some way of communicating with one another but in the end failed to find a common ground for negotiating their disagreements." As I argue in this essay, however, I believe Blake exaggerates the level of personal animosity between the two. See Casey Nelson Blake, "Private Life and Public Commitment: From Walter Rauschenbusch to Richard Rorty," in *A Pragmatist's Progress?: Richard Rorty and American Intellectual History*, ed. John Pettegrew (Lanham, Md.: Rowman & Littlefield, 2000), 85–101.

14. *Christianity and the Social Crisis* (New York: Macmillan, 1907; reprint, Louisville, Ky.: Westminster/John Knox Press, 1991), 421.

15. Rauschenbusch, *Christianizing the Social Order*, 262.

16. For details on Rauschenbusch's parents and on Pauline Rauschenbusch, see Paul Minus, *Walter Rauschenbusch: American Reformer* (New York: Macmillan, 1988).

17. See, for example, Leonard I. Sweet, *The Minister's Wife: Her Role in Nineteenth-Century American Evangelicalism* (Philadelphia: Temple University Press, 1983), 220–236.

18. Susan Curtis, *A Consuming Faith: The Social Gospel and Modern American Culture* (Baltimore and London: Johns Hopkins University Press, 1991), 112.

19. Letter WR to Winifred Rauschenbusch, 19 July 1910, WRP, box 143.

20. Letter WR to family, 7 January 1911, WRP, box 108.

21. Letter WR to Hilmar (Stephen) Rauschenbusch, 19 July 1910, WRP, box 108.

22. Letter WR to family, 9 March 1911, WRP, box 108.

23. Rauschenbusch Diary Book, WRP, box 143.

24. Letter WR to Winifred Rauschenbusch, 8 September 1908, WRP, box 143.

25. Letter WR to Winifred Rauschenbusch, 19 July 1910, WRP, box 143.

26. Letter WR to Winifred Rauschenbusch, 17 March 1914, WRP, box 180.

27. Letter WR to Winifred Rauschenbusch, 14 February 1916, WRP, box 144.

28. Letter WR to Winifred Rauschenbusch, 16 July 1915, WRP, box 180.

29. Letter WR to Winifred Rauschenbusch, 14 February 1916, WRP, box 144.

30. Letter WR to Winifred Rauschenbusch, 15 November 1912, WRP, box 180.

31. Letter Winifred Rauschenbusch to WR, 10 February 1914, WRP, box 143.

32. Letter WR to Winifred Rauschenbusch, 25 February 1916, WRP, box 144.

33. Letter WR to Winifred Rauschenbusch, 29 January 1917, WRP, box 180.

34. See, for example, letter WR to Winifred Rauschenbusch, 26 October 1917, WRP, box 143.

35. Letter Winifred Rauschenbusch to WR, 24 October 1916, WRP, box 144.

36. Letter WR to Winifred Rauschenbusch, 4 November 1916, WRP, box 144.

37. Letter WR to Winifred Rauschenbusch, 8 March 1917, WRP, box 144.

38. Letter WR to Winifred Rauschenbusch, 10 March 1918, WRP, box 143.

39. Letter Pauline Rauschenbusch to WR, 14 July 1918, WRP, box 37.

40. Feminist historians have pointed to the gender dualism of many social gospel proponents, whose "liberal" theological pronouncements were often undercut by their own resistance to social change. For a fuller discussion on this point, see Janet Fishburn's essay in this book. At the same time, further research is needed on selected male and female church leaders to ascertain more fully how gender was understood as a justice issue in twentieth-century American Protestantism.

41. Letter Winifred Rauschenbush to Dores Sharpe, 8 October 1941, WRP, box 155.

42. Casey Nelson Blake argues that part of the significance of the conflict between Walter and Winifred was that it accentuated the deep divide that was developing in America between old-school social gospelers like Rauschenbusch and emerging liberal, more secular, progressives, like Winifred. Blake, however, ignores the popularity Rauschenbusch enjoyed as a leading speaker on college campuses throughout the 1900s and how increasing numbers of social gospel adherents after World War I embraced emerging secular currents related to pragmatist philosophy and functionalist social psychology (leaders who shared the same generational identity as Winifred). See, for example, William McGuire King, "The Emergence of Social Gospel Radicalism: The Methodist Case," *Church History* 50 (December 1981): 436–449.

43. Rauschenbusch, *A Theology for the Social Gospel* (New York: Macmillan, 1917; reprint, Nashville: Abingdon,1978), 227.

Chapter 5. Women Creating Communities—
and Community—in the Name of the Social Gospel

1. Isabella Horton, *High Adventure: Life of Lucy Rider Meyer* (New York: Methodist Book Concern, 1928), 76.

2. *Deaconess Advocate* (March 1911), 8.

3. Mary Agnes Dougherty, *My Calling To Fulfill: Deaconesses in the United Methodist Tradition* (New York: General Board of Global Ministries, The United Methodist Church, 1997), 6.

4. Reverend Christian Golder, *History of the Deaconess Movement in the Christian Church* (Cincinnati: Jennings & Pey, 1903), chap. 14.

5. Susanna M.D. Frey, "Ancient and Modern Sisterhoods," *The Ladies Repository* (October 1872), 245, quoted in Dougherty, xv.

6. Isabella Horton, *The Burden of the City* (New York: Fleming H. Revell, 1904), 145, 146, quoted in Catherine Prelinger and Rosemary Keller, "The Function of Female Bonding," in *Women in New Worlds*, vol. 2, eds. Rosemary Keller, Louise Queen, and Hilah Thomas (Nashville: Abingdon, 1982), 327.

7. Golder, *History of the Deaconess Movement*, 579, quoted in Dougherty, 14.

8. Horton, *High Adventure*, 169, 136.

9. Ibid., 138.

10. Ibid., 109, 110.

11. *Deaconess Advocate* (September 1912), 9, quoted in Dougherty, 17.

12. *Message and Deaconess Advocate* (December 1895), 8, quoted in *Women and Religion in America, vol. I: The Nineteenth Century*, eds. Rosemary Radford Ruether and Rosemary Skinner Keller (San Francisco: Harper & Row, 1982), 281.

13. *The Heathen Woman's Friend* (May 1869), 2, quoted in *Women and Religion in America*, 243.

14. Willard Larkin, "Our Literature Work," *Lutheran Missionary Journal* (February 1890), 43, quoted in *Women and Religion in America*, 261.

15. Editorial, *The Woman's Evangel* (January 1882), 6, quoted in *Women and Religion in America*, 260.

16. "Laborers Wanted," *The Heathen Woman's Friend* (October 1869), 32, quoted in *Women and Religion in America*, 264.

17. "Suggestions for the Formation of Auxiliaries," *The Missionary Helper* (July 1878), 83, quoted in *Women and Religion in America*, 265.

18. J. L. Phillips, "Our Needs," *Missionary Helper* (July 1878), 74, quoted in *Women and Religion in America*, 262, 246.

19. Evelyn Brooks Higginbotham, *Righteous Discontent: The Women's Movement in the Black Baptist Church, 1880–1920* (Cambridge: Harvard University Press, 1993), 157.

20. Ibid., 176.

21. Jane Addams, *Twenty Years at Hull-House* (New York: New American Library, 1960; originally published 1910) 115.

22. Horton, *High Adventure*, 183. Eleanor Stebner, *The Women of Hull House: A Study in Spirituality, Vocation, and Friendship* (Albany: SUNY Press, 1997), 79.

23. Kathryn Kish Sklar, *Florence Kelley and the Nation's Work: The Rise of Women's Political Culture, 1830–1900* (New Haven: Yale University Press, 1995), 126.

24. Stebner, *The Women of Hull House*, 126.

25. Ibid., 107.

26. Ibid., 128.

27. Ibid., 125.

28. Ibid., 130.

29. Sklar, *Florence Kelley*, 175, 176, 183.

30. Ibid., 183.

31. Ibid., 185.

32. Ibid., 185, 183.

33. Ibid., 196.

34. *The Message and Deaconess Advocate* (November 1895), 3, 4, quoted in Ruether and Keller, *Women and Religion in America*, vol. 1, 282.

Chapter 6. Giving Patterns and Practices among Church Women in the Methodist Episcopal and the Colored Methodist Episcopal Churches, 1870–1920: A Social Gospel Perspective

1. Lawrence Mamiya, "A Social History of the Bethel African Methodist Episcopal Church in Baltimore: The House of God and the Struggle for Freedom," *American Congregations*, vol. 1, eds. James P. Wind and James W. Lewis (Chicago: University of Chicago Press, 1994), 246.

2. Ibid., 247.

3. Robert Wood Lynn, "Why Give?: Stewardship, A Documentary History of One Strand in American Protestant Teachings About Giving," unpublished manuscript, xii.

4. Robert Wood Lynn, "Why Give?," *Financing American Religion*, eds. Mark Chaves and Sharon Miller (Walnut Creek, Calif.: Alta Mira Press, 1999), 58.

5. Ibid., 59.

6. Ibid., citing Ben Primer, *Protestants and American Business Methods* (Ann Arbor: UMI Research Press, 1979).

7. Ibid.

8. Ibid.

9. Ibid.

10. Ibid., 60. 1 Cor. 16:2 reads as follows: "On the first day of every week, each of you is to put aside and save whatever extra you earn, so that collections need not be taken when I come."

11. Ibid.

12. Washington Gladden, *The Christian Pastor and the Working Church* (New York: Charles Scribner's Sons, 1898), 378.

13. Lynn, "Why Give?" unpublished manuscript, 234.

14. H. Shelton Smith, Robert T. Handy and Lefferts A. Loetscher, *American Christianity: An Historical Interpretation with Representative Documents*, Vol. II (New York: Charles Scribner's Sons, 1963), 368.

15. Lynn, "Why Give?" unpublished manuscript, 215.

16. Ibid., xiv.

17. Ibid., 216.

18. Earl Kent Brown, "Women in Church History: Stereotypes, Archetypes and Operational Modalities," *Methodist History*, 18 (January 1980), 109–32.

19. Rosemary Skinner Keller, "Creating a Sphere for Women," *Women in New Worlds*, eds. Hilah F. Thomas and Rosemary Skinner Keller (Nashville: Abingdon, 1981), 246.

20. Ibid., 255.

21. Earl Kent Brown, "Women in Nineteenth Century Methodism" (a lecture given at Boston University School of Theology, April 16, 1986).

22. Dana L. Robert, *American Women in Mission: A Social History of Their Thought and Practice* (Macon: Mercer University Press, 1996), 144.

23. Ibid., 129.

24. Thomas and Keller, *Women in New Worlds*, 255.

25. Robert, *American Women in Mission*, 133.

26. Ibid.

27. James Thoburn, *Life of Isabella Thoburn* (New York: Jennings and Pye, 1903), 368.

28. Earl Kent Brown, "Isabella Thoburn," *Methodist History* 22 (July 1984), 219.

29. For the official history of the Colored (later Christian) Methodist Episcopal

Church, see Othal Hawthorne Lakey, *The History of the CME Church*, revised (Memphis: The CME Publishing House, 1996).

30. Othal Lakey and Betty Stephens, *God in My Mama's House: The Women's Movement in the CME Church* (Memphis: The CME Publishing House, 1994), 73.

31. Ibid., 79.

32. Ibid.

33. Ibid.

34. Ibid., 80.

35. Ibid.

36. Ibid.

37. Lakey, *The History of the CME Church*, 303.

38. Lakey and Stephens, *God in My Mama's House*, 94.

39. Ibid., 82.

40. Ibid., 88.

41. Lakey, *The History of the CME Church*, 413f.

42. Dean Hoge, Charles Hoge, Patrick McNamara, and Michael J. Donahue, *Money Matters: Personal Giving in American Churches* (Louisville, Ky.: Westminster John Knox Press, 1996), 130–43.

43. Walter Rauschenbusch, *Christianizing the Social Order* (New York: Macmillan, 1912), 464–65.

PART II: THE SOCIAL GOSPEL TODAY

Chapter 7. Social Salvation: The Social Gospel as Theology and Economics

1. Walter Rauschenbusch, *A Theology for the Social Gospel* (1st ed.: 1917; Louisville: Westminster John Knox Press, 1997), 23–30.

2. For informative discussions of race and the social gospel movement, see Ralph E. Luker, *The Social Gospel in Black and White: American Racial Reform, 1885–1912* (Chapel Hill: University of North Carolina Press, 1991); and Ronald C. White Jr., *Liberty and Justice for All: Racial Reform and the Social Gospel (1877–1925)* (New York: Harper & Row, 1990). Washington Gladden was one of the social gospel leaders who welcomed black speakers to his pulpit and who worked for many years to create new educational and industrial opportunities for blacks, especially through the programs of the American Missionary Association.

3. See Washington Gladden, *Being a Christian: What It Means and How to Begin* (Boston: Congregational Publishing Society, 1876); Gladden, *The Christian Way: Whither It Leads and How to Go On* (New York: Dodd, Mead & Co., 1877).

4. See Charles H. Hopkins, *The Rise of the Social Gospel in American Protestantism, 1865–1915* (New Haven: Yale University Press, 1940), 113–117, 175–176, 194–195, 260; Henry F. May, *Protestant Churches and Industrial America* (New York: Harper & Brothers, 1949), 254; Jacob Henry Dorn, *Washington Gladden: Prophet of the Social Gospel* (Columbus: Ohio State University Press, 1967), 200–201; Josiah Strong, *Our Country* (New York: Baker & Taylor, 1885), 138–139; Richard T. Ely, *Ground Under Our Feet: An Autobiography* (New York: Macmillan, 1938), 140–143.

5. Washington Gladden, *Applied Christianity: Moral Aspects of Social Questions* (Boston: Houghton Mifflin, 1889), 8–32; see Gladden, *Recollections* (Boston: Houghton Mifflin, 1909), 300–304.

6. Washington Gladden, *Working People and Their Employers* (New York: Funk and Wagnalls, 1894), 44–45; "industrial system" quote in Gladden, *Applied Christianity*, 32–33.

7. Gladden, *Applied Christianity*, 34–35. See Richard T. Ely, ed., *A History of Cooperation in America* (Baltimore: Johns Hopkins University Press, 1888); Nicholas Paine

Gilman, *Profit Sharing Between Employer and Employee: A Study in the Evolution of the Wages System* (London: Macmillan, 1890); Gladden's thinking on profit sharing was strongly influenced by Sedley Taylor, *Profit-Sharing Between Labor and Capital, Six Essays* (New York: Humboldt, 1886).

8. Gladden, *Applied Christianity*, 53–101; quotes, 98, 100.

9. Washington Gladden, *Tools and the Man: Property and Industry Under the Christian Law* (Boston: Houghton Mifflin, 1893), quotes, 214, 124; discussion of cooperative ownership, 190–203.

10. Ibid., 130, 271.

11. Ibid., 264–265; closing quote in Washington Gladden, *Christianity and Socialism* (New York: Eaton & Mains, 1905), 141.

12. Gladden, *Christianity and Socialism*, 102–138, right to property statement, 92; Gladden, *Social Facts and Forces* (New York: G. P. Putnam's Sons, 1897), 80–86; Gladden, *Recollections*, 308–309; Gladden, *Tools and the Man*, 294–302; quotes, 299, 300.

13. Washington Gladden, *The Labor Question* (Boston: Pilgrim Press, 1911), 3–55, 98–110; quote, 55; Gladden, *Recollections*, 306–308; Gladden, *Social Facts and Forces*, 81–82; unidentified "vindictive opposition" quote in *Recollections*, 305; see John L. Shover, "Washington Gladden and the Labor Question," *Ohio Historical Quarterly* 68 (October 1959), 344–345.

14. Gladden, *Tools and the Man*, 1–2.

15. Ibid., 3–4, 6; see Washington Gladden, *Social Salvation* (Boston: Houghton Mifflin, 1902), 1–31; Gladden, *Burning Questions of the Life That Now Is, and of That Which Is to Come* (London: James Clarke, 1890), 223–248; Gladden, *The Church and the Kingdom* (New York: Fleming H. Revell, 1894).

16. For his early struggles with the question, see Shailer Mathews, "The Social Teaching of Paul, 1: The Social Content of Early Messianism," *The Biblical World* 19 (1902), 34–46; "II: The Social Content of Messianism in New Testament Times," 113–121; "III: The Apocalyptic Messianism of the Pharisees," 178–189; Mathews, "The Gospel and the Modern Man," *Christendom* 1 (1903), 300–302, 352–353, 399–401, 446–449, 489–491, 537–539; for his verdict, see Mathews, *The Messianic Hope in the New Testament* (Chicago: University of Chicago Press, 1905).

17. Gladden conversation with Carl S. Patton quoted in *First Church News: The Gladden Centennial* 6 (February 1936), 6–7.

18. Lyman Abbott, *The Twentieth Century Crusade* (New York: Macmillan, 1918), 62; Shailer Mathews, *Patriotism and Religion* (New York: Macmillan, 1918), 4; Ray H. Abrams, *Preachers Present Arms* (New York: Round Table Press, 1933), 54–55; Jacob Henry Dorn, *Washington Gladden*, 429; see Thomas J. Knock, *To End All Wars: Woodrow Wilson and the Quest for a New World Order* (Princeton: Princeton University Press, 1992), 108–122; Ronald Schaffer, *America in the Great War: The Rise of the Welfare State* (New York: Oxford University Press, 1991), xiv–xvii.

19. "All that is needed" text in Washington Gladden, "Loyalty," reprinted in Gladden, *The Interpreter* (Boston: Pilgrim Press, 1918), 81–96; quote, 96; "this war" in Gladden, "Making the World Safe for Democracy," sermon (April 29, 1917), Gladden Papers, Ohio State University.

20. Walter Rauschenbusch, *Christianity and the Social Crisis* (New York: Macmillan, 1907), 400–401.

21. Jacob Henry Dorn, *Washington Gladden: Prophet of the Social Gospel*, 431.

22. Washington Gladden, "A New Heart for the Nation," in Gladden, *The Interpreter*, 131–147; quotes, 145.

23. Ernst Troeltsch, *The Social Teaching of the Christian Churches*, 2 vols., trans. Olive Wyon (1st ed.: 1912; Louisville: Westminster John Knox Press, 1992), II: 1011.

24. See Walter Raushenbusch, *Christianizing the Social Order* (New York: Macmillan, 1912), 361–362; parts of this section are adapted from Gary Dorrien, *Soul in Society: The Making and Renewal of Social Christianity* (Minneapolis: Fortress, 1995), 290–292; and Dorrien, "Rethinking the Theory and Politics of Christian Socialism," *Democratic Left* (January 2000), 23–26.

25. See David Miller, *Market, State and Community: Theoretical Foundations of Market Socialism* (Oxford: Clarendon, 1990); Alec Nove, *Socialism, Economics, and Development* (London: Allen & Unwin, 1986); Julian Le Grand and Saul Estrin, eds., *Market Socialism* (Oxford: Oxford University Press, 1989); Frank Roosevelt and David Belkin, eds., *Why Market Socialism: Voices from Dissent* (Armonk, N.Y.: M. E. Sharpe, 1994).

26. See Gary Dorrien, *Reconstructing the Common Good: Theology and the Social Order* (Maryknoll, N.Y.: Orbis Books, 1992); Dorrien, *The Democratic Socialist Vision* (Totowa, N.J.: Rowman & Littlefield, 1986); Dorrien, *Soul in Society.*

Chapter 8. The Reawakening of the Evangelical Social Consciousness

1. Donald E. Miller, *Reinventing American Protestantism: Christianity in the New Millennium* (Berkeley: University of California Press, 1997); Christian Smith, *American Evangelicalism: Embattled and Thriving* (Chicago: University of Chicago Press, 1998).

2. Norris Magnuson, *Salvation in the Slums: Evangelical Social Work 1865–1920* (Metuchen, N.J.: Scarecrow Press, 1977).

3. George Marsden, *Fundamentalism and American Culture* (New York: Oxford University Press, 1980); Leonard I. Sweet, "The Evangelical Tradition in America," in *The Evangelical Tradition in America*, ed. Leonard I. Sweet (Macon, Ga.: Mercer University Press, 1984).

4. Timothy Weber, "Premillennialism and the Branches of Evangelicalism" in *The Variety of American Evangelicalism*, eds. Donald W. Dayton and Robert K. Johnson (Knoxville, Tenn.: University of Tennessee Press, 1991), 13.

5. Donald W. Dayton, *Theological Roots of Pentecostalism* (Scarecrow Press and Francis Asbury Press of Zondervan, 1987). See also Donald W. Dayton, "The Limits of Evangelicalism: the Pentecostal Tradition," in *The Variety of American Evangelicalism*, 36–56.

6. Donald W. Dayton, "Some Doubts about the Usefulness of the Category 'Evangelical'" in *The Variety of American Evangelicalism*, 245–51.

7. Evangelical alliance with neo-conservatism, as attested to by the impact of conservative Christians upon the Republican Party vis-à-vis the organizing efforts of the Christian Coalition and the political positions taken by Focus on the Family and the Family Research Council, represents, to some degree, an effort to "apply" their understanding of Christian faith to society.

8. Ronald J. Sider, *Just Generosity: A New Vision for Overcoming Poverty in America* (Grand Rapids: Baker, 1999), 217.

9. Joel Carpenter, *Revive Us Again: The Reawakening of American Fundamentalism* (New York: Oxford University Press, 1997), 6, 245.

10. Gary Dorrien, *The Remaking of Evangelical Theology* (Louisville, Ky.: Westminster John Knox, 1998). For fundamentalism's impact on defining gender roles, see Margaret Lamberts Bendroth, *Fundamentalism and Gender: 1875 to the Present* (New Haven: Yale University Press, 1993).

11. Carl F. H. Henry, *The Uneasy Conscience of Modern Fundamentalism* (Grand Rapids: Wm B. Eerdmans, 1947), 84.

12. Henry, *The Uneasy Conscience of Modern Fundamentalism*, 38.

13. George Marsden, *Reforming Fundamentalism: Fuller Seminary and the New Evangelicalism* (Grand Rapids: Eerdmans, 1987).

14. In 1965, evangelical leaders organized a Consultation on Christian Unity. This was followed by the Congress on the Church's Worldwide Mission (Wheaton, Illinois) and the World Congress on Evangelism (Berlin, Germany) in 1966, the U.S. Congress on Evangelism in 1969, KEY '73, and Lausanne (1973).

15. Mary A. Wilson, "Evangelical Voices: Attitudes Toward the Vietnam War" (master's thesis, California State University, Dominguez Hills, 1997), 28.

16. Kenneth T. Jackson, *Crabgrass Frontier: The Suburbanization of the United States* (New York: Oxford University Press, 1985).

17. Magnuson, *Salvation in the Slums*.

18. Henry, *The Uneasy Conscience of Modern Fundamentalism*, preface.

19. Virginia L. Brereton, *Training God's Army: The American Bible School, 1880–1940* (Bloomington, Ind.: Indiana University Press, 1990), xvii.

20. Larry J. McKinney, "The Fundamentalist Bible School as an Outgrowth of the Changing Patterns of Protestant Revivalism, 1882–1920," in *Religious Education*, 84:1, 605.

21. Charles Y. Furness, "Report to Council on Social Work Education," (1973).

22. Philadelphia College of Bible, publicity material (1963).

23. Douglas B. MacCorkle, interview with Margaret S. Furness, March 1995.

24. Larry J. McKinney, "Equipping for Service: A Historical Account of the Bible College Movement in North America" (Fayetteville, Ark.: AABC, 1997), 184.

25. Brereton, *Training God's Army*, 103, 104.

26. Charles Y. Furness, *Christianity Today*, (June 1965), reprinted with permission by Philadelphia College of Bible.

27. Charles Y. Furness, *The Christian and Social Action* (Old Tappan, N.J.: Fleming H. Revell, 1972), 171.

28. The Carver School closed in 1997 after the fundamentalist resurgence at Southern Seminary declared that social work was incongruent with its theological position.

29. *Integrating Faith and Practice: A History of The North American Association of Christians in Social Work 1950–1993* (St. Davids, Pa.: North American Association of Christians in Social Work, 1994), 21.

30. *Wheaton Declaration: Subscribed by the Delegates to the Congress on the Church's Worldwide Mission* (Washington, D.C.: Evangelical Missions Information Service, 1966), 24.

31. Carl F. H. Henry, *Evangelicals at the Brink of Crisis* (Waco, Tex.: Word Books, 1967), 72.

32. Richard Pierard calls Rufus Jones one of the "most forward looking thinkers" and a "real role model" who spoke out on social issues as far back as the 1950s. Timothy Tseng interview with Richard Pierard, May 24, 2000.

33. Rufus Jones, "What Programs and Activities Should Evangelicals Be Promoting and Implementing?" Billy Graham Center archives (Wheaton, Ill., May 1965) RG 37:1.

34. David O. Moberg, *Inasmuch: Christian Social Responsibility in the Twentieth Century* (Grand Rapids: Eerdmans, 1965). This was followed by *The Great Reversal: Evangelicalism and Social Concern* (Philadelphia: Lippincott, 1972).

35. Rufus Jones to Lewis Smedes, Dec. 13, 1972, Billy Graham Center archives (Wheaton, Ill.), RG 37:10.

36. Richard Pierard to W. T. Miller, Nov. 15, 1972, Billy Graham Center archives (Wheaton, Ill.), RG 37:3. See Robert Clouse, Robert Linder, and Richard Pierard, *The Cross and the Flag* (Carol Stream, Ill.: Creation House, 1972) and Richard Pierard, *The Unequal Yoke* (Philadelphia: J. B. Lippincott, 1970).

37. Donald W. Dayton, "The Radical Message of Evangelical Christianity" in *Churches in Struggle: Liberation Theologies and Social Change in North America*, ed. William K. Tabb (New York: Monthly Review Press, 1986), 211–222. Donald W. Dayton, *Discovering an Evangelical Heritage* (New York: Harper & Row, 1976).

38. Richard Pierard to W. T. Miller, Nov. 15, 1972, Billy Graham Center archives (Wheaton, Ill.), RG 37:3. Members of the EFM Board of Reference included such better known evangelicals like Tom Skinner, Ronald J. Sider, Lewis Smedes, David O. Moberg, Robert Webber, Stephen Monsma, and Anthony Campolo.

39. Circular letter from Walden Howard, undated. Billy Graham Center archives (Wheaton, Ill.), RG 37:3.

40. Ronald J. Sider to Stephen Charles Mott, Nov. 14, 1972 (circular letter), Billy Graham Center archives (Wheaton, Ill.), RG 37:4. Sider reported that 358 people contributed $5,762 to McGovern for president through Evangelicals for McGovern. Billy Graham Center archives, RG 37:10.

41. Ibid.

42. David O. Moberg to Lewis B. Smedes, Oct. 25, 1972; Lewis B. Smedes to Rufus Jones, Nov. 6, 1972; Rufus Jones to Lewis B. Smedes, Nov. 13, 1972. Billy Graham Center archives, Wheaton, Ill.

43. Stephen Mott recalls that the conference was essentially a conversation between John Howard Yoder's Anabaptist and Calvin College's Reformed views. Mott found that Yoder's *Politics of Jesus* was not the best way to understand his theology, since he sounded like a separatist with political criticism. At the conference, it became clear to Mott that Yoder was more deeply involved in politics. Timothy Tseng interview with Stephen C. Mott, May 31, 2000.

44. "The Chicago Declaration," in *The Social Gospel: Religion and Reform in Changing America*, eds. Ronald C. White Jr. and C. Howard Hopkins (Philadelphia: Temple University Press, 1976), 279–280.

45. Among the original signers were John Alexander (editor, *The Other Side*), William Bentley (president, National Black Evangelical Association), Donald Dayton, James Dunn, Samuel Escobar, Frank Gaebelain, Vernon Grounds, Nancy Hardesty, Mark Hatfield, Carl F. H. Henry, Paul B. Henry, Rufus Jones, David Moberg, Stephen Mott, Richard Mouw, William E. Pannell, John Perkins, Richard Pierard, Clark Pinnock, Ron Sider, Lewis Smedes, Foy Valentine, and Jim Wallis (editor, *The Post-American* [now *Sojourners*]).

46. This affirmation was strengthened at the Lausanne-sponsored "Consultation on the Relationship between Evangelism and Social Responsibility" at Grand Rapids in 1982 and again in *The Manila Manifesto* (1989). See The Lausanne Covenant, paras. 4 and 5; *Evangelism and Social Responsibility: An Evangelical Commitment: The Grand Rapids Report* (Paternoster, 1982); *The Manila Manifesto: An Elaboration of the Lausanne Covenant 15 Years Later* (Lausanne Committee for World Evangelization, 1989).

47. Rufus Jones to Lewis Smedes, Dec. 13, 1972, Billy Graham Center archives (Wheaton, Ill.), RG 37:10.

48. John R. W. Stott, *The Contemporary Christian: Applying God's Word to Today's World* (Downers Grove, Ill.: InterVarsity Press, 1992), 338.

49. Ibid., 350. It is interesting to note that evangelicals like John Stott say very little

about the social gospel other than repeating evangelical stereotypes of it. Walter Rauschenbusch, despite his evangelical piety, is considered anathema to many evangelicals. Perhaps unfairly, Richard Foster does not even mention Rauschenbusch in his survey of social justice spirituality in his book *Streams of Living Water: Celebrating the Great Traditions of Christian Faith* (San Francisco: Harper & Row, 1998).

50. Ibid., 339–349.

51. Stephen Mott interview with Timothy Tseng (May 31, 2000).

52. Ronald J. Sider, *Just Generosity: A New Vision for Overcoming Poverty in America* (Grand Rapids: Baker Books, 1999). Though *Sojourners* is not as eager to support school vouchers or Charitable Choice, there are indications of similar rethinking about an uncritical embrace of "secular left" policies in Jim Wallis's *The Soul of Politics: A Practical and Prophetic Vision for Change* (Maryknoll, N.Y.: Orbis Press, 1994).

53. Ronald Sider interview with Timothy Tseng (May 31, 2000).

54. As a Baptist who jealously guards the separation of church and state, Richard Pierard disagrees with ESA's support of vouchers and Charitable Choice. Richard Pierard interview with Timothy Tseng (May 23, 2000).

Chapter 9. The Social Gospel, Gender, and Homosexuality: Then and Now

1. Charles Stelzle, *A Son of the Bowery: The Life Story of an East Side American* (New York: Fleming H. Revell, 1924), 244.

2. Tom W. Smith, "The Emerging 21st Century American Family," *National Opinion Research Center* GSS Social Change Report No. 42 (November 24, 1999): 7–8.

3. Gender refers to whether a person is a woman or a man. Sexual orientation refers to the primary erotic and sexual attraction of a person to another of the same gender (homosexual), the other gender (heterosexual), or both genders (bisexual).

4. Charles Stelzle, *A Son of the Bowery*, 168.

5. Elizabeth Osborn Thompson, ed., *Charles Lemuel Thompson, An Autobiography* (New York: Fleming H. Revell, 1924), 153.

6. William Adams Brown, *A Teacher and His Times: A Story of Two Worlds* (New York: Charles Scribner's Sons, 1940), 135.

7. Ibid., 115.

8. There is a much fuller account of denominational politics around social gospel issues in Donald K. Gorrell, *The Age of Social Responsibility: The Social Gospel in the Progressive Era, 1900–1920* (Macon, Ga.: Mercer University Press, 1988), chap. 14.

9. Henry F. May, *Protestant Churches and Industrial America with a New Introduction by the Author* (rpt. New York: Octagon Books, 1977), 189–190.

10. Harry F. Ward, *The Social Creed of the Churches* (New York: Abingdon, 1914), 192.

11. Ibid., 7.

12. For a complete account of his position, see "Horace Bushnell on Women in Family, Church and Nation in Nineteenth Century Christian America," a dissertation submitted by Michiyo Morita to the Caspersen School of Graduate Studies of Drew University, Madison, N.J., October 1999.

13. Betty A. DeBerg, *Ungodly Women: Gender and the First Wave of American Fundamentalism* (Minneapolis: Fortress, 1990), 126–127.

14. Anna Adams Gordon, *The Life of Frances E. Willard* (Cambridge: Belknap, 1970), 128.

15. Carolyn DeSwarte Gifford, ed., *The Debate in the Methodist Episcopal Church Over Laity Rights for Women* (New York: Garland, 1987), introduction. This was a great blow

to Willard, provoking her to threaten that she would start a new denomination, one in which women would enjoy equality in church governance.

16. "From Parlor to Politics," Smithsonian National Museum of American History, November 1999.

17. Steven M. Buechler, *Women's Movements in the United States: Woman Suffrage, Equal Rights, and Beyond* (New Brunswick: Rutgers University Press, 1990), 171.

18. Ibid., 171–172.

19. Ibid., 184.

20. Ibid., 179.

21. For an excellent detailed description of fundamentalist antisuffrage positions and publications, see chapter 2 in Betty A. DeBerg, *Ungodly Women*. This chapter also contains descriptions of the "two spheres."

22. Theodore Roosevelt, "Women's Rights; And The Duties of Both Men and Women," *The Outlook* (February 3, 1912): 262–266.

23. Walter Rauschenbusch, "Some Moral Aspects of The 'Woman Movement'", *The Biblical World* XLII (October 1913): 198.

24. Ibid., 197.

25. Ibid., 195.

26. James Buckley, ed., *The New York Christian Advocate* (January 1, 1912).

27. Charles Stelzle, *A Son of the Bowery*, 170–171.

28. "Church and Society at Eighty," *Church and Society* 80, no. 1 (Sept./Oct. 1989): 6.

29. Betty A. DeBerg, *Ungodly Women*, 81, fn. 32.

30. Lois A. Boyd and R. Douglas Brackenridge, *Presbyterian Women in America: Two Centuries of a Quest for Status* (Westport, Conn.: Greenwood, 1983), 52.

31. John Patrick McDowell, *The Social Gospel in the South: The Woman's Home Mission Movement in the Methodist Episcopal Church, South, 1886–1939* (Baton Rouge: Louisiana State University Press, 1982), 139.

32. James E. Will, "Ordination of Woman" in *Women in New Worlds, Volume II*, eds. Rosemary Skinner Keller, Louise L. Queen, and Hilah F. Thomas (Nashville: Abingdon, 1982), 295.

33. Tom W. Smith, "The Emerging 21st Century American Family," 7.

34. Robert Wuthnow, *The Restructuring of American Religion: Society and Faith Since World War II* (Princeton, N.J.: Princeton University Press, 1981), 226.

35. Ibid., 230.

36. Steven M. Buechler, *Women's Movements in the United States*, 190.

37. Leonora Tubbs Tisdale, "Book Review of Clergy Women: An Uphill Calling," *The Princeton Seminary Bulletin* vol. XX, no. 3 (New Series, 1999): 345.

38. Mary P. Ryan, *Cradle of the Middle Class: The Family in Oneida County, New York, 1790–1865* (Cambridge: Cambridge University Press, 1981), 241–242.

39. "United Methodist News Service Backgrounder on Homosexuality," http://www.umc.org/umns/backgrounders/homosexuality.html.

40. Paul H. Sherry, "Now, No Condemnation, a Pastoral Letter to the United Church of Christ," (November 1998), 4.

41. The narration of legislative actions that follows can be found in more detail under "Homosexuality" at http://www.pcusa.org/pcusa/info/homosexu.htm.

42. For a fuller account of the extent to which the two sides were talking past each other, see Janet F. Fishburn, "The Presbyterian Sexuality Task Force: Confusing the Language of Moral Discourse," in *The Sexuality Debate in North American Churches, 1988–1993: Controversies, Unresolved Issues, Future Prospects*, ed. John J. Carey (Lewiston, N.Y.: Edward Mellen Press, 1995), 59–103.

43. Robert Moats Miller, *American Protestantism and Social Issues: 1919–1939* (Chapel Hill: The University of North Carolina Press, 1958), 348.

44. Lewis C. Daly, researcher, *A Moment to Decide: The Crisis in Mainstream Presbyterianism* (New York: Institute for Democracy Studies, May 2000), v.

45. "The Promotion of Social Righteousness" in *The Great Ends of the Church* (Louisville: Curriculum Publishing, Presbyterian Church (U.S.A.), 1997), 23.

46. Charles Stelzle, *A Son of the Bowery*, 257. Stelzle differs in many ways from most of his social gospel counterparts, including having more sympathetic views of women. He relates his successful ministry at Labor Temple to his childhood in a Bowery tenement. Unlike peers who were often patronizing in attempts to minister to tenement dwellers, he knew their life first-hand.

47. Benton Johnson, "From Old to New Agendas: Presbyterians and Social Issues in the Twentieth Century," in *The Confessional Mosaic: Presbyterians and Twentieth-Century Theology*, eds. Milton J. Coalter, John M. Mulder, and Louis B. Weeks (Louisville: Westminster/John Knox Press, 1990), 202–235. Although his topic is a close study of General Assembly social proclamations and agendas, Johnson notes the role of social activists inspired by the writing of Reinhold Niebuhr and a militant "new breed" of leaders inspired by black religious leaders of the Civil Rights movement in the 1960s. Yet, even when he claims liberal dominance in key positions within the denomination, the result is not Presbyterian public activism. It is a more highly politicized denomination (230–231).

48. Although sociologists have treated "changing family" as a topic since the early 1960s, the Presbyterian Church (U.S.A.) only acknowledged this as a topic worthy of reflection when a Task Force to study the subject was appointed in 1999.

49. Tom W. Smith, "The Emerging 21st Century American Family," 8. Smith says that between the mid-70s and 1985, attitudes toward homosexuality became less tolerant, but since 1991 "disapproval began falling away." However, most people remain opposed to homosexuality as a lifestyle and to same-sex marriages in particular.

Chapter 10. The Fifth Social Gospel and the Global Mission of the Church

1. See my "Jesus and Economics: A Century of Christian Reflection on the Economic Order," in *The Bible in American Law Politics and Political Rhetoric*, ed. J. T. Johnson et al., SBL Centennial Series, No. 5 (Lanham, Md.: Scholars Press, 1985), 107–152.

2. See the new introduction to the republished volume by Walter Rauschenbusch, *The Righteousness of the Kingdom* (Lewiston, N.Y.: Edwin Mellen Press, 1999). There, I credit Ronald C. White Jr., *Liberty and Justice for All* (San Francisco: Harper, 1990), and Ralph E. Luker, *The Social Gospel in Black and White* (Chapel Hill, N.C.: University of North Carolina Press, 1991), with clarifying previous questions about the relationship of the social gospel to racial issues.

3. See Reinhold Niebuhr, "Why the Christian Church Is Not Pacifist" in *Christianity and Power Politics* (New York: Charles Schribner's Sons, 1948), and his earlier, *Moral Man and Immoral Society* (New York: Charles Scribner's Sons, 1932).

4. See Charles Howard Hopkins, *The Rise of the Social Gospel in American Protestantism: 1865–1915* (New Haven, Conn.: Yale University Press, 1940). These motifs had parallels in Roman Catholic Christian thought, as can be seen in Paul Misner, *Social Catholicism in Europe: From the Onset of Industrialization to the First World War* (New York: Crossroad Press, 1991). For a "Neo-Conservative" effort to recover these motifs through conversation between Protestants and Catholics, see R. J. Neuhaus and G. Weigel, eds., *Being Christian Today: An American Conversation* (Washington: Ethics and Public Policy Center, 1992).

5. Martin Luther King Jr.'s *Stride Toward Freedom* (New York: Harper, 1958) is a kind of commentary on the two sides of the earlier legacy. His analysis of the power realities in the Montgomery City Council is fully "Niebuhrian," while his strategy for mobilizing the movement without provoking violent reaction is "active pacifism."

6. Perhaps the meeting of the World Council of Churches in Africa in 1965 was the chief emblem of that.

7. Portions of this section of the paper are drawn from my "General Introduction" to the four-volume study *God and Globalization: Theological Ethics and the Spheres of Life* (Harrisburg, Pa.: Trinity Press International, 2000).

8. The remarkable new volume by British scholars David Held and Anthony McGrew, et al., *Global Transformations: Politics, Economics and Culture* (Stanford, Calif.: Stanford University Press, 1999) joins the more journalistic treatment by Thomas L. Friedman, *The Lexus and the Olive Tree: Understanding Globalization* (New York: FSG Press, 1999) as summarizing the state-of-the-art work on globalization from the standpoint of non-theological perspectives.

9. Examples of all of these motifs are present in Scott Paeth, T. Dearborn, et al., *The Local Church in a Global Era* (Grand Rapids: Eerdmans, 2000).

10. G. Arrighi and B. Silver, *Chaos and Governance in the Modern World System* (Minneapolis: University of Minnesota Press, 1999), 21.

11. "The Backlash Against Globalism," *The Futurist* (March 1999), 27.

12. Ibid. We can sometimes see this abroad before we recognize it at home. See Mark Juergensmeyer, *The New Cold War: Religious Nationalism Confronts the Secular State* (Berkeley: University of California Press, 1993); and Peter van der Veer, *Religious Nationalism: Hindus and Muslims in India* (Berkeley: University of California Press, 1994).

13. This is true of Christian voices as well as those indifferent to religion. See M. D. Litonjua, "Global Capitalism," *Theology Today*, 56/2 (July 1999), 210 ff.; *The Cultures of Globalization*," ed. F. Jameson and M. Miyoshi (Durham, N.C.: Duke University Press, 1998), or Paul Helyer, *Stop: Think* (Toronto: Chimo Media, 1999). Helyer lists the best available bibliography of Western attacks on globalization, understood as the increasing influence of the World Bank, the IMF, and all who cooperate with "the multinationals" and "capitalism." "Third World" attacks can be represented by J. Mohan Razu, *Transnational Corporations as Agents of Dehumanization in Asia: An Ethical Critique of Development* (Delhi: CISRS/ISPCK, 1999).

14. Peter Berger, ed., *The Desecularization of the World: Resurgent Religion and World Politics* (Grand Rapids: Eerdmans, 1999) represents a major trend in current scholarship on this point. From the standpoint of the philosophical and historical analysis of cultures, see also the remarkable *The Human Condition and Ultimate Realities*, vol. 3, ed. Robert Cummings Neville (Albany, N.Y.: SUNY Press, forthcoming); and the discerning review of major new studies in anthropology that signal a return of interest in religion after several generations of nonreligious or antireligious focus by Sarah Caldwell, "Transcendence and Culture: Anthropologists Theorize Religion," *Religious Studies Review* 28/3 (July 1999), 227–232.

15. See my "Public Theology and Ethical Judgment," *East & West: Religious Ethics: Proceedings of the Third Symposium of Sino-American Philosophy and Religious Studies*, Zhang Zhegang & Mel Stewart (Beijing: University of Beijing, 1998), 132–147; English edition in *Theology Today*, vol. 54, no. 2 (July 1997), 165–179; and "Human Rights and Public Theology: The Basic Validation of Human Rights," *Religion and Human Rights: Competing Claims?*, ed. Carrie Gustafson and Peter Juviler (New York: M. E. Sharp, 1999), 12–30.

16. See Peter Byrne, *The Moral Interpretation of Religion* (Grand Rapids: Eerdmans, 1998); and Franklin I. Gamwell, *The Divine Good: Modern Moral Theory and the Necessity*

of God (San Francisco: HarperCollins, 1990). These volumes not only review the contributions of mutually critical thinking in theology and ethics since the Enlightenment, but show the contemporary state of their discussion.

17. When globalization began is an open question and laden with tensions between naturalist and historical perspectives. Jared Diamond, *Guns, Germs and Steel* (New York: W. W. Norton, 1998), suggests that it is built into the universal evolutionary process; while David Landis, *The Wealth and Poverty of Nations* (New York: W. W. Norton, 1998), treats it as a European phenomenon, rooted in the deep social and cultural history of the West—often resisted by political decisions in other parts of the world; and Saskia Sasson, *Losing Control? Sovereignty in an Age of Globalization* (New York: Columbia University Press, 1996), sees it as the wider empowerment of the United States after the collapse of the USSR, obvious in the global hegemony of U.S. popular culture and in the new instruments of world governance backed by the United States and its closest allies. These are not the only, uncontroverted, or mutually exclusive theories.

18. I have elsewhere identified the ways in which a great number of the social gospel authors utilized a set of categories to define the foundational institutions of society as necessary to the common life—religion, family, economy, politics, and culture (sometimes also, science), and did so in ways that accorded with liberal Lutheran, conservative Calvinist, Roman Catholic, and Humanist attempts to identify the main spheres of life (see my "Introduction," especially pp. xxiv–xxv, mentioned in note 1 above). Today, a number of scholars prefer to rely on Niklas Luhmann's treatment of the various social systems of communications media: truth, love, money, power, and art (see his *Religious Dogmatics and the Evolution of Societies*, trans. P. Beyer (New York: Edwin Mellen Press, 1984). I prefer, following Rauschenbusch's treatment of the "superpersonal forces of good and evil," to speak not only of religion, but of eros, mammon, Mars, and the muses as "powers" in globalization today. See *God and Globalization*.

19. In fact, Rauschenbusch was quite alert to these professions and their significance. He does not treat them very extensively in his major books, but they appear with nuanced awareness in his *For God and the People: Prayers of the Social Awakening* (Cleveland: Pilgrim Press, 1910).

20. S. P. Huntington, *The Clash of Civilizations and the Remaking of World Order* (New York: Simon & Schuster, 1997). A great number of highly informative volumes on globalization ignore religion or treat it simply as a subordinate function of culture. Huntington's argument, not beyond criticism by any means, has forced religion onto the table of discussion of social and political life in a global era, much as has already been the case in global discussions of human rights and ecological concerns.

21. I have documented some of these convergences in my contributions "Christian Social Movements" and "Missionary Activity" in Mircea Eliade, et al., eds., *The Encyclopedia of Religion* (New York: Macmillan, 1987), vol. 3, pp. 446–52, and vol. 9, pp. 563–69.

22. This is amply documented in, for example, Arthur Vidich and S. M. Lyman, *American Sociology* (New Haven, Conn.: Yale University Press, 1987).

23. See especially W. C. Smith, *Towards a World Theology* (Maryknoll, N.Y.: Orbis, 1981), part III. This commonality, of course, is directly opposed to both Huntington's sense of inevitable "clash" and to Christian dogmatic approaches, such as that of Karl Barth.

24. See especially P. F. Knitter, *No Other Name? A Critical Survey of Christian Attitudes Toward the World Religions* (Maryknoll, N.Y.: Orbis, 1985). He is especially critical of Evangelical Protestant and Catholic Exclusivist approaches, but also of positions such as Smith's, which are prematurely inclusivist, as though real differences are simply incidental, historical accretions.

25. See H. Küng, et al., *Christianity and the World Religions* (New York: Doubleday, 1986); F. Fukuyama, *Trust: The Social Virtues and the Creation of Prosperity* (New York: The Free Press, 1995); and Daniel Elazar, *The Covenant Tradition in Politics*, vol. 4 (New Brunswick: Transaction Press, 1994–1998).

26. With contributions from Lamin Sanneh of Yale, Diane Obenchain of Beijing, Thomas Thangaraj of Emory, John Mbiti of Berne, Kosuke Koyama of Union, Szekar Wan of Andover Newton, and Justo González of Columbia, I am presently editing a volume that will attempt to extend, refine, and integrate such perspectives. See *Christ and the Dominions of the World*, vol. 3 of *God and Globalization* (Harrisburg, Pa.: Trinity Press International, forthcoming 2001).

Chapter 11. The Social Gospel and Pastoral Care Today

1. See the continued use of the term *social gospel* for the social witness of the United Methodist Church in Walter G. Muelder, *Methodism and Society in the Twentieth Century* (New York: Abingdon, 1961). My review of library holdings shows that the term *social gospel* is used constructively in publications until about 1977, after which publications focus on the history of the social gospel movement of the late nineteenth and early twentieth centuries. (Student theses and dissertations at Colgate Rochester Divinity School/Crozer Theological Seminary continue to use the term constructively into the 1990s.) My hunch is that the language of *public church* that was made popular by Martin E. Marty and *The Christian Century* becomes the constructive term that substitutes for *social gospel* after 1980, but the Library of Congress subject headings did not allow me to trace the use of this phrase.

2. Charles V. Gerkin, *An Introduction to Pastoral Care* (Nashville: Abingdon, 1997), 57–60; E. Brooks Holifield, *A History of Pastoral Care in America: From Salvation to Self-Realization* (Nashville: Abingdon, 1983), 201–209.

3. See Carolyn De Swarte Gifford, "'My Own Methodist Hive': Frances Willard's Faith as Disclosed in Her Journal, 1855–1870," and Emilie M. Townes, "Because God Gave Her Vision: The Religious Impulse of Ida B. Wells-Barnett," in *Spirituality and Social Responsibility*, ed. Rosemary Skinner Keller (Nashville: Abingdon, 1993), and Pamela D. Couture, "Beyond Private and Public Patriarchy," in *Religion, Feminism, and the Family* (Louisville: Westminster/John Knox Press, 1996).

4. Pamela D. Couture and Rodney Hunter, eds., *Pastoral Care and Social Conflict: Essays in Honor of Charles V. Gerkin* (Nashville: Abingdon, 1995), 7.

5. A selected bibliography of pastoral care and pastoral theology texts that specifically deal with these social contexts is provided at the conclusion of this book.

6. This list forms a basis for further study by a working group studying "traditional and emerging practices of ministry" of Consultation on Teaching the Practices of Ministry, June 7–11, 2000. The working group consists of Virstan Choy, Christie Neuger, and me.

7. See Pamela D. Couture, *Seeing Children, Seeing God: A Practical Theology of Children and Poverty* (Nashville: Abingdon, 2000); Larry Kent Graham, "Pastoral Theology as Public Theology in Relation to the Clinic," in *The Journal of Pastoral Theology* 10 (June 2000), 2–6; "Family Counseling in the Context of Poverty: Experiences from Brazil," Christoph Schneider-Harpprecht, in *The Journal of the Society for Pastoral Theology* 7 (Summer, 1997), 129–148.

8. See Dorothy Bass, ed. *Practicing Our Faith* (San Francisco: Jossey-Bass, 1997).

9. I reach this conclusion based on interviews with United Methodist bishops that were conducted by James Wood, a colleague on the United Methodist denominational team for the Organizing Religious Work project, Hartford Theological Seminary, funded by the Lilly Endowment.

10. Keith Clements, *Learning to Speak: The Church's Voice in Public Affairs* (Edinburgh: T & T Clark, 1995), 146–172.

11. Clements, 51–79.

12. Clements, 73.

13. Clements, 185.

Conclusion. Toward a New Social Gospel?

1. Christopher Lasch, "Religious Contribution to Social Movements: Walter Rauschenbusch, the Social Gospel, and its Critics," *The Journal of Religious Ethics* 18 (Spring 1990): 20; see also Lasch, *The True and Only Heaven: Progress and its Critics* (New York: W. W. Norton, 1991).

2. Charles Clayton Morrison, *The Social Gospel and the Christian Cultus* (New York: Harper & Brothers, 1933).

Selected Bibliography

Introduction. Historical Integrity and Theological Recovery: A Reintroduction to the Social Gospel

Curtis, Susan. *A Consuming Faith: The Social Gospel and Modern American Culture.* Baltimore: Johns Hopkins University Press, 1991.

Dorrien, Gary J. *Soul in Society: The Making and Renewal of Social Christianity.* Minneapolis: Fortress, 1995.

Fogel, Robert William. *The Fourth Great Awakening & the Future of Egalitarianism.* Chicago and London: University of Chicago Press, 2000.

Handy, Robert T., ed. *The Social Gospel in America: 1870–1920.* New York: Oxford University Press, 1966.

Hopkins, Charles Howard. *The Rise of the Social Gospel in American Protestantism, 1865–1915.* New Haven: Yale University Press, 1940.

Hutchison, William R. *The Modernist Impulse in American Protestantism.* Cambridge: Harvard University Press, 1976.

———, ed. *Between the Times: The Travail of the Protestant Establishment.* Cambridge: Cambridge University Press, 1989.

Johnson, F. Ernest. *The Social Gospel Re-Examined.* New York and London: Harper & Brothers, 1940.

King, William McGuire. "'History as Revelation' in the Theology of the Social Gospel." *Harvard Theological Review* 76:1 (1983): 109–29.

———. "An Enthusiasm for Humanity: The Social Emphasis in Religion and its Accommodation in Protestant Theology." In *Religion and Twentieth-Century American Intellectual Life*, edited by Michael J. Lacey. Cambridge: Cambridge University Press, 1989.

Lindley, William D. "Introduction: Taking a New Look at the Social Gospel." In *Shailer Mathews's Lives of Jesus: The Search for a Theological Foundation for the Social Gospel.* Albany, N.Y.: State University of New York Press, 1997.

Luker, Ralph E. "Interpreting the Social Gospel: Reflections on Two Generations of Historiography." In *Perspectives on the Social Gospel*, edited by Christopher H. Evans, 1–13. Lewiston, N.Y.: Edwin Mellen, 1999.

Phillips, Paul T. *A Kingdom on Earth: Anglo-American Social Christianity, 1880–1940.* University Park, Pa.: Pennsylvania State University Press, 1996.

Visser 'T Hooft, W. A. *The Background of the Social Gospel in America.* St. Louis: Bethany Press, 1962.

White, Ronald Jr. and Charles Howard Hopkins, eds. *The Social Gospel: Religion and Reform in Changing America.* Philadelphia: Temple University Press, 1976.

PART I: HISTORICAL AND THEOLOGICAL LEGACY

Chapter 1. Deciding Who Counts:
Toward a Revised Definition of the Social Gospel

Fishburn, Janet Forsythe. *The Fatherhood of God and the Victorian Family: The Social Gospel in America*. Philadelphia: Fortress, 1981.

Gifford, Carolyn De Swarte, ed. *The American Deaconess Movement in the Early Twentieth Century*. New York and London: Garland, 1987.

Lindley, Susan Hill. "'Neglected Voices' and *Praxis* in the Social Gospel." *Journal of Religious Ethics* 18 (Spring 1990): 75–101.

Luker, Ralph E. *The Social Gospel in Black and White: American Racial Reform, 1885–1912*. Chapel Hill: University of North Carolina Press, 1991.

McDowell, John Patrick. *The Social Gospel in the South: The Woman's Home Mission Movement in the Methodist Episcopal Church, South, 1886–1939*. Baton Rouge: Louisiana State University Press, 1982.

White, Ronald C. Jr. *Liberty and Justice for All: Racial Reform and the Social Gospel, 1875–1925*. San Francisco: Harper & Row, 1990.

Chapter 2. The Social Gospel Movement and the Question of Race

Curtis, Susan. "The Social Gospel and Race in American Culture." In *Perspectives on the Social Gospel*, edited by Christopher H. Evans, 15–31. Lewiston, N.Y.: Edwin Mellen, 1999.

Harding, Vincent. *Martin Luther King: The Inconvenient Hero*. Maryknoll, N.Y.: Orbis, 1997.

King, Martin Luther Jr. *Strength to Love*. Philadelphia: Fortress, 1981.

Morris, Calvin. "Reverdy Ransom, the Social Gospel and Race." *Journal of Religious Thought* 41 (Spring–Summer 1984): 21.

Smith, Kenneth L. and Ira G. Zepp. *Search for the Beloved Community: The Thinking of Martin Luther King, Jr.* Valley Forge: Judson, 1974.

Townes, Emilie. "Because God Gave Her a Vision: The Religious Impulse of Ida B. Wells-Barnett." In *Spirituality and Social Responsibility: Vocational Vision of Women in the United Methodist Tradition*, edited by Rosemary S. Keller. Nashville: Abingdon, 1993.

Williams, Preston N. "The Social Gospel and Race Relations: A Case Study of a Social Movement." In *Toward a Discipline of Social Ethics: Essays in Honor of Walter George Muelder*, edited by Paul Deats, 232–256. Boston: Boston University Press, 1972.

Chapter 3. The Kingdom of God, the Church, and the World:
The Social Gospel and the Making of Theology in
the Twentieth-Century Ecumenical Movement

Best, Thomas and Martin Robra, eds. *Ecclesiology and Ethics: Ecumenical Ethical Engagement, Moral Formation and the Nature of the Church*. Geneva: World Council of Churches, 1997.

Ellingsen, Mark. *The Cutting Edge: How Churches Speak on Social Issues*. Geneva: World Council of Churches, 1993.

Kinnamon, Michael and Brian Cope, eds. *The Ecumenical Movement: An Anthology of Key Texts and Voices*. Geneva: World Council of Churches/Grand Rapids: Eerdmans, 1997.

Chapter 4. Gender and the Kingdom of God: The Family Values of Walter Rauschenbusch

Blake, Casey Nelson. "Private Life and Public Commitment: From Walter Rauschenbusch to Richard Rorty." In *A Pragmatist Progress? Richard Rorty and American Intellectual History*, edited by John Pettegrew, 85–101. Lanham: Rowman & Littefield, 2000.

Edwards, Wendy J. Deichmann, ed. *Women, Gender, and the Social Gospel*. Urbana: University of Illinois Press, forthcoming.

Hudson, Winthrop. *Walter Rauschenbusch: Selected Writings*. New York: Paulist Press, 1984.

Minus, Paul. *Walter Rauschenbusch: American Reformer*. New York: Macmillan, 1988.

Rauschenbusch, Walter. *A Theology for the Social Gospel*. New York: Macmillan, 1917. Reprint, Nashville: Abingdon, 1978.

———. *Christianizing the Social Order*. New York: Macmillan, 1912.

———. *Dare We Be Christians? A Classic Treatise on Love*. Cleveland: Pilgrim Press, 1914. Reprint, Pilgrim, 1993.

———. *Christianity and the Social Crisis*. New York: Macmillan, 1907. Reprint, Louisville, Ky.: Westminster/John Knox, 1991.

Chapter 5. Women Creating Communities— and Community—in the Name of the Social Gospel

Higginbotham, Evelyn Brooks. *Righteous Discontent: The Women's Movement in the Black Baptist Church, 1880-1920*. Cambridge: Harvard University Press, 1993.

Horton, Isabella. *High Adventure: Life of Lucy Rider Meyer*. New York: Methodist Book Concern, 1828.

Prelinger, Catherine and Rosemary Keller. "The Function of Female Bonding." In *Women in New Worlds: Historical Perspectives on the Wesleyan Tradition*. Vol. 2. Edited by Rosemary Skinner Keller, Louise L. Queen, and Hilah F. Thomas. Nashville: Abingdon, 1982.

Sklar, Kathryn Kish. *Florence Kelley and the Nation's Work: The Rise of Women's Political Culture, 1830–1900*. New Haven: Yale University Press, 1995.

Stebner, Eleanor J. *The Women of Hull House: a Study in Spirituality, Vocation, and Friendship*. Albany, N.Y.: State University of New York Press, 1997.

Chapter 6. Giving Patterns and Practices among Church Women in the Methodist Episcopal and the Colored Methodist Episcopal Churches, 1870–1920: A Social Gospel Perspective

Brown, Earl Kent. "Women in Church History: Stereotypes, Archetypes, and Operational Modalities." *Methodist History* 18 (January 1980): 109–32.

Gladden, Washington. *The Christian Pastor and the Working Church*. New York: Charles Scribner's Sons, 1898.

Hoge, Dean, Charles Zech, Patrick McNamara, and Michael J. Donahue. *Money Matters: Personal Giving in American Churches*. Louisville, Ky.: Westminster John Knox, 1996.

Keller, Rosemary Skinner. "Creating a Sphere for Women." *Women in New Worlds*. Edited by Hilah F. Thomas and Rosemary Skinner Keller. Nashville: Abingdon, 1981.

Lakey, Othal and Betty Stephens. *God in My Mama's House: The Women's Movement in the CME Church*. Memphis: CME Publishing House, 1994.

Lynn, Robert Wood. "Why Give?" *Financing American Religion*. Edited by Mark Chaves and Sharon Miller. Walnut Creek, Calif.: Alta Mira Press, 1999.

Robert, Dana L. *American Women in Mission: A Social History of Their Thought and Practice*. Macon, Ga.: Mercer University Press, 1996.

Wind, James P. and James W. Lewis, eds. *American Congregations. Volume I: Portrait of Twelve Religious Communities*. Chicago: University of Chicago Press, 1994.

PART II: THE SOCIAL GOSPEL TODAY

Chapter 7. Social Salvation:
The Social Gospel as Theology and Economics

Dombrowski, James. *The Early Days of Christian Socialism in America*. New York: Columbia University Press, 1936.

Dorn, Jacob Henry. *Washington Gladden: Prophet of the Social Gospel*. Columbus: Ohio State University Press, 1967.

Ely, Richard T., ed. *A History of Cooperation in America*. Baltimore: Johns Hopkins University Press, 1888.

Gladden, Washington. *Applied Christianity: Moral Aspects of Social Questions*. Boston: Houghton, Mifflin and Co., 1886.

——. *Tools and the Man*. Boston: Houghton, Mifflin and Co., 1893.

Taylor, Sedley. *Profit-Sharing Between Labor and Capital*. New York: Humboldt Publishing, 1886.

Chapter 8. The Reawakening of the Evangelical Social Consciousness

Brereton, Virginia. *Training God's Army: the American Bible School, 1880–1940*. Bloomington, Ind.: Indiana University Press, 1990.

Furness, Charles Y. *The Christian and Social Action*. Old Tappan, N.J.: Fleming Revell, 1971.

Henry, Carl F. H. *The Uneasy Conscience of Modern Fundamentalism*. Grand Rapids: Eerdmans, 1947.

Hunter, James Davison. *Evangelicalism: The Coming Generation*. Chicago: University of Chicago Press, 1987.

Magnuson, Norris. *Salvation in the Slums: Evangelical Social Work, 1865–1920*. Metuchen, N.J.: Scarecrow Press, 1977.

Marsden, George. *Fundamentalism and American Culture: The Shaping of Twentieth-Century Evangelicalism, 1870–1925*. New York: Oxford University Press, 1980.

McKinney, Larry. *Equipping for Service: A Historical Account of the Bible College Movement in North America*. Fayetteville, Ark.: Accrediting Association of Bible Colleges, 1997.

Moberg, David O. *The Great Reversal: Evangelicalism and Social Concern*. Philadelphia: Lippincott, 1972.

Sider, Ronald J. *Completely Pro-Life: Building a Consistent Stance on Abortion, the Family, Nuclear Weapons, the Poor*. Downers Grove, Ill.: InterVarsity Press, 1987.

——. *Just Generosity: A New Vision for Overcoming Poverty in America*. Grand Rapids: Baker Books, 1999.

Smith, Timothy L. *Revivalism and Social Reform in Mid-Nineteenth Century America*. New York: Abingdon, 1957.

Wallis, Jim. *The Soul of Politics: a Practical and Prophetic Vision for Change*. Maryknoll, N.Y.: Orbis, 1994.

Chapter 9. The Social Gospel, Gender, and Homosexuality: Then and Now

Boyd, Lois A. and R. Douglas Brackenridge, *Presbyterian Women in America: Two Centuries of a Quest for Status.* Westport, Conn.: Greenwood, 1983.

Buechler, Steven. *Women's Movements in the United States: Woman Suffrage, Equal Rights, and Beyond.* New Brunswick, N.J.: Rutgers University Press, 1990.

Coalter, Milton J., John M. Mulder, Louis B. Weeks, eds. *The Confessional Mosaic: Presbyterians and Twentieth-Century Theology.* Louisville, Ky.: Westminster/John Knox, 1990.

Daly, Lewis C., researcher. *A Moment to Decide: The Crisis in Mainstream Presbyterianism.* New York: Institute for Democracy Studies, 2000.

DeBerg, Betty A. *Ungodly Women: Gender and the First Wave of American Fundamentalism.* Minneapolis: Fortress, 1990.

Gorrell, Donald K. *The Age of Responsibility: The Social Gospel in the Progressive Era, 1900–1920.* Macon, Ga.: Mercer University Press, 1988.

May, Henry. *Protestant Churches and Industrial America.* Rev. ed. New York: Octagon Books, 1977.

Chapter 10. The Fifth Social Gospel and the Global Mission of the Church

Fukuyama, Francis. *Trust: The Social Virtues and the Creation of Prosperity.* New York: Free Press, 1995.

Huntington, Samuel P. *The Clash of Civilizations and the Remaking of World Order.* New York: Simon & Schuster, 1996.

Knitter, Paul F. *No Other Name? A Critical Survey of Christian Attitudes Toward the World Religions.* Maryknoll, N.Y.: Orbis, 1985.

Küng, Hans et al. *Christianity and the World Religions: Paths of Dialogue with Islam, Hinduism, and Buddhism.* New York: Doubleday, 1986.

Niebuhr, Reinhold. *Moral Man and Immoral Society.* New York: Charles Scribner's Sons, 1932.

Paeth, Scott, T. Dearborn et al. *The Local Church in a Global Era.* Grand Rapids: Eerdmans, 2000.

Rauschenbusch, Walter. *The Righteousness of the Kingdom.* Revised edition with new introduction by Max L. Stackhouse. Lewiston, N.Y.: Edwin Mellen, 1999.

Stackhouse, Max L., ed. *God and Globalization Volume 1: Theological Ethics and the Spheres of Life.* Harrisburg, Pa.: Trinity Press International, 2000.

———, ed. *God and Globalization, Volume 2: The Spirit and the Modern Authorities.* Harrisburg, Pa.: Trinity Press International, 2001.

———, ed. *God and Globalization, Volume 3: Christ and the World's Civilizations and Godly Covenants: Transforming Global Society.* Harrisburg, Pa.: Trinity Press International, forthcoming.

Chapter 11. The Social Gospel and Pastoral Care Today

Augsburger, David W. *Conflict Mediation Across Cultures: Pathways and Patterns.* Louisville: Westminster/John Knox Press, 1992.

Clinebell, Howard. *Ecotherapy: Healing Ourselves, Healing the Earth.* New York: The Haworth Press, 1996.

Couture, Pamela D. *Seeing Children, Seeing God: A Practical Theology of Children and Poverty.* Nashville: Abingdon, 2000.

Couture, Pamela D. and Rodney J. Hunter. *Pastoral Care and Social Conflict*. Nashville: Abingdon, 1995.

Furniss, George M. *The Social Context of Pastoral Care: Defining the Life Situation*. Louisville, Ky.: Westminster/John Knox, 1994.

Gerkin, Charles V. *Prophetic Pastoral Practice: a Christian Vision of Life Together*. Nashville: Abingdon, 1991.

Graham, Larry Kent. *Care of Persons, Care of Worlds: a Psychosystemic Approach to Pastoral Care and Counseling*. Nashville: Abingdon, 1992.

Kornfield, Margaret Zipse. *Cultivating Wholeness: a Guide to Care and Counseling in Faith Communities*. New York: Continuum, 1998.

Poling, James Newton. *Deliver Us From Evil: Resisting Racial and Gender Oppression*. Minneapolis: Fortress, 1996.

Steinhoffsmith, Roy Herndon. *The Mutuality of Care*. St. Louis: Chalice, 1999.

Conclusion. Toward a New Social Gospel?

Beckley, Harlan. *Passion for Justice: Retrieving the Legacies of Walter Rauschenbusch, John A. Ryan, and Reinhold Niebuhr*. Louisville: Westminster/John Knox, 1992.

Lasch, Christopher. "Religious Contributions to Social Movements: Walter Rauschenbusch, the Social Gospel, and its Critics." *The Journal of Religious Ethics* 18 (Spring 1990): 7-23.

Morrison, Charles Clayton. *The Social Gospel and the Christian Cultus*. New York: Harper & Brothers, 1933.

Index of Names

Index of Subjects